Democracies and dictatorships

Europe and the world 1919–1989

Allan Todd

CAMBRIDGE
UNIVERSITY PRESS

For my parents

PUBLISHED BY THE PRESS SYNDICATE OF THE UNIVERSITY OF CAMBRIDGE
The Pitt Building, Trumpington Street, Cambridge, United Kingdom

CAMBRIDGE UNIVERSITY PRESS
The Edinburgh Building, Cambridge CB2 2RU, UK
40 West 20th Street, New York, NY 10011–4211, USA
477 Williamstown Road, Port Melbourne, VIC 3207, Australia
Ruiz de Alarcón 13, 28014 Madrid, Spain
Dock House, The Waterfront, Cape Town 8001, South Africa

http://www.cambridge.org

First published 2001
Third printing 2003

Printed in the United Kingdom at the University Press, Cambridge

Typeface Minion 10.5pt.   *System* QuarkXPress®

A catalogue record for this book is available from the British Library

ISBN 0 521 77797 6   paperback

Text design by Newton Harris Design Partnership

Map illustrations by Kathy Baxendale

The cover shows a photograph of people walking on the Berlin Wall, in front of the
Brandenburg Gate, 10 November 1989. The photograph is reproduced courtesy of
Associated Press.

ACKNOWLEDGEMENTS
Photo AKG-London: pp.24, 130, 191; Bildarchiv Preussischer Kulturbesitz: p.32; Camera Press
Limited: p.162; David Low/The Evening Standard: cartoons supplied by the Centre for the Study of
Cartoons and Caricatures, University of Kent, Canterbury: pp.20, 35, 41, 118; Bettmann/Corbis:
pp.207, 256; Hulton|Archive: pp.14, 74, 91, 217; The Illustrated London News Picture Library, London:
p.10; David King Collection: pp.47, 57, 68, 78, 89, 107; NOVOSTI (London): p. 109; Peter Newark's
Military Pictures: p.128; Popperfoto: pp.106, 181, 229; Rex Features Limited: p.182; Associated Press/
Topham: pp.177, 238.

We have been unable to trace the copyright holders of the images on pp.145 and 164, and would be
grateful for any information that would enable us to do so.

Picture Research by Sandie Huskinson-Rolfe of PHOTOSEEKERS.

Contents

International relations, 1919–39

1

The Treaty of Versailles

Focus questions

◆ What were the aims of the Big Three?

◆ What problems did they face?

◆ Was Germany treated unfairly?

Significant dates

1918   *January*   Wilson's Fourteen Points peace plan
       4 October   German government asks for armistice based on Wilson's Fourteen Points
       November   Allies agree to armistice based on the Fourteen Points; Wilson loses control of Congress to Republicans
       11 November   Germany and Allies sign armistice
       December   Lloyd George's Liberal–Conservative coalition wins 'make Germany pay' election

1919   *January*   Peace conferences begin in Paris
       May   Germany makes many criticisms of the draft Treaty of Versailles
       28 June   Germany signs Treaty of Versailles
       September   Austria signs Treaty of St Germain
       November   Bulgaria signs Treaty of Neuilly

1920   *March*   Republican-dominated US Senate rejects Treaty of Versailles, so USA signs separate peace with Germany
       June   Hungary signs Treaty of Trianon
       August   Turkey signs Treaty of Sèvres (replaced in July 1923 by Treaty of Lausanne)

An **armistice** is a ceasefire which puts a temporary end to the fighting, while treaty terms are agreed – a treaty officially ends a war.

A *diktat* is an imposed or 'dictated' peace. The German delegation that represented the new democratic government of Germany were not allowed to take part in the peace negotiations. They were handed the treaty on 7 May 1919 and were given 15 days (extended later by 7 days) to comment on its 440 clauses. Their detailed criticisms – especially that it was too harsh and not based on Wilson's Fourteen Points – persuaded the British to press for some amendments, but few changes occurred.

Overview

In November 1918, after four years of conflict, an **armistice** was signed to halt the fighting of the First World War. In January 1919, the leaders of the winning Allied countries met in Paris to decide how to deal with Germany and the other defeated powers. The three main leaders were Wilson (USA), Clemenceau (France) and Lloyd George (Britain). They became known as the Big Three. (Though Italy had been an ally since 1915, the Italian prime minister Orlando was now largely ignored.) These three leaders had different aims: Wilson wanted a fair peace, Clemenceau a harsh peace and Lloyd George a compromise peace. In all, five separate peace treaties were signed between the Allies and the defeated powers, the main one being the Treaty of Versailles which dealt with Germany. This treaty imposed significant military restrictions on Germany and resulted in the loss of some of its European territory and all its overseas colonies. Germany was also forced to accept total blame for the war (the 'war guilt' clause) and to pay huge compensation, mainly to France and Britain. The Treaty of Versailles was presented to Germany on a 'take it or leave it' basis – rejection would have meant the resumption of war. Both contemporaries and historians have debated whether this was an unfair treaty and a harsh '*diktat*'.

What were the aims of the Big Three?

By September 1918, the German High Command realised they were losing the war and ordered the civilian government to begin peace negotiations based on Wilson's Fourteen Points peace plan. France and Britain had reservations about some of these points, but Wilson threatened to make a separate peace with Germany if they did not accept his plan as the basis for an armistice. On 9 November 1918, the **kaiser** abdicated and on 11 November a new provisional civilian German government signed the armistice. However, this armistice, which was negotiated by the Allied military commanders, differed in many respects from Wilson's Fourteen Points.

The United States of America

From as early as 1917, President **Wilson** clearly intended to use US power, both financial and military, to create a new order in international relations once the First World War was over. He wanted an end to traditional European 'Great Power' diplomacy, based on secret treaties and military alliances; instead, he wanted open diplomacy, new principles of international law and the creation of a new international organisation to ensure world peace.

On 8 January 1918, he presented his Fourteen Points, which outlined the kind of peace settlement he wanted, to the US Congress. Significantly, he had not discussed this plan beforehand with Britain or France – Wilson knew both of these countries disagreed with some of his general aims and that France, in particular, wanted a harsher peace imposed on Germany.

France

Unlike the USA and Britain, France had been invaded during the First World War and much French agriculture and industry had been destroyed. This,

The German emperor was known as the **kaiser**. Before 1918, he controlled the government, foreign affairs and the armed forces; parliamentary democracy – especially in the First World War – had been very limited.

Woodrow **Wilson** was born in 1856. He was elected Democratic president of the USA in 1912 and re-elected in 1916. His Fourteen Points, issued in January 1918, were the basis on which German civilian governments sued for peace in October and November 1918. His main aim was to establish a League of Nations to settle disputes peacefully and to end secret diplomacy, but he was forced to make many concessions to Britain and France. In the end, despite strong campaigning, the US Senate rejected the Treaty of Versailles and membership of the new League of Nations. Instead, the USA made its own separate peace with Germany and, under the Republicans, adopted a policy of isolation in relation to much of European diplomacy, though economic and trade developments continued to be of interest.

Demilitarisation means that all troops and military equipment have to be removed from an area.

The **Rhineland** was the area to the west of the River Rhine, between France and Germany. The Treaty of Versailles finally decided that the demilitarised zone (DMZ) should extend to 50 km wide along the east bank of the Rhine, as well as all land to the west.

> What were France's main aims once Germany had been defeated?

Georges **Clemenceau**, known as 'the Tiger', was born in 1841. In 1871 he was elected as a Radical deputy to the French National Assembly. He was prime minister from 1906 to 1909 and from 1917 to 1920. Though he pushed hard for France's security concerns at Versailles, he was not as harsh on Germany as some historians have claimed. He was particularly worried that Russia was no longer a potential powerful ally, so he pushed for the demilitarisation of the Rhineland and severe military restrictions on Germany.

Born in 1863, David **Lloyd George** was a Liberal. He was chancellor of the exchequer from 1908 to 1915 and in 1916 replaced Asquith as prime minister of the wartime coalition government. In December

together with the earlier invasion of France by Germany during the Franco-Prussian War (1870–71), led France to want Germany to be permanently weakened. The French wanted the **demilitarisation** of the **Rhineland** and most of Germany's military equipment to be surrendered. To ensure this, they wanted the Allied naval blockade of Germany to continue until a peace treaty had been signed.

Clemenceau and Marshal Foch (Allied commander-in-chief towards the end of the war) have been traditionally portrayed by historians as being determined to punish Germany and to make it pay compensation for the damage it caused during the war. However, Clemenceau only insisted on massive compensation from Germany *after* the USA and Britain had rejected his call for cancellation of France's war debts (incurred for the First World War).

Britain

Lloyd George (like Clemenceau) was also under considerable pressure from the popular press and the general public to 'make Germany pay'. However, Britain did not want to see France replace Germany as the dominant power in Europe – relations between Britain and France had often been very tense during the last quarter of the nineteenth century. Lloyd George was also keen to rebuild Germany as a trading partner and, most importantly, to maintain control of Britain's empire.

Lloyd George thus attempted to push for a compromise peace, something between the idealistic aims of Wilson and the punitive aims of Clemenceau.

What problems did they face?

In addition to the significant differences between the Allies over what kind of peace treaty should be drawn up, the situation was further complicated by the results of the US mid-term **elections** in November 1918. The Republicans defeated Wilson's Democratic Party in both the House of Representatives and the Senate. Most Americans – especially Republicans – were opposed to Wilson's Fourteen Points and rejected any US involvement in the proposed League of Nations. Thus by the time peace negotiations opened in Paris in January 1919, France and Britain knew Wilson's bargaining position was considerably weakened. (In fact the only point of the fourteen to be accepted was his call for a League of Nations to be set up; Wilson was forced by Britain and France to give way on many of the others.)

Apart from these difficulties, the peacemakers of 1919 faced several serious problems, of which the three biggest were:
- the current situation in Germany;
- the future role of Germany in Europe;
- the instability in central and eastern Europe.

The situation in Germany

Early in October 1918, following the failure of their spring offensive and then the successful Allied counter-attack in August, the German military commanders, Ludendorff and Hindenburg, handed power over to a civilian government to avoid the army being directly blamed for any peace settlement. They then secretly instructed this government to apply for peace. However, the German people had been told that Germany was still winning and were shocked to learn of these peace negotiations. By early November mutinies and revolutionary unrest were spreading across Germany. In many areas, factories were occupied by workers and workers' councils were set up, in direct imitation of the 1917 November Revolution in Russia. However, these actions were also a protest against the continuation of the war, the months of food shortages and rapid inflation.

On 9 November, the head of the civilian government, Prince Max of Baden, resigned and the kaiser abdicated and fled to the Netherlands. A new democratic socialist provisional government, made up of **SPD** and **USPD** ministers, took over and signed the armistice two days later.

However, many Germans saw these politicians as traitors for signing the armistice (they became known as the 'November criminals'), while the army was seen as 'undefeated heroes', especially as Germany had not been invaded. Many soon came to believe that Germany had been betrayed by communists, socialists and Jews who, in the autumn of 1918, had 'stabbed Germany in the back'. This myth, advanced by the far right, seriously undermined the new democratic government of Germany. In addition, the abdication of the kaiser left a political vacuum in a Germany that had never before experienced complete political democracy.

Most Germans expected their government to be directly involved in drawing up peace terms, which they believed would be based on Wilson's Fourteen Points. In particular, they expected the principle of self-determination for all national groups to be equally applied to all Germans (in other words, that German citizens would be able to decide which country they wanted to be in).

The role of Germany in Europe

Following German unification after the Franco-Prussian War, Germany had rapidly developed into a major new power in Europe. Its population rose from 49 million in 1890 to 66 million in 1914 and its economy grew faster than that of any other European power. By the start of the First World War in 1914, German steel production was greater than the combined figures for Britain, France and Russia, while its coal production was second only to Britain's. More significantly, Germany had a tremendous lead in the new electrical and chemical industries. It was this economic growth that had enabled Germany's

1918, he was re-elected as leader of a Liberal–Conservative coalition. The coalition had won a big majority and was under pressure from press and public to 'make Germany pay'. However, as head of the British peace delegation, he tried to limit some of France's more extreme demands.

Elections for Congress and the Senate are held both mid-way between and at the same time as presidential elections.

The **SPD** was the Social Democratic Party and the **USPD** was the Independent SPD, a left-wing breakaway group from the SPD.

What was the 'stab in the back' myth?

Why did most Germans see the Treaty of Versailles as a *diktat*?

military and naval expansion. Many Germans felt their country had an important economic role to play in Europe and saw Germany as a barrier to the spread of communism. To others, the collapse of the Austro-Hungarian and Russian empires in central and eastern Europe presented opportunities for future German expansion.

However, the First World War had a negative impact on Germany's economic power – as it did on the rest of Europe. By 1918, manufacturing output in Europe as a whole was 30 per cent lower than it had been in 1914, but it was much worse in Germany and Austria, where it fell by 60 per cent. In addition Germany was forced to sell all its foreign investments. The war had forced all countries to borrow – Britain and France, in particular, had borrowed heavily from the USA. As a consequence, European currencies in general were weaker after 1918 and there was high inflation. Again, this was worse in Germany: the national debt rose from 5,000 million marks in 1914 to 154,000 million in 1918. By then, the German mark had dropped in value by 75 per cent and by 1920 was worth only 10 per cent of its value in 1914.

Germany's particularly severe problems slowed down any general European recovery in the 1920s. Some contemporaries, such as J. M. Keynes, in his *Economic consequences of the peace* (1920), argued that German economic recovery was essential for the recovery of European trade in general. However, rebuilding the German economy made many (especially in France) fear a future revival of German military power.

Instability in central and eastern Europe

The Austro-Hungarian empire had also been an important economic component of central and eastern Europe. The impact of the First World War combined with nationalism to break up the pre-1914 Habsburg (Austro-Hungarian), Ottoman (Turkish) and Romanov (Russian) empires. The break-up of these three empires added to the general economic disruption in Europe after 1918.

They were replaced by a large number of small states (the **successor states**) demanding national self-determination, but the peace treaties with these countries failed to solve all their ethnic and national demands. Hungary lost 66 per cent of its territory and 40 per cent of its population; for example, the 3.5 million German speakers of the Sudetenland (part of Moravia) were given to the newly created state of Czechoslovakia, which also contained other minority ethnic groups. The new state of Yugoslavia and the restored state of Poland were both made up of various minority groups, with resultant tensions. Most of these states, with the exception of Czechoslovakia, soon became right-wing dictatorships of one kind or another and most had territorial claims against their neighbours.

The **successor states** were the new states in central and eastern Europe which were created – or, in Poland's case, re-created – by the peace treaties of 1919 and 1920. Apart from Poland (which had in the past been shared between the old German, Austro-Hungarian and Russian empires), the new states were Czechoslovakia and Yugoslavia, with Austria and Hungary becoming two separate states. Finland and the Baltic States of Estonia, Latvia and Lithuania also gained their independence, having previously been part of Tsarist Russia. Most of these states were economically and militarily weak and many had significant minority ethnic groups (which often wanted to be ruled by another country, or felt unfairly treated) as part of their population.

In addition to this considerable political instability, was the ideological and possible military threat posed by the new **Bolshevik** government of Soviet Russia. Equally significant was the fact that the disappearance of these three empires and the subsequent exclusion of Soviet Russia from the ranks of the great powers (for the time being) meant that Germany alone remained as a united and intact state.

Though the German army had failed to win the First World War, it had not been seriously defeated or destroyed. Furthermore, as we have seen, many politicians in Europe came to see Germany, in view of the political unrest in central and eastern Europe, as the main barrier to the spread of Bolshevism into war-devastated Europe.

What impact did the First World War have on the countries of central and eastern Europe?

The **Bolsheviks** were a revolutionary Russian political party, led by Lenin, which followed the communist ideas of Karl Marx. They led the overthrow of Russia's provisional government in November 1917, and changed their name to the Russian Communist Party in 1918. They hoped there would be other victorious workers' revolutions in the rest of Europe.

Was Germany treated unfairly?

The differing war aims of the Big Three made it impossible to draw up a provisional peace settlement for detailed negotiation with German representatives. Instead, the Allies produced a hastily drafted treaty which was handed over to the Germans for acceptance or rejection. Rejection, however, was not an option for the German delegation as this would have meant the resumption of war – German commanders had already informed the new democratic civilian government that the German army was incapable of resistance. So the humiliated German delegation was forced to accept the terms. Scheidemann, the German chancellor (elected in January 1919), resigned in protest but his successor, Bauer, signed on 28 June 1919.

The terms of the Treaty of Versailles

As with the other treaties, the first 26 articles of the treaty dealt with the establishment of the League of Nations. The remaining articles, which dealt specifically with Germany, have long been seen by historians as forming a harsh *diktat* imposed on a weak Germany. More recently, however, revisionist historians have argued that it was relatively moderate – and certainly much more moderate than the Treaty of Brest–Litovsk, imposed by the kaiser's government on Soviet Russia in March 1918. The Treaty of Versailles was designed to limit the military and political power of Germany.

Military restrictions
These included:
- banning the German army from having tanks, heavy artillery or military aircraft;
- limiting the army to 100,000, with no conscription;
- limiting the German navy to 6 battleships, 6 light cruisers, 12 destroyers and 12 torpedo boats and not allowing it to have any submarines or

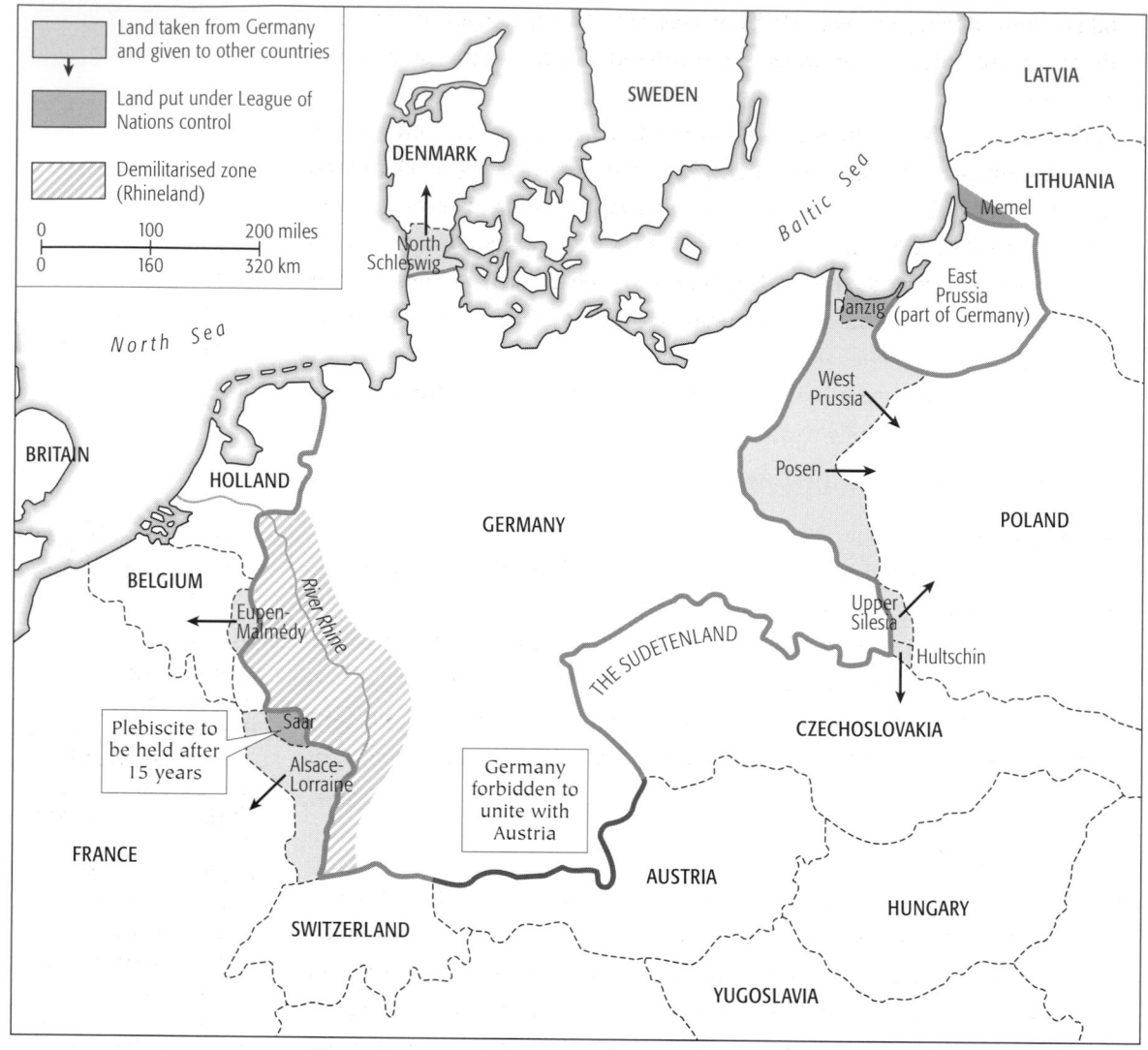

The main territorial changes brought about by the Treaty of Versailles.

military aircraft – the rest of the German navy was to be handed over and divided among the Allies, but it was scuttled by the German commanders at Scapa Flow, on 21 June;

- demolishing the Heligoland fortifications and opening the Kiel Canal to all nations' shipping;

- demilitarising the Rhineland indefinitely, with Allied troops in occupation for 15 years (France had wanted the Rhineland to become a separate independent state, but Wilson had refused).

Territorial changes

These included:

- handing over all overseas colonies – Britain, France and Japan had already

What were the main military restrictions placed on Germany by the Treaty of Versailles?

taken these during the war (Wilson was able to get agreement that, in theory, these colonies would be administered under League of Nations' mandates);

- reducing German's continental territory: Alsace-Lorraine was returned to France, Eupen-Malmédy went to Belgium, North Schleswig to Denmark, the small area of Hultschin to Czechoslovakia, and Poland received West Prussia and Posen, giving Poland a 'corridor' to the sea (although this cut off East Prussia from the rest of Germany), as well as parts of Silesia, while Gdansk (Danzig) became an International Free City (under the League of Nations);
- allowing France to administer the Saar (important for coal) for 15 years, technically under League of Nations' supervision;
- banning any union (*Anschluss*) with Austria.

What were the territorial changes imposed on Germany by the Treaty of Versailles?

The war guilt clause

In addition, Germany was forced to accept Article 231, which stated that Germany alone was totally responsible for causing the First World War. This war guilt clause committed Germany to paying **compensation**, but because of Allied disagreements the final figure (of £6,600 million) was only agreed by the special Reparations Committee in 1921. Before then, in 1919, all Germany's foreign currency and assets abroad were seized by the Allies and were not returned.

Why was the war guilt clause so significant?

Impact of the treaty

Most Germans were angered by the terms of the treaty and blamed the new Weimar government for accepting it. During the 1920s and 1930s, resentment of the Treaty of Versailles was a major factor in the rise of extreme nationalism and the far right. At the same time, British governments came increasingly to see the treaty as harsh – this, in part, explains the policy of appeasement that was followed in the 1930s.

In practice, the treaty was more leniently applied. Disarmament, for example, was to be carried out by the Germans, under the supervision of the Allied commissions of control. These frequently pointed out that throughout the 1920s Germany was not complying, and restrictions on Germany's armed forces were later evaded by military agreements with Soviet Russia. In addition, the German army commanders retained their positions, thus ensuring that the army remained an extremely powerful force in the young Weimar Republic.

Furthermore, though the treaty resulted in Germany losing approximately 13 per cent of its economic production capacity and about 10 per cent of its population, Germany was left largely intact, with a population almost double that of France.

Reparations, **compensation** or indemnity. In the First World War Britain suffered 750,000 deaths and France 1.4 million; France also lost 52,000 factories, 5,600 km of railway lines and 4,800 km of roads. Public opinion in both Britain and France wanted Germany to be made to pay in full ('squeeze the German lemon till the pips squeak'). However, the British delegation were less harsh than the French, and Allied differences prevented any agreement on a final figure in June 1919. Instead, a special Reparations Committee was set up to decide, but it took until 1921 to agree a total.

PEACE AND FUTURE CANNON FODDER

1940 CLASS

PEACE TREATY

The Tiger: "Curious! I seem to hear a child weeping!"

A British cartoon of 1919, predicting that the terms of the Treaty of Versailles would lead to another world war. Clemenceau, Wilson, Lloyd George and Orlando (of Italy) are shown looking at a weeping child. The cartoonist predicts 1940 as the date for the next war.

Also significant was the fact that Germany was not invaded, while France's ten richest departments (provinces) were devastated by the fighting. When we consider the reparations burden in Chapter 3 it will be seen that the 'final' figure was progressively reduced and the payments were rescheduled over a longer period during the 1920s, to the extent that in the 1930s Germany was able to finance large-scale rearmament. Overall, the basic strength of the German economy was not seriously weakened by the treaty and Germany was soon restored to being the most successful European economy. By 1925, Germany's steel production was already twice the size of Britain's.

When compared to the other peace treaties of 1919–20, especially the Treaties of St Germain and Trianon with Austria and Hungary respectively, the Treaty of Versailles seems quite lenient. Even so, almost from the start, Britain began to favour revision of some of its terms, with Lloyd George supporting some of the German objections even before the treaty was finally signed. In particular, British governments did not want to prevent the revival of an important pre-war trading partner or to weaken Germany's ability to 'contain' communism.

Historical sources

1 Erzberger, leader of the faction in the German cabinet in favour of signing the treaty, speaking at a cabinet meeting in June 1919

There was no dishonour if we signed under duress, provided we announced the fact that we were signing under duress. Suppose somebody tied my arms and placed a loaded pistol against my chest, and asked me to sign a paper obligating me to climb to the moon within 48 hours. As a thinking man I would sign to save my life, but at the same time would say openly that the demand simply could not be fulfilled. The moral situation presented by [the Entente demand to sign] the treaty was exactly of the same kind.

K. Epstein, *Matthias Erzberger: a dilemma of German democracy*, Princeton, 1957, p. 138

2 The view of a US delegate at the Treaty of Versailles conference

The magnitude of the reparations demanded of Germany under the treaty . . . placed great strain upon credit. Largely on this account there was a widespread collapse of the entire pre-war system of goods and services and investments . . . The reparations clauses contributed largely toward a German psychology which has changed the political complexion of much of the world.

J. F. Dulles, 'Foreword', in P. Burnett, *Reparations at the Paris peace conference*, New York, 1940

Historical-source questions

1 What do you understand by the term 'entente' in Source 1?
2 What is Erzberger's view on Germany's signing of the Treaty of Versailles?
3 What do you understand by the term 'reparations' in Source 2?
4 What, according to J. F. Dulles, was the economic impact of reparations?
5 What considerations should be made before accepting as fact the claims of Source 2?

Summary questions

1 Identify and explain any *two* differences between the aims of the Big Three.

2 Compare the importance of at least *three* ways in which Germany was affected by the Treaty of Versailles.

2 The League of Nations, 1919–29

Focus questions

◆ What were the initial weaknesses of the League?

◆ How successful was the League in solving disputes in the period 1919–29?

Significant dates

1919–20	Peace treaties' first 26 articles set up the League of Nations' Covenant
1920	*January* League of Nations meets, with headquarters at Geneva; prevents Yugoslavia from invading Albania
	September War between Turkey and Greece begins
1920–21	Åland dispute between Finland and Sweden; dispute between Poland and Lithuania over Vilna; Russo-Polish War
1921	*March* Dispute over Upper Silesia between Germany and Poland
1922	Austrian financial crisis
	December War between Turkey and Greece ends
1923	*January* Invasion of Ruhr by France and Belgium
	August Corfu crisis between Italy and Greece; failure of draft Treaty of Mutual Assistance; dispute over Memel
1924	*September* Geneva Protocol drawn up
1924–25	Dispute over the Mosul between Iraq and Turkey
1925	*October* Geneva Protocol rejected; war between Greece and Bulgaria
1926	*September* Germany allowed to join League of Nations

Sanctions are actions taken to put pressure on a country (or individual) to force them to do or to stop doing something; economic sanctions, for example, might include a trade ban or boycott, especially of vital products such as armaments or coal.

Overview

The need for a League of Nations had been raised by President Wilson before the peace negotiations began in 1919. His hope was that world peace could be maintained through collective security, with members of the League acting together to prevent one country from attacking another. This would be done by member countries applying economic or, if necessary, military **sanctions**. However, because the Republican Party (which favoured isolationism as regards European diplomatic developments) won the 1918 US mid-term elections, the USA never joined the League. In addition, Germany was not allowed to join and communist Russia was not invited to join. As a result, Britain and France were the League's main members. This made the League appear as a 'victors' club' to the defeated countries.

Britain and France, however, did not always agree; yet, for any action to be taken, decisions of the Council of the League had to be unanimous. Any member could raise problems, but the Assembly had little real power. As well as preventing conflicts, the League was intended to carry out humanitarian work, dealing with refugees, health and working conditions.

Where conflicts arose between relatively weak states, the League had some success in the years 1919–29. However, where the interests of a strong country clashed with those of a weaker one, the League was much less successful.

What were the initial weaknesses of the League?

The League was intended to be the first global peace-keeping organisation, designed to ensure that no conflict such as the First World War would occur again. However, the League of Nations was not just a response to the First World War. After the Napoleonic Wars, the more powerful nineteenth-century European states had held conferences to try to settle disputes between smaller states, but no machinery was set up for this to happen on a regular basis. At the start of the twentieth century a few countries (such as Russia) had begun to call for disarmament, while technical and scientific developments (such as the telegraph and shipping) had also created the need for greater international co-operation.

Wilson was convinced that the traditional secrecy of European diplomacy had been a major factor in causing the First World War (see Chapter 1). Consequently, his Fourteen Points included a call for the establishment of a 'general association of nations' to guarantee the 'political independence' and 'territorial integrity' of all nations. He believed the USA should use its new global economic and military power to create a 'new international order' which would 'make the world safe for democracy'. In part, however, his plans were also a result of concerns arising from the Bolshevik Revolution in Russia.

Covenant, organisation and membership

In January 1919, a commission was set up to draft a constitution for the League. Fourteen states were involved: the USA, Britain, France, Italy and Japan (the Big Five) had two delegates each and nine other minor states were represented by one delegate each. Though all agreed that the prevention of future wars should be the main aim of the League, there was disagreement on

Who were the Big Five?

A photograph of the first meeting of the Council of the League of Nations, August 1920.

how this should be achieved. However, by February 1919, it was agreed that a new international body should be established and its constitution (or Covenant) became the first 26 articles (points) in all of the peace treaties, signed in 1919–20.

The commission agreed that the League should be a permanent international conference, with a variety of functions. The four most important ones were:

- to guarantee the territory of states via collective security;
- to prevent conflicts;
- to settle disputes peacefully; and
- to act as an agency for disarmament.

The League's administrative system, based at Geneva in neutral Switzerland, can be seen in the diagram on page 15. The Assembly met once a year and was attended by all member countries, which had one vote each. Any member with a dispute was to bring the matter to the Assembly, instead of resorting to violence. The original founder members were made up of 32 Allied states and 13 neutral powers, all of which had their own national interests.

If the Assembly was unable to prevent a conflict breaking out, then a smaller body called the Council would take action to implement collective security, initially by imposing economic sanctions on the offending powers. This Council had four permanent members (Britain, France, Italy and Japan – the Big Four) as well as four smaller countries elected at intervals by the Assembly.

The routine administration and secretarial work was to be carried out by the Secretariat, which acted as the League's civil service.

A system of mandates (powers to supervise) was set up to administer the former territories of the defeated central powers; they were to be operated by League members (mostly Britain, the British **dominions**, France and Japan) on agreed conditions and had to submit annual reports to the League. The League also set up special commissions to administer special treaty areas such as Danzig and the Saar (see map on page 8).

Finally, in order to carry out its economic and social roles, the League established various bodies such as the International Labour Organisation (to establish fair and humane conditions of labour); a permanent Court of International Justice was also set up. Based in The Hague in the Netherlands, its function was to settle legal disputes between countries. Other bodies to end slavery, drugs and the arms trade, to prevent and control the spread of disease, and to maintain the freedom of trade and communications were also established.

Though the number of Council members elected by the Assembly increased to six in 1926 and nine in 1929, it was essentially seen as a European

What happened to the former colonies and provinces of the defeated central powers after 1918?

The **dominions** were the former British colonies of Australia, Canada, New Zealand and South Africa which, since 1910, had been given internal self-government. Britain, however, remained responsible for foreign policy and defence, and the British sovereign was still head of state.

What were the main bodies of the League of Nations?

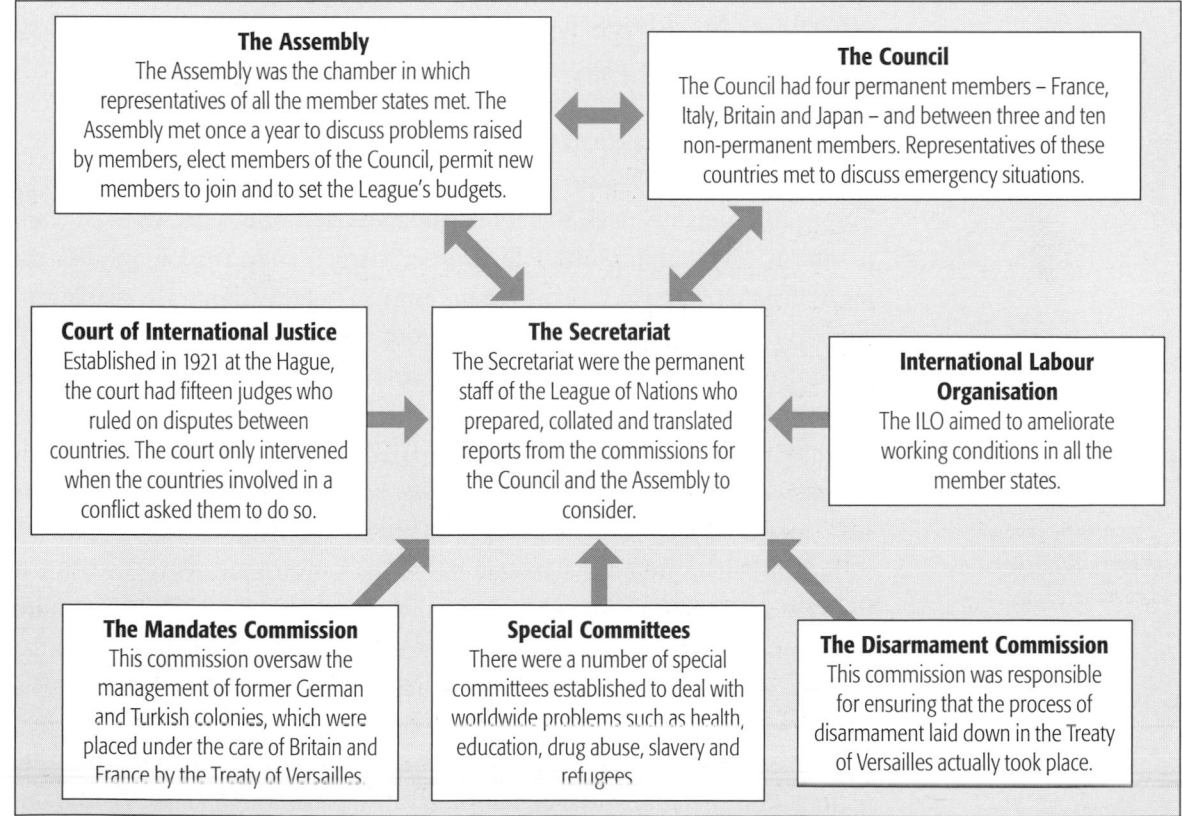

The Assembly
The Assembly was the chamber in which representatives of all the member states met. The Assembly met once a year to discuss problems raised by members, elect members of the Council, permit new members to join and to set the League's budgets.

The Council
The Council had four permanent members – France, Italy, Britain and Japan – and between three and ten non-permanent members. Representatives of these countries met to discuss emergency situations.

Court of International Justice
Established in 1921 at the Hague, the court had fifteen judges who ruled on disputes between countries. The court only intervened when the countries involved in a conflict asked them to do so.

The Secretariat
The Secretariat were the permanent staff of the League of Nations who prepared, collated and translated reports from the commissions for the Council and the Assembly to consider.

International Labour Organisation
The ILO aimed to ameliorate working conditions in all the member states.

The Mandates Commission
This commission oversaw the management of former German and Turkish colonies, which were placed under the care of Britain and France by the Treaty of Versailles.

Special Committees
There were a number of special committees established to deal with worldwide problems such as health, education, drug abuse, slavery and refugees.

The Disarmament Commission
This commission was responsible for ensuring that the process of disarmament laid down in the Treaty of Versailles actually took place.

The main bodies and functions of the League of Nations.

club. Similarly, despite Germany being allowed to join as one of the permanent council members in 1926, it was also seen as a 'victors' club'. This was because, until then, Germany and its former allies were not allowed to join the League. This early weakness was compounded by the fact that the fear of communism meant Soviet Russia was also not allowed to join (in fact, the Russian government condemned the League as a capitalist club dominated by imperialist powers). Especially significant was the refusal of the USA to join the League (see Chapter 1). Thus, from its beginning, three of the great world powers were not members of the League.

Which important states were not founder members of the League?

Problems in practice

Wilson believed that the main purpose of the League was to guarantee the 'territorial integrity and existing political independence of all members' against external aggression and that this could be achieved by the collective action of all member states (Article 10). In practice this meant peaceful revision of the new frontiers drawn by the 1919–20 treaties would be difficult. Several states (including Britain) tried unsuccessfully to get Wilson to drop this article, as they had no desire to become the 'policemen of the world'.

Furthermore, Article 8, which dealt with disarmament, proved extremely contentious. Nevertheless, its inclusion showed how many countries believed that the build up of armaments before 1914 had created insecurity in Europe and had thus been a major factor in the outbreak of the First World War. Article 8 was contentious partly because the 1920s were very unstable – the existence of communist Russia and the power vacuum in central and eastern Europe meant many states, such as Poland and Czechoslovakia, were reluctant to disarm. More importantly, France was extremely concerned about disarming as Britain refused to give the League any real military powers to enable it to enforce League decisions; in addition, both Britain and the USA refused to guarantee support for France in any future conflict in Europe. France's fears were also linked to the fact that Germany possessed greater industrial resources and had a population of 66 million compared to France's 39 million. Though Britain was willing to reduce its level of weapons, the non-membership of the USA meant disarmament talks often bypassed the League (see Chapter 3). Although Britain urged the League to set up a disarmament convention, a Preparatory Disarmament Commission was not established at Geneva until 1926. Serious differences emerged before it finally ended in 1930.

Why was France so strongly opposed to attempts by the League to bring about general disarmament in Europe?

The League's procedures to prevent aggression also had several practical weaknesses. First, while members of the Assembly could bring any issue that threatened a military conflict to the League and could discuss any 'international considerations' that endangered world peace, the Assembly could not insist on the discussion of any problem. More importantly, should a dispute arise, member states were to submit the dispute to the Council and avoid all use of force until three months after the League had made its report. Meanwhile, the League had six months to investigate (usually by setting up a committee of inquiry) and report to the Council. Any decision reached by the Council had to be unanimous and if no agreement was reached after another three months the members in dispute could resort to force. As the Council was dominated by Britain and France and as these two countries had quite different views about the role of the League, unanimous agreement often proved difficult to reach.

Second, if a member failed to comply with the time-limits of the League, economic sanctions (such as trade boycotts and the banning of financial relations with an aggressor) could be imposed. Many members were hesitant about becoming involved in trade boycotts in case non-member states (such as the USA) simply took over the trade. If economic sanctions failed, the Council could recommend military sanctions, using troops which member states agreed to provide. France, in particular, wished the League to have its own armed forces, so that it could undertake direct military intervention, but Britain, among others, opposed this. Thus, in practice, if a country refused to abide by the rules of the League or simply refused to join or left, there was little the League could do to prevent military aggression.

> Why was it often difficult, in practice, for the League's Council to take action?

Finally, another potential problem was that, at the same time that the League was established, a Conference of Ambassadors, comprising Britain, France, Italy and Japan, was set up to supervise the peace treaties. This body met at regular intervals and often resulted in clashes of responsibility with the League of Nations.

How successful was the League in solving disputes in the period 1919–29?

The League formally began its work in January 1920. Despite its various problems, examined in the previous section, the League was able to achieve several successes:

- In a dispute between Yugoslavia and Albania in 1920, the League was able to persuade Yugoslavia to withdraw its troops from Albania.
- In 1920 Britain brought a dispute between Finland and Sweden over the Åland Islands to the attention of the League. The islands were owned by Finland, although the majority of their population was Swedish. The League settled the dispute peacefully in Finland's favour. Finland was, however, ordered to keep the islands demilitarised.
- In 1921 the League successfully resolved a dispute between Poland and Germany over Upper Silesia. The Treaty of Versailles had decided that the

people of this territory should vote in a **plebiscite** to decide whether they wished to be part of Poland or Germany. The result was close and resulted in rioting, so the League decided to step in. The League finally decided to divide the area between Poland and Germany, though the drawing of the borders was extremely complicated and Germany received the greater share.

- In 1925 the League resolved a dispute between Iraq and Turkey over the important oil-rich area of the Mosul in Iraq's favour. (At this time, Iraq was a British mandate area.)
- The League was able to settle a conflict between Greece and Bulgaria in 1925. Greece was ordered to withdraw its troops, and to pay compensation to Bulgaria for the damage it had caused.

The League was also successful in administering the Saar and Danzig and was able to assist the Austrian and Hungarian economies in the 1920s by stabilising their currencies. In addition, the League Secretariat helped to revive the world economy by arranging world conferences on **tariffs** and trade agreements, while in the late 1920s it also examined proposals from France's **Aristide Briand** for closer European economic and political co-operation. Its humanitarian work with refugees and prisoners of war (especially after the Russo-Polish war, 1920–21, and the Greco-Turkish War, 1920–22) was also a significant achievement. The League also did much to deal with tropical diseases such as leprosy, yellow fever and malaria, and the spread of infection; the International Labour Organisation actively worked to improve workers' rights and working conditions across the world.

However, even during the period 1920–29, the League of Nation's success as a peace-keeping organisation was limited. Its failures included:

- When Lithuania (formerly part of Tsarist Russia) was recreated as one of the independent Baltic states in 1919, it wanted Vilna to be its new capital, as it had been in the past. Because Vilna had a large Polish population, Poland seized it in 1920. Lithuania asked the League to intervene, but Poland ignored the League's overtures; eventually the Conference of Ambassadors agreed to Polish control in 1922.
- Poland was not content with its eastern border (the Curzon Line) as decided by the peace treaties of 1919–20. In 1920, after minor armed clashes, Poland crossed the Curzon Line to seize White Russia and the Ukraine, thus starting the Russo-Polish War. The League was unable to prevent this war; in fact, Poland was backed by Britain and France which, along with the USA, Italy, Japan and several other countries, also intervened in the civil war in Russia, against the communist government.
- The 1920 Treaty of Sèvres had given most of Turkey's European lands to

Greece. Turkish nationalists overthrew their sultan for signing the treaty. Greece then invaded Turkey in order to overthrow the new nationalist government which was determined to overturn the Treaty of Sèvres. The Turkish army defeated the Greeks and then threatened the British forces occupying parts of Turkey. Further warfare was avoided by Britain agreeing that a new treaty should be signed (Lausanne, 1923). The League had been unable to either prevent or halt this war, in large part because Britain supported Greece, while France supported Turkey.

- The port of Memel (see map on page 8) and the land around it was mainly inhabited by Lithuanians and had been put under League administration by the Treaty of Versailles. The League was unable to prevent Lithuania from seizing Memel in 1923 and the Conference of Ambassadors' attempts to resolve the problem were also unsuccessful. Eventually Lithuania accepted the port becoming an 'international zone', on condition that it was given the surrounding area.

- The League was unable to prevent France and Belgium from invading the Ruhr in 1923, after Germany failed to pay its second reparations instalment (see also page 23). In fact, France did not even consult the League before it took action.

- Later in the year, the League also failed to stop another of its leading members – this time Italy – from invading the Greek island of Corfu after five Italians (sent by the Conference of Ambassadors to help survey a disputed border between Greece and Albania) were killed in an ambush (see also page 26). Greece asked the League for help, but Mussolini ignored the League as he argued this was a matter for the Conference of Ambassadors. The Conference of Ambassadors finally supported Italy and ordered Greece to pay 50 million lire in compensation; Italian troops then withdrew from Corfu. This incident clearly revealed serious weaknesses in the League's ability to resolve disputes involving more powerful nations. France, which saw Italy as an important potential ally against Germany, did not want to upset Italy (which had earlier co-operated with France over its invasion of the Ruhr) and so blocked any action by the League. The British government was reluctant to become involved as it had been advised that applying economic or naval sanctions against Italy would damage British interests. So both the unanimous-decision process and the use of sanctions (see pages 16–17) were shown to be wanting in practice when effective collective action was required.

- The League also had only limited success in effectively supervising the mandates given to Britain, France and Japan to administer the former German and Turkish territories. Similarly, the League was able to do very little to protect the rights of ethnic minorities in the new central and

Why did France not favour strong action against Italy over the Corfu Incident in 1923?

A British cartoon highlighting Italy's use of force in the Corfu Incident, 1923. The smiling figure in the middle is Mussolini.

What was the intention behind both the draft Treaty of Mutual Assistance (1923) and the Geneva Protocol (1924)?

Born in 1866, **Ramsay MacDonald** was a Labour politician who opposed British policy in the First World War. He supported the League of Nations and, in the December 1923 election campaign, said Labour's foreign policy would be based on the League's Covenant. After the fall of a minority Conservative government in January 1924, he became Britain's first Labour prime minister. He also acted as foreign secretary and was nicknamed 'Mac the peacemaker'.

eastern European states. More importantly, attempts to strengthen the League's ability to guarantee the terms of the 1919–20 peace treaties also failed. In 1923, a draft Treaty of Mutual Assistance, suggested by France to give the League powers to take rapid military action in the event of unprovoked aggression, was blocked by Britain. France tried again in 1924 with the Geneva Protocol, which aimed to commit all members to undertake collective military action. This was supported by the new Labour prime minister of Britain, **Ramsay MacDonald**, but he fell from power later in 1924. In March 1925, Austen Chamberlain, on behalf of the new Conservative government, blocked this scheme as well. This effectively left the League unable to protect the territorial integrity of nations.

Despite these problems and failures, however, the League did help to promote a greater level of international co-operation than had existed before 1914. These aspects will be examined in Chapter 3.

Historical sources

1 Marcel Cachin, a French politician, speaking in 1920 about the USA's decision not to join the League of Nations

The defeat suffered by Wilsonism in the United States strikes at the very existence of the League of Nations. America's place will remain empty at Geneva, and the two countries that dominate, France and Great Britain, are divided on almost every one of the topics to be discussed.

T. McAleavy, *Modern world history*, Cambridge, 1996, p. 32

2 Criticisms of the French made by George Saunders, a British official, in 1919

At the back of all this is the French scheme to suck Germany and everybody else dry and to establish French military and political control of the League of Nations. The French see the League of Nations as an organisation for the restoration of France to a supreme position in Europe and her maintenance in that position.

T. McAleavy, *Modern world history*, Cambridge, 1996, p. 32

Historical-source questions

1 What does the term 'Wilsonism' in Source 1 refer to?

2 What 'defeat' is Source 1 referring to?

3 Show how Sources 1 and 2 present a similar view of the relationship between Britain and France in the years 1919–20.

4 In what ways did the non-membership of the USA weaken the League of Nations?

Summary questions

1 Identify and explain the importance of *two* successful resolutions of international disputes by the League of Nations in the years 1920–29.

2 Compare the importance of *three* factors which explain the weaknesses of the League of Nations.

3 International diplomacy, 1919–29

Focus questions

◆ What were the main diplomatic developments in the period 1919–29?

◆ What problems remained unresolved?

Significant dates

1919 *June* Conference of Ambassadors set up

1921–22 Washington Naval Conference

1922 *February* Washington Naval Treaty
March Genoa Conference on Disarmament
April Treaty of Rapallo

1923 *August* Corfu Incident

1924 *January* Alliance between France and Czechoslovakia
August Dawes Plan

1925 *October* Locarno Treaty

1928 *August* Kellogg–Briand Pact (Pact of Paris)

1929 *June* Young Plan

Overview

Despite the uneven performance of the League of Nations in preventing or solving conflicts in the years 1919–29, it did help to promote greater international discussion and diplomacy. Much work was done independently of the League by other international organisations or conferences. In particular, the Allied Conference of Ambassadors frequently settled disputes or negotiated agreements during this period. Thanks to their combined efforts, the 1920s can be seen as a time of improving international relations, marked by several important agreements, such as the 1922 Washington Naval Treaty (to limit the navies of the great powers) and the Dawes and Young Plans (to help Germany with its reparations payments and to rebuild its economy). Other diplomatic attempts to guarantee the peace of Europe (such as the Locarno Treaty and the Kellogg–Briand Pact) were less successful.

What were the main diplomatic developments in the period 1919–29?

For most of this period, direct negotiations between states and diplomacy were more significant than the work of the League of Nations. In particular, much was done by the Conference of Ambassadors.

This body was set up to resolve any problems arising from the peace treaties of 1919–20. It consisted of Britain, France, Italy and Japan (the Big Four) and met in Paris throughout the 1920s. It frequently made decisions independently of the League. This was largely because of the League's weaknesses (see Chapter 2). The League was soon further undermined in the 1920s when it became clear that both Italy and Japan were determined to follow expansionist policies in defiance of the League.

As the Conference was a smaller body, it was able to focus on specific problems and was often able to reach limited practical agreements on issues which the League found difficult to resolve. As well as the Conference of Ambassadors, the normal direct diplomacy between countries also resulted in some practical agreements during the 1920s, as outlined below.

What was the main purpose of the Conference of Ambassadors?

How did the existence of the Conference of Ambassadors affect the work of the League?

The Washington Naval Treaty, 1922

This treaty was largely the result of the initiative by the USA, which was concerned about growing tensions with Japan in the Pacific Ocean. In theory, this was the sort of issue the League was designed to resolve but, as the USA had not joined the League, direct diplomacy was the only way to approach the situation. In 1921 and 1922, conferences took place in Washington between the USA, Britain and Japan along with some other nations. The main points of the resulting treaty, signed in February 1922, allowed the USA and Britain to have navies of equal size, while Japan's was to be limited in comparison, on the basis of a 5:5:3 ratio. Later, both France and Italy also agreed to limit their navies – again, the League was not involved in this decision.

The Dawes Plan, 1924

When Germany failed to make its second reparations payment in December 1922, France and Belgium invaded the Ruhr in January 1923 (see page 19). The German government responded by calling for passive resistance and Ruhr workers responded to this call. Then, with the economy in tatters, they began to print extra money. This contributed to hyperinflation which caused severe economic and political problems in Germany. In particular, the resultant economic distress led many middle-class Germans to blame the **Weimar Republic** for their problems and greatly contributed to the growth of nationalist and far-right political movements. It also began to have negative effects on the French economy.

The **Weimar Republic** was the name given to the new German system of government established in 1919, after the abdication of the kaiser. The name 'Weimar' was used because Germany's new democratic constitution was drawn up and approved in the small German town of Weimar. Weimar Germany lasted until 1933, when Hitler set up the Nazi dictatorship.

How did the Dawes Plan of 1924 improve both the diplomatic and economic situation in Europe?

The USA, concerned about the impact of this situation on its international trade and global economic power, then became involved. A US banker, Charles Dawes, drew up a plan which froze German reparations payments for two years, scaled down the level of Germany's repayments and made huge loans available to German industry. These loans enabled Germany to resume its reparations payments to France and Britain and it was this, not the League of Nations, which persuaded France to withdraw its troops. From 1924 to 1929, the USA loaned Germany about $2 billion, with German reparations payments for the same period totalling about $1 billion.

The Locarno Treaty, 1925

The Dawes Plan resulted in improved diplomatic relations between France and Germany, although this was also due to the policies and work of Briand of France and **Gustav Stresemann** of Germany, rather than the League. In 1925, Stresemann, in an attempt to pacify French fears, contacted Britain and France and offered to guarantee Germany's acceptance of its western frontiers, as established by the Treaty of Versailles. In September 1925, the Locarno Conference took place, at which Germany, France and Belgium promised not to use force to change their borders with each other. Germany also promised to accept the demilitarisation of the Rhineland. Britain and Italy then agreed to act as guarantors of this pact which, however, gave no guarantees concerning German acceptance of its eastern frontiers. Though it had been negotiated outside the League, the Locarno Treaty played a big part in Germany being allowed to join the League in September 1926.

What was the significant omission from the terms of the Locarno Treaty of 1925?

Gustav Stresemann was born in 1878. He acted first as chancellor (prime minister) and then as foreign minister of Germany from 1923 to 1929. As a result, he became the most significant German statesman of the Weimar Republic. He worked closely with France's Aristide Briand to improve relations between Germany and the Allies in this period. Although a conciliator, he was also a firm nationalist who believed that, because of Germany's military weakness, it was necessary

A photograph of the signing of the Locarno Treaty, 1925. Stresemann is signing on behalf of Germany.

The Kellogg–Briand Pact, 1928

In 1926, following the easing of tensions after Germany's admission to the League, the USA and France (represented by Kellogg, the US secretary of state, and Briand respectively) agreed to renounce the use of force for national objectives. They invited other countries to sign the agreement and, in 1928, 15 countries, including Britain and Germany, signed the Kellogg–Briand Pact. Attempts to have this agreement incorporated into the League of Nations Covenant failed. Another of the pact's weaknesses was that it made no provision for enforcing its objectives.

The Young Plan, 1929

The Dawes Plan was supposed to have solved the question of German reparations but, although Germany had promised to keep to the revised payments schedule, this did not happen. Stresemann continued to press for the renegotiation of reparations, creating further tensions.

The Young Plan, devised by the USA and not by the League, was agreed in 1929. Its terms were that further large US loans would be made to Germany and a considerably reduced reparations scheme of payments was to be spread over the next 50 years. Germany accepted this; in return the Allies agreed to end their occupation of the Rhineland five years earlier than set down by the Treaty of Versailles.

After the **Wall Street Crash** of October 1929 and the start of the **Great Depression**, this revised scheme of reparations was ignored by later German governments.

What problems remained unresolved?

Although direct diplomacy was frequently more successful than attempts by the League to resolve disputes, three main underlying problems emerged during the 1920s. These were:

- resolving armed conflicts involving at least one strong power;
- the attempt to achieve disarmament; and
- the security of the borders between Germany and the successor states in central and eastern Europe (see page 6).

Armed conflicts

Two major incidents of armed force occurred in 1923; one involved France and the other Italy. Both these countries were important members of the League and the Conference of Ambassadors. Both cases were resolved by direct diplomacy (and not by the League) and they revealed the League's serious underlying problems and growing irrelevance, which became more apparent in the Depression-hit Europe of the 1930s.

to co-operate with the Allies in order to revise the Treaty of Versailles. His long-term aims were to get all Allied troops removed from Germany; to readjust Germany's eastern borders with Czechoslovakia and Poland; to end reparations completely; to make Austria part of a 'Greater Germany'; and even to get back Alsace-Lorraine and Eupen-Malmédy. However, Stresemann did not plan to achieve these objectives by force.

Wall Street was, and still is, the location of the US Stock Exchange. Because of over-speculation and then panic, share prices plummeted dramatically in October 1929. The **Wall Street Crash** caused a severe economic depression in the USA, which ended its loans to other countries and caused demands for repayment of those already made. Germany was particularly badly affected.

The **Great Depression** refers to the global economic distress characterised by high unemployment, inflation, industrial decline in production and trade, and poverty which hit most capitalist countries in the 1930s, following the Wall Street Crash of 1929. Communist Russia was unaffected and actually experienced tremendous economic growth (see Chapter 7).

The invasion of the Ruhr

Disputes between France and Germany over the question of German reparations and disarmament led to 23 summit meetings between Germany, Britain, France, Italy and Belgium between January 1920 and December 1922. In March 1922, Britain called an international conference to be held in Genoa in an attempt to find a solution to these problems (see page 27). Germany was present at the conference but, because it was not a member of the League, the conference was held without League involvement. Britain tried to persuade France to soften the provisions on reparations, but France was only prepared to make minor concessions, and then only on condition that Britain agreed to Allied occupation of German territory to obtain compliance should Germany default. (In 1920 and 1921, Britain had reluctantly agreed to support French occupation of some towns in the Ruhr.) This conference was also a failure and the problems continued until, in January 1923, France and Belgium invaded the Ruhr, the most important industrial area of Germany, in order to seize reparations in kind.

France's invasion was also intended to encourage the possibility of a Rhineland separatist movement and the eventual creation of a state totally independent of Germany. This failed, but France's actions worried Britain and led to a further widening of the gap between the polices of these two countries.

How did the invasion of the Ruhr in 1923 affect relations between Britain and France?

The Corfu Incident, 1923

As we saw on page 19, the League had been unable to deal with this issue and both Britain and France had agreed it should be dealt with by the Conference of Ambassadors instead, as insisted on by **Mussolini**. As a result of Britain and France's differing interests, Mussolini was able to pressurise the Conference of Ambassadors into devising a solution along the lines he desired.

Born in 1883, Benito **Mussolini** quickly abandoned his earlier socialist polices in the First World War. He moved to a far-right ultra-nationalistic position which was violently opposed to socialism and communism. In 1919–21, he formed Europe's first Fascist Party and, after becoming prime minister in 1922, turned Italy into a Fascist dictatorship. He pursued an aggressive and expansionist foreign policy, invading Abyssinia in 1935 and Albania in 1939. In the 1930s, he also moved closer to Nazi Germany, finally becoming an ally. After the Allied invasion of Italy, he was captured by communist partisans in 1945 and executed.

Disarmament

Disarmament was one of the League's major objectives and it was closely linked to the problems that arose from enforcing the terms of the peace treaties. At the time of the peace negotiations in 1919, France's concerns about future German attacks led it to push for the transformation of the Rhineland into a separate state. Britain and the USA had overcome this by supporting the demilitarisation of the Rhineland and by offering guaranteed military support, under League supervision, if France suffered unprovoked aggression. However, Britain already doubted US ratification, so the draft Treaty of Versailles contained an escape clause, cancelling guarantees should the USA not ratify. In the event, the US Senate rejected the treaty, so there was no secure military support for France in the event of future attacks from Germany. As a result, France was reluctant to consider any significant disarmament.

Another unsuccessful attempt to address France's security fears was made in March 1925 following the failure of the draft Treaty of Mutual Assistance in 1924 and the Geneva Protocol in 1925 (see page 20) – both would have given the League military teeth with which to impose observance of the peace treaties, which France saw as an acceptable alternative to a military commitment from Britain. The Preparatory Disarmament Commission, set up by the League in 1926, failed to produce an agreed agenda for discussion until 1931.

These two attempts, emanating from League committees on disarmament, were blocked by Britain which, more concerned about its empire, did not see Germany as a threat to European peace and was therefore more worried about France's refusal to consider disarmament, conciliation and treaty revision in general. The British foreign secretary, **Austen Chamberlain**, suggested to his cabinet that Britain should offer a military alliance with France, but this was rejected.

Differing aims of Britain and France

As the 1920s progressed, it became increasingly clear that Britain and France had very different aims and policies. Britain, like France, was facing economic competition from a strengthened USA and was also having to deal with rising nationalism in its empire, especially in the key colonies of Egypt and India. The dominions were also beginning to demand greater independence. For these reasons, Britain wanted political and economic stability in Europe, so that its financial and military resources could be devoted to protecting its empire.

Successive British governments believed the best way of ensuring German acceptance of the main terms of the Treaty of Versailles was to agree to the revision of its less important terms. In the absence of any firm Anglo-American military commitment, France saw even the slightest changes as increasing Germany's strength.

Genoa and Rapallo, 1922

In March 1922, some success regarding naval disarmament was achieved outside Europe, in the Washington Naval Treaty of 1922 (see page 23). From 1920 to 1925, France refused to consider disarmament unless it received guaranteed military support from Britain, as had been promised in 1919 by the USA and Britain. A draft treaty, agreed by Lloyd George and Briand at Cannes in January 1922, failed when Britain refused to make clear and firm commitments concerning military assistance. As we have seen, the 1922 Genoa Conference also ended in failure.

At the same time, Germany and Russia met and signed the Treaty of Rapallo which, besides establishing friendly relations between these two

Austen Chamberlain, born in 1863, was the half-brother of Neville Chamberlain. A British Conservative politician, he held various government posts, before acting as foreign secretary from 1924 to 1929. Though opposed to the Geneva Protocol of 1924, he was one of the main architects of the Locarno Treaty. Along with the American Charles Dawes he received the Nobel Peace Prize for his efforts. Later, in 1931, he acted as first lord of the admiralty.

Why did the diplomatic aims of Britain and France differ in the 1920s?

countries, had secret clauses on military co-operation. As a result Germany was able to get hold of most of the weapons it was banned from having by the Treaty of Versailles. Stresemann also concluded the Treaty of Berlin with Soviet Russia in 1926 which, like the Treaty of Rapallo, allowed Germany to develop banned weapons and to rearm. This undermined the whole question of disarmament as well as, once again, the League and the peace terms. One consequence of this treaty was to increase British concerns about stability in Europe and thereby strengthen its willingness to make concessions to Germany. This made France even more determined to keep Germany weak and to reject calls for disarmament.

What was the significance of the 1922 Treaty of Rapallo between Germany and Russia?

Even after Locarno in 1925, France remained concerned about its security and therefore opposed any serious disarmament. These fears multiplied in the period 1926–29 and during the Depression, when German statesmen – Stresemann included – repeatedly indicated their desire to revise many other aspects of the Treaty of Versailles.

The assessment of historians of France's security concerns has altered in recent years, with many now viewing them as quite valid. Not only was France not given any real help to restore its war-devastated provinces, but the USA pressed France hard over repayment of its war debts in the early years after the war when its economy was still weak. In addition, France was given no real help in pressing Germany for reparations due to it, while its frequent proposals for military and economic co-operation to strengthen the treaties were always rejected by Britain and the USA.

France's continuing concerns about security and the peace settlements were not really answered by the Treaty of Locarno in 1925, which dealt only with Germany's western frontiers. Significantly, there was no similar agreement about its borders with the successor states.

The successor states

As well as having a disruptive effect on trade, the collapse of the Habsburg and Ottoman empires in central and eastern Europe led to fragmentation, disorder and a political vacuum in this area. This situation was further complicated by the political threat posed by the existence of communist Russia. With the League of Nations denied real military capability and the refusal of Britain and the USA to give France the military guarantees it felt it needed, French governments turned more and more to direct diplomacy and military pacts with countries on Germany's eastern borders.

Czechoslovakia and Poland, in particular, owed their existence to the defeat of Germany and the break-up of the Austro-Hungarian and Russian empires and contained large minorities of former German or Austrian citizens. These states were not in favour of any increase in Germany's military or even economic strength and, like France, did not favour revisions of the peace treaties. As early as 1921, Czechoslovakia, Romania and Yugoslavia had formed the 'Little **Entente**' (this was also in response to growing hostility from Hungary).

Unlike France, Britain was in favour of revisions in the east, especially as Britain felt a stronger Germany would be more able to resist the spread of communism and revolutions than the small, weak and often divided states of eastern Europe. However, with the loss of Russia as an ally, France felt that the successor states' determination to uphold the borders established in 1919–20 would provide some sort of check on Germany. Consequently, a series of treaties of mutual assistance were signed by France with Poland in 1921, Czechoslovakia in 1924, Romania in 1926 and Yugoslavia in 1927.

Entente is French for 'understanding' or 'agreement' and is applied to diplomatic agreements between states.

How did France view the newly created successor states of central and eastern Europe?

Conclusion

According to some historians, the Locarno agreements and general diplomacy in the years 1925–29 failed to resolve the main sources of bitterness and rivalry between the major powers – even after 1925, there was still no agreement about what Germany's power, position and role in Europe should be.

This was, in part, a reflection of the fact that in many ways the economies of Britain and especially France were more damaged by the First World War than Germany's, which had not been invaded (Britain had had to sell approximately 25 per cent of its foreign investments, while for France the figure was 50 per cent). Consequently, there was a partial return to the old pre-war diplomacy aimed to create and maintain a balance of power. This even took place in the forum of the League of Nations, where individual states attempted to pursue and defend their own national interests. However, though the diplomacy of the 1920s did not solve all the problems of post-war Europe, it had helped to reduce the risk of war. It took the impact of the Depression and the rise of Hitler and the Nazis to plunge Europe into a second world war.

Historical sources

1 Commentary from the British historian J. Joll in 1983

The Locarno agreements gave new hope that the League of Nations might assume the role which Wilson had expected of it and that, in spite of the bitterness of the post-war years, a new international order in Europe might be attainable . . . If one tries to look at the European scene between 1925 and 1929 as it appeared at the time, and without the knowledge of what came after, there seemed to be some grounds for hope.

B. Walsh, *Modern world history*, London, 1996, p. 196

2 Gustav Stresemann, the German foreign minister, commenting on his motives in a confidential letter just before the Locarno Conference in September 1925

In my view the foreign policy of Germany has for the short-term future three main objectives: First, a solution to the Rhine question favourable to Germany, and peace, without which Germany will not be able to regain its strength. Second, protection for the ten to twelve million Germans living under the foreign yoke. Third, the alteration of our eastern frontiers, so that we recover Danzig and the Polish Corridor. In the more distant future the reuniting of Austria with Germany.

T. McAleavy, *Modern world history*, Cambridge, 1996, p. 41

Historical-source questions

1   What was the 'Rhine question' referred to in Source 2?
2   To what extent do the comments by Stresemann (Source 2) conflict with the more positive image of the Locarno Treaty given by Joll (Source 1)?
3   In what way does Source 2 seem to offer justification for the optimism displayed in Source 1?

Summary questions

1   Identify and explain *two* reasons for the reduction of tension in Europe in the period 1920–29.

2   Compare the importance of *three* factors which contributed to diplomatic instability in Europe during the 1920s.

4 The decline of international co-operation, 1929–32

Focus questions

◆ How significant was the Depression in the decline of co-operation?

◆ How successful was the League in the years 1929–32?

Significant dates

1929   *October* Death of Stresemann; Wall Street Crash

1931   *September* Japanese invasion of Manchuria
December Lytton Commission; Conference of Ambassadors dissolved; Britain blocks League attempt to ban bombing

1932   War between Bolivia and Paraguay
February League of Nations' disarmament conference
November Roosevelt wins US presidential elections; border dispute between Colombia and Peru

Overview

The hopes for continued European peace raised by the Kellogg–Briand Pact of 1928 and the Young Plan of 1929 were soon shattered by the impact of the Depression. Starting with the collapse of the US economy in October 1929, the Depression soon affected most countries to varying degrees. Several countries – especially Japan and Italy – began to pursue aggressive foreign policies as a way of solving their economic problems. Other countries tended to ignore foreign developments as they concentrated on dealing with their own internal economic situation. As a result, the League of Nations became increasingly ineffective, proving unable to exert any meaningful pressure on aggressive countries.

How significant was the Depression in the decline of co-operation?

The collapse of the US stock market, which began with the Wall Street Crash on 24 October 1929 (see page 25), not only caused economic chaos in the

A photograph, taken in 1930, of German children scavenging for food during the economic crisis provoked by the Wall Street Crash of 1929.

How did the Great Depression affect international diplomacy in the 1930s?

Protectionism refers to the measures taken by governments to help protect their country's manufacturers from competition from goods imported from other countries. Customs duties, or tariffs, are usually imposed to make foreign goods more expensive than home-produced ones. When other countries take similar measures in retaliation, exports and world trade are affected.

The *Mittelstand* refers to the middle classes of Germany; it includes the 'old' middle class such as small retailers, self-employed craftsmen, peasant farmers, pensioners, etc. and the 'new' middle class such as white-collar, non-manual employees. These tended to compare the Weimar Republic unfavourably with the German imperial period and increasingly turned to the Nazis after the Depression set in.

USA, it also began an economic crisis that affected the whole world in what became known as the (Great) Depression. Its impact on international diplomacy as well as on countries' internal politics was tremendous. In general, most countries tended to ignore diplomatic developments as they tried to deal with the economic effects of the Depression. Many of the countries affected soon moved away from free trade towards **protectionism** and foreign affairs increasingly took second place to domestic political and economic concerns.

Although the international trade and currency problems stemming from the First World War appeared to have been resolved by the end of the 1920s, underlying weaknesses remained because much of the world's economic activities had become dangerously dependent on the globally dominant US economy.

In the USA national income dropped by almost 50 per cent in the years 1929–32. At the same time, US foreign policy (at least regarding Europe) became even more isolationist than it had been before 1929. Elsewhere, the impact of the Depression was even greater, especially in Germany, which had been rebuilt in large part by US loans arranged by the Dawes Plan and the Young Plan. During 1924–29, Germany had received £9,000 million in loans and had only paid out £5,000 million in reparations. When the loans ended, the German economy collapsed: by 1932, Germany's industrial production had dropped by 60 per cent and unemployment (which had been 1.4 million in 1928) had soared to 12 million (an unemployment rate of 33 per cent). German farmers, like their American counterparts, were also badly hit – by 1932, their income had declined by 50 per cent. Germany's middle classes – the *Mittelstand* – felt particularly affected by the Depression. Politically, the impact of the Depression was one of the main factors contributing to the rise of the Nazis. In 1928, they had only 12 seats in the **Reichstag**; this had risen to 107 by September 1930 (making them the second largest party) and, though their rise was checked slightly in the November 1932 elections, by January 1933 Hitler had been appointed chancellor.

The **Reichstag** was the German parliament.

In 1931, Chancellor Brüning attempted to distract attention from the domestic impact of the Depression by focusing on foreign affairs – he proposed the idea of economic *Anschluss* with Austria. This was blocked by the International Court of Justice and by the French. Then, in 1932, Brüning unilaterally stopped making all reparations payments. This was accepted by Britain and France at the International Conference of Lausanne later in 1932, in view of the impact of the Depression. In fact, Germany never made any more reparations repayments. (A request from Britain and France that they should scale down their war debts to the USA was refused.) A more nationalist government, headed by von Papen, increased tariffs on British goods by 300 per cent and demanded the return of Germany's former colonies and the Saar in 1932.

What foreign policy initiatives were attempted by Chancellors Brüning and von Papen of Germany in the years 1931–32?

Britain was also badly hit by the Depression – iron and steel production (important indicators of economic strength) dropped by 50 per cent and the value of the pound was significantly reduced. In 1932, the Ottawa Agreements established protectionism for the British dominions and empire. Successive British governments dealt with the crisis by cutting government spending – including spending on defence. In 1932, Neville Chamberlain, as chancellor of the exchequer, drew up the lowest arms estimates for the entire period 1919–39. In the main, British governments after 1929 were more concerned about protecting the British empire (Japan's growth was seen as a serious threat) than with risking involvement in any conflict in Europe.

France too was badly hit – though the effects of the Depression were not felt as early as in Britain, as France was less dependent on international trade. Italy presented a similar picture.

Another country hit badly early on by the worldwide Depression was Japan. Although Japan's industry had been modernising and expanding, it was not self-sufficient in coal, iron, oil, tin or rubber. So Japan, like the USA and European powers before it, was increasingly seeking an empire to supply its industries with raw materials. By 1931, the Depression resulted in 50 per cent of Japan's factories closing down, and hit Japan's rice farmers badly. Japan's main export, silk, had declined sharply, with prices less than a third of what they had been in 1925. Given Japan's geographical position, Asia seemed the natural area into which it could expand. However, this brought Japan into potential conflict with European nations. Britain, France and the Netherlands already had Asian colonies and the USA was also trying to expand its influence in the Pacific.

The *zaibatsu* were the large industrial companies in Japan in the interwar period. Many had close links to those army officers who saw military conquest as a way of solving the problems caused by the Depression.

What potential issues of conflict existed between Japan and countries such as the USA, Britain and France before 1931?

The **Guomindang** was the Chinese nationalist party, set up by Sun Yatsen, which overthrew the last Manchu emperor in the 1911 revolution. Sun wanted to unite China under one government, which would be free of warlords and foreign rule. In 1922, following the refusal of western European powers to give help, he turned to Soviet Russia. In addition, he made an alliance with the Chinese Communist Party, newly founded in 1921. When Sun died in 1925 the party was taken over by Jiang Jieshi, who moved it rapidly to the right, and there was soon conflict with the Chinese Communist Party.

Japan had been on the Allied side in the First World War, but had been disappointed with its gains from the 1919–20 peace settlements. Once the Depression began and the slump became established, Japanese goods were hit by tariffs and Japanese emigration was restricted by racist immigration laws. In particular, Japan was increasingly denied full access to markets and sources of raw materials. These developments led Japanese nationalists to press for Japanese conquests and expansion.

The Japanese army (already a powerful force in Japan by the late 1920s) was linked to the *zaibatsu* and they both pressed for a more aggressive foreign policy. The army increasingly dominated or ignored the civilian governments of Japan, especially after 1930 when the serious drop in exports caused by the Depression led to a political crisis. This, in turn, led to the military factions exercising greater influence. Earlier attempts at parliamentary democracy collapsed and extreme nationalists resorted to the assassination of liberal political leaders.

How successful was the League in the years 1929–32?

Although the League of Nations continued to have occasional successes in this period, the impact of the Depression on international diplomacy resulted in League weaknesses becoming increasingly apparent. Its main success, significantly, was not in Europe but in Latin America where, in 1932, it was able to prevent a border dispute between Colombia and Peru from erupting into war. On the whole, however, the years 1929–32 were largely years of failure.

The Manchurian Crisis, 1931–32

Technically, Manchuria (see map on page 205) was part of China but, because of the political situation in China, where civil war had broken out between the **Guomindang** and the Chinese Communist Party, there was little stability there. This harmed Japanese trade and economic interests in Manchuria, which had allowed the Japanese to have a small military force to protect their interests. By 1927, Japan was in control of most of Manchuria's mines, factories and ports; to protect these, they had a large army stationed in the Kwantung area of southern Manchuria. At this time, Manchuria was ruled by an ineffective Chinese warlord (military ruler), but Japan feared the new nationalist government of China, set up by Jiang Jieshi in 1928, might soon provide effective control over Manchuria.

On 18 September 1931, officers of the Japanese Kwantung army in Manchuria (allied to economic interests which had long wanted to control Manchuria) staged the Mukden (Shenyang) Incident in order to justify sending in a Japanese army of occupation. The Japanese officers claimed that

A British cartoon about the invasion of Manchuria, depicting Japan as a criminal defying the judges of the League of Nations and the Lytton Report.

Chinese soldiers had tried to blow up the Japanese-owned South Manchurian Railway near the town of Mukden or Shenyang (the latter is the correct Chinese name), when it was they themselves who had arranged the incident.

Though the civilian government of Japan tried to get the military to withdraw, the army refused and continued their invasion. Eventually, in February 1932, Manchuria was renamed Manzhouguo (Manchukuo), with Puyi, the last **Manchu** emperor of China, as a nominal figurehead of a puppet government.

Both China and Japan were League members and the Japanese invasion was clearly in breach of the League's collective security system. The invasion of Manchuria also violated the Washington Naval Treaty of 1922, in which Japan had promised not to attack China. China's **Jiang Jieshi** quickly appealed to the League's Council to stop this Japanese aggression.

The League set up the **Lytton Commission** (on Japan's suggestion) to investigate the situation and collect facts. This committee did not submit its report until October 1932 – by then, Japan had been in complete control of Manchuria for almost a year. Its report criticised both China and Japan and did not recommend either economic or military sanctions. The League accepted the report, agreeing the Japanese claims were valid, but indicated that Japan was wrong to have used force and should therefore withdraw its troops. As a result, in 1933, Japan left the League. The Manchurian Crisis clearly showed how ineffective collective security was.

The **Manchu** was the last imperial dynasty to rule China. It was overthrown by the 1911 Double Tenth Revolution which began on 10 October 1911. The last emperor, Puyi, was a young boy, so his uncle ruled as regent. He and his uncle finally abdicated in February 1912.

Born in 1887, **Jiang Jieshi** was an early member of the Guomindang (Nationalist) Party and was Sun's brother-in-law. After he seized control in 1925, following Sun's death, he began the March to the North campaign in 1926 to re-establish central control over all China. By 1927, after discussions with foreign businesses, he turned on his communist allies and a civil war between nationalists and communists began and continued, on and off, until 1949, when the communists finally won. Jiang then fled to Taiwan (Formosa) where he set up an anti-communist government, with US backing. He died in 1975.

The **Lytton Commission** was the commission of inquiry sent by the League of Nations in December 1931 to investigate the facts of the Japanese invasion of Manchuria. It was headed by Lord Lytton of Britain.

What action did the League take over Japan's invasion of Manchuria?

Reasons for the League's ineffectiveness

According to some later historians, the reason for the League's inability to solve the Manchurian Crisis was because of its timing – it happened in 1931–32, when the Depression was at its peak. At this time, European countries and the USA were more concerned with the problems created by the Depression. The League might have been more effective if both the USA and the **Soviet Union** had been members, especially as both had interests in Asia. (It is important to note that Germany's membership of the League, if anything, tended to complicate the League's decision-making, simply because yet another state was involved in the decision-making process.) The USA, which had significant trade with Japan, was led by **Hoover** and the Republicans, who were reluctant to get involved in the conflict between China and Japan (despite their own growing disagreements with Japan) and refused to consider the idea of economic sanctions (though they did state the USA would not accept any territorial changes resulting from military aggression). As a result, especially given the widespread impact of the Depression, most League members feared any trade ban imposed on Japan would result in losing that trade to the USA.

The USSR viewed Japan's aggression as a threat to its Asian territories and was willing to act against Japan, even though the country was in turmoil resulting from Stalin's forced collectivisation of agriculture (see Chapter 7). However, no western European state was prepared to co-operate with the communist regime in any military action and the Soviet Union was not prepared to risk any unilateral intervention.

As regards the important League members, there were clear divisions between them. Neither Italy nor Germany really objected to the Japanese invasion. In fact, Mussolini was so encouraged by the lack of effective League action during the Manchurian Crisis that, from 1932, he began detailed planning of the conquest of Abyssinia. Germany, despite significant investments in China, was waiting to see what the League would do in response to Japan's use of force.

Britain and France remained divided. Britain did not want to risk a naval conflict as, under the Washington Naval Treaty, Japan had naval superiority in the Far East and military advisers informed the British government that such a conflict might be lost, endangering important imperial territories, such as India, Singapore and Hong Kong. Britain also had important trade links with Japan so that, despite concern over Japan's long-term plans, its immediate fear was of losing that trade to the USA. However, the government, under MacDonald, did ban the sale of arms to both sides but, when it became clear that the boycott was hitting China harder than Japan, it was ended.

France, which had its own colonies in **Indochina** (where, in 1931, Ho Chi Minh began an armed communist–nationalist insurrection for independence; see Chapter 18), disapproved of Japan's actions. At this stage, however, France

Communist Russia refers to the country in the period 1917–24; thereafter it became known as the **Soviet Union** or the USSR.

Born in 1874, Herbert **Hoover** was a Republican. He began his working life as a mining engineer and ended it as a multi-millionaire businessman, able to retire at 40. He was president from 1929 to 1933 and was thus in power when the Wall Street Crash and Depression took place. As regards foreign affairs, Hoover (like many Republicans) tended to be an isolationist – although this applied more to European diplomacy than to developments in Central and Latin America or in the Pacific; he did involve the USA in various economic and disarmament conferences.

Indochina refers to the French colonies of Vietnam, Laos and Cambodia which were formed into a union in the years 1887–93. Other countries in this area of south-east Asia include Burma and Thailand.

was more concerned about the possible threat from Germany (in 1930, the French had begun to build fortifications known as the **Maginot Line**) and so wished to avoid any conflict with Japan. Although France publicly condemned the Japanese aggression, it sent a secret note to Japan stating that it sympathised with the 'difficulties' Japan was in.

Although the crisis over Manchuria led to continuing instability in the Asian and Pacific regions, some historians now consider this was not necessarily significant for later developments in Europe.

The **Maginot Line** was a series of fortifications built by France along its north-eastern border with Germany during the years 1929–31. It did not cover France's border with Belgium, through which Germany later invaded in 1940.

The World Disarmament Conference, 1932

This conference, organised by the League, was an attempt to agree limits on army, naval and airforce weapons. It was attended by 61 member nations and 5 non-members, including both the USA and the USSR. France again unsuccessfully attempted to introduce the idea of the League having its own army. A British proposal to limit offensive weapons such as tanks, bombs, submarines and chemical weapons obtained a 41-vote majority, but both Germany and the USSR refused to ban such weapons.

More immediately important was the fact that Germany insisted that either all nations should disarm to the German level set by the Treaty of Versailles or Germany should be allowed to rearm up to the levels of other major powers. In fact, Germany had never fully complied with the disarmament restrictions of Versailles and had begun some limited rearmament through the Treaties of Rapallo and Berlin with Soviet Russia. German delegates walked out of the conference and said they would not return until they had been granted 'equality of treatment'.

How had the Treaties of Rapallo and Berlin allowed Germany to evade the military restrictions imposed by the Treaty of Versailles?

What did the German delegates at the World Disarmament Conference mean by 'equality of treatment'?

The Chaco War, 1932–35

The League was also unable to prevent or solve long-standing border tensions between Bolivia and Paraguay over the Chaco border area. In 1932, a full-scale war broke out; it continued until 1935, by which time both sides were unable to continue. The failure of the League to deal with this issue, involving two minor states, underlined its growing ineffectiveness.

In what way did the Chaco War between Bolivia and Paraguay reveal the serious weaknesses of the League of Nations by the mid 1930s?

Historical sources

1 Extract from an article in the *Manchester Guardian* in December 1931 discussing the failure of the League to deal with Japan's invasion of Manchuria

The League Covenant can apparently be ignored with impunity. Japan has ignored it by invading Manchuria; the nations represented on the League Council have ignored it by refusing to insist on the withdrawal of Japanese troops. The Covenant has failed to save China from aggression as completely as a signed and ratified treaty failed to save Belgium from German aggression in 1914. The Great Powers, despite all their fine gestures, have to their great shame not even seriously protested against, let alone resisted, such a state of affairs.

T. McAleavy, *Modern world history*, Cambridge, 1996, p. 53

2 Von Papen, speaking in 1932, on the impact of the Wall Street Crash on Germany

The German problem is the central problem of all the world's difficulties . . . Unemployment, which is relatively more widespread than in any other country whatever, and constitutes from 20 to 25 per cent of the population, is a burden on public funds.

What is particularly fatal is that an ever-growing number of young people have no possibility of finding employment and earning their livelihood. Despair and the political radicalisation of the youthful section of the population are the consequences of this state of things.

S. Pollard and C. Holmes (eds.), *Documents of European history: the end of old Europe, Vol. 3*, London, 1973, pp. 329–31

Historical-source questions

1 What do you understand by the term 'League Council' referred to in Source 1?
2 What was the 'Wall Street Crash' referred to in Source 2?
3 Why did the Wall Street Crash have such an adverse effect on Germany?
4 What considerations should be made before deciding whether to accept Source 2 as an accurate assessment of the situation?

Summary question

1 Identify and explain *two* reasons why the League of Nations failed to take action against Japan's invasion of Manchuria in 1931.

2 Compare the importance of at least *three* factors which contributed to the growing ineffectiveness of the League in the early 1930s.

5 The road to war, 1933–39

Focus questions

◆ How effective was the League in the years 1933–37?

◆ Why was the policy of appeasement followed?

◆ Did Hitler plan the Second World War?

Significant dates

1933   *January*   Hitler becomes chancellor of Germany
       February   Japan leaves the League of Nations
       October   USA gives diplomatic recognition to USSR; Germany leaves World Disarmament Conference and League of Nations
       November   Germany begins rearmament

1934   *January*   Disarmament Conference ends in failure; Germany and Poland sign a non-aggression pact
       July   Hitler attempts *Anschluss* with Austria
       September   USSR joins League of Nations

1935   *March*   Saarland votes to return to Germany; Hitler reintroduces conscription
       April   Stresa Front between Britain, France and Italy
       June   Anglo-German Naval Treaty
       October   Italy invades Abyssinia
       December   Hoare–Laval Pact

1936   *March*   Hitler orders reoccupation of the Rhineland
       August   Hitler and Mussolini support Franco as Spanish Civil War begins; Hitler's four-year war plan
       October   Rome–Berlin Axis
       November   Anti-Comintern Pact between Germany and Japan

1937   *May*   Neville Chamberlain becomes British prime minister
       July   Japan attacks China
       October   Italy signs Anti-Comintern Pact (Rome–Berlin–Tokyo Axis)
       November   The Hossbach Memorandum
       December   Italy leaves the League of Nations

1938   *March*   *Anschluss* between Germany and Austria
       September   Sudeten crisis and Munich Conference

Adolf **Hitler** was born in 1889 in Austria. After the First World War, he took over the small German Workers Party in Munich, making it the Nationalist Socialist German Workers Party (NSDAP, or Nazi Party for short). An attempt at an armed takeover in 1923 (the Beer-Hall Putsch) failed and he was briefly imprisoned. While in prison, he set out his extreme racist and nationalist views in his book, *Mein Kampf*. On his release in 1924 he decided to use mainly parliamentary methods to obtain power. The Nazis did very badly in elections, but after the Depression hit Germany the Nazis soon became the largest single party in the German Reichstag (parliament). Invited to be chancellor in January 1933, he destroyed the democracy of Weimar Germany in just over a year and set up the Third Reich (a Nazi dictatorship intended to last 1,000 years). As well as launching programmes of rearmament and conscription, and pursuing an aggressive foreign policy, he also unleashed a programme of anti-Semitism against Jewish people in Germany (and, later, the occupied countries) which culminated in the Holocaust.

Appeasement refers to Chamberlain's policy of avoiding war through attempting to negotiate peaceful revisions of the Treaty of Versailles in line

1939	*March* Hitler invades rest of Czechoslovakia; Lithuania gives Memel to Germany; Britain and France refuse Soviet offer of anti-Nazi pact
	May Pact of Steel between Germany and Italy; rejection of second Soviet offer of anti-Nazi pact
	August Nazi–Soviet Non-Aggression (Molotov–Ribbentrop) Pact
	September Invasion of Poland

Overview

In a series of crises from 1934 onwards – in particular the invasion of Abyssinia, the Spanish Civil War and **Hitler**'s many violations of the Treaty of Versailles – the League was shown to be increasingly powerless and irrelevant. At the same time the major European nations (Britain, France and the Soviet Union) pursued quite different foreign policy objectives, with Britain following a policy of **appeasement**. The foreign policy of the USA varied – some **Axis** aggressions were condemned, but certain legitimate German grievances were recognised. However, its main aim was to avoid involvement in any new European war and to this end several Neutrality Acts were passed in the 1930s. Within seven years of Hitler's appointment as chancellor in January 1933, Europe – and the world – was involved in another major war. From 1938, when the resolution of the Czech crisis failed to satisfy Hitler's growing demands, it became clear that the next crisis would be over Poland. In September 1939, Germany invaded Poland, thus beginning the Second World War (though, technically, it did not become a truly world or global war until the second half of 1941, when Germany invaded the Soviet Union and Japan attacked the US naval base in Pearl Harbor).

How effective was the League in the years 1933–37?

The significance of Hitler

Undoubtedly, the rise of Hitler and the Nazis had a tremendous impact on international affairs in this period. Until 1934, Hitler was mostly concerned with establishing internal control; soon after, he began to adopt a more aggressive foreign policy. Initially this involved taking Germany out of the World Disarmament Conference and the League of Nations. His policies were, at first, essentially cautious and his aims were not much wider than those of previous German statesmen, including those of Gustav Stresemann (see pages 24–25).

At the World Disarmament Conference held in October 1933, Hitler stressed Germany's desire for peace and suggested that either all countries disarm to Germany's level or Germany be allowed to arm to the level of other countries. MacDonald, the British prime minister, urged France to agree; however, the

"MY FRIENDS, WE HAVE FAILED. WE JUST COULDN'T CONTROL YOUR WARLIKE PASSIONS."

DISARMAMENT CONFERENCE

COMMON PEOPLE OF THE WORLD

A British cartoon, commenting on the World Disarmament Conference, which ended in failure in 1934.

French insisted that the Germans guarantee that the Versailles limitations would be respected for the next four years. Hitler complained that Germany was not being treated equally and withdrew from the conference and then from the League.

In 1934, Hitler signed a non-aggression pact with Poland. As well as easing general European concerns over Germany's intentions, it prevented closer Polish ties with France and brought Poland under greater German influence. Britain welcomed this development, but France remained suspicious and felt it would have to ensure its security independently of Britain.

Though Germany's departure from the League was a setback both for the League and for international relations in general, a new member – the Soviet Union – joined in 1934. The Soviet Union, increasingly disturbed by Hitler's rise to power, had begun to fear Nazi Germany's intentions.

Hitler's first aggressive foreign policy action was an attempt in 1934 to bring about *Anschluss* with Austria by supporting an attempted coup by Austrian Nazis. However, the coup was blocked, not by the League, but by Italy, supported by Britain and France. Hitler backed down as, at this stage, the German army was not ready for a serious military conflict. After the **Night of the Long Knives** in June 1934, which made Nazi power secure within Germany, Hitler focused increasingly on foreign policy. In January 1935, the important Saar area voted to return to Germany. In March, Hitler announced Germany was no longer bound by the military terms of Versailles and began openly rearming; this included naval expansion and the reintroduction of

with German wishes. This continued even after several acts of German aggression.

In the Second World War, Germany and its allies were known as the **Axis** Powers.

Why did Hitler sign a non-aggression pact with Poland in 1934?

The **Night of the Long Knives** took place on 29–30 June 1934, when Hitler ordered the SS to arrest and execute the main SA leaders. They wanted the SA to become Germany's new army and also for the Nazi government to begin a 'second revolution' against big business. After this event, and the death of President Hindenburg, the army agreed to swear an oath of loyalty to Hitler. In return, Hitler promised to make Germany a great military power again through rearmament and conscription.

How did the Night of the Long Knives in Germany, in June 1934, affect the future conduct of Nazi foreign policy?

conscription. The German army was already 400,000 strong, well beyond the 100,000 limit set by Versailles; now Hitler announced he intended to increase its size to 550,000.

Britain, France and Italy then formed the Stresa Front in April 1935, with the intention of opposing any further German actions which might endanger Austrian independence or peace in general. Significantly, this was done independently of the League, which took no action against Germany's clear breaches of the peace settlements.

Hitler took steps to weaken the Stresa Front. He made speeches stating how Germany wanted both peace and rearmament. It had the effect of further widening the gulf between British and French policies – Britain was impressed by these statements, but France remained unconvinced. As a result, France negotiated a mutual assistance pact with the Soviet Union, which included a joint promise to protect Czechoslovakia from German aggression.

Why did Britain sign the Anglo-German Naval Treaty in 1935?

What impact did this treaty have on the Stresa Front?

Britain disapproved of these links with Soviet Russia and, in June 1935, signed the Anglo-German Naval Treaty in an attempt to limit Hitler's planned naval expansion. It was agreed that the German navy could expand to 35 per cent of the size of the British navy and have submarines. This recognition of Germany's right to ignore the Treaty of Versailles angered both France and Italy, thus weakening the recently formed Stresa Front.

The invasion of Abyssinia

In October 1935, with Allied foreign policy already undermined by the Anglo-German Naval Treaty, Italy invaded Abyssinia (now known as Ethiopia); this was the first serious act of aggression by a major European power since 1920.

The League imposed economic sanctions on Italy, but did not include oil in the list of banned goods. Oil was thus allowed to pass through the British- and French-owned Suez Canal to the Italian invasion force, enabling Italy to continue their invasion. In addition, many non-League members continued to trade with Italy. France, in particular, was reluctant to provoke an argument with Mussolini, as it wished to maintain the Stresa Front in order to resist future German threats to Austria. This action again demonstrated the weaknesses of the League and its irrelevance in solving serious crises.

The Hoare–Laval Pact

The result of French reluctance to take serious action against Italy was the secret Hoare–Laval Pact which offered Italy the bulk of Abyssinia. However, the contents of the pact were leaked to the press and the resulting uproar forced Hoare to resign and the pact to be abandoned. Instead, the League, supported by Britain and France, began to take a tough line with Italy – in March 1936, they decided to ban the sale of oil and petrol to Italy, but the ban was not fully operable until May 1936. By then the Italian conquest was complete. However, the British and French reaction had succeeded both in alienating Mussolini (and so destroying the Stresa Front) and in discrediting the League which, even though it was supposed to take action to prevent the success of such aggression, ended all sanctions against Italy in July.

What was the significance of the Hoare–Laval Pact concerning the Abyssinian crisis?

Italian foreign policy

In Europe, Mussolini was concerned about Hitler's ambitions in eastern Europe and the likely implications for the Austro-Italian border. It was for this reason that Italy had sent Italian troops to the Austrian border when Hitler had threatened to take over Austria in 1934.

Despite their alliances in the 1930s, it was Britain's and France's inability to approve Mussolini's invasion of Abyssinia that led him to move away from the Allies and closer to Germany. As early as January 1936, Mussolini let Hitler know that he no longer had any objections to Austria coming under German control and hinted that he would not move to prevent any reoccupation of the Rhineland. Then on 6 March 1936, he withdrew Italy from the League of Nations and began to move closer to Nazi Germany. In October 1936, Hitler and Mussolini formed the Rome–Berlin Axis, making Italy's move away from Britain and France quite clear. With the loss of Italy as an ally, Britain and France were forced to rely on one another.

The Rhineland

On 7 March 1936, Hitler ordered German troops to enter the Rhineland which, according to the Treaty of Versailles, was to remain a demilitarised zone. Following the collapse of the Stresa Front, Britain and France were now on their own and yet they continued to follow quite separate policies. Eden, the British foreign secretary, was prepared to 'appease' what were seen as justifiable German grievances.

Though Britain gave a promise to support France in the event of an unprovoked German attack, France felt isolated. This was compounded by the USA ignoring France's request to President Roosevelt to condemn this German action. France therefore felt unable to oppose the reoccupation – although, as we now know, the German High Command had secured Hitler's permission to withdraw if the French made a stand over this issue, as the German army was not in a position to deal with any armed opposition.

What was the significance of Germany's re-occupation of the Rhineland in March 1936?

As for the League, it took no action at all and was becoming clearly irrelevant to international and even European events. When a civil war broke out in Spain in October 1936, the League was once again shown to be ineffective. Despite German and Italian military help given to Franco against the elected **Popular Front** government, the response of Britain and France was to form an

The **Popular Front** was a coalition of socialists which won elections in Spain in 1936. The term was later used to describe any anti-fascist alliance or coalition, usually involving communists.

Germany and Japan signed the **Anti-Comintern Pact** against the Soviet Union in 1936; Italy joined later in 1937. 'Comintern' is an abbreviation for the Communist International, set up by the Bolsheviks in 1919 to help spread socialist revolution throughout Europe.

What was the main implication of the Japanese 'Fundamentals' policy as stated in 1936?

Born in 1868, **Neville Chamberlain** was a Conservative politician, first elected in 1918. He served as chancellor of the exchequer (1923–24) and minister of health (1924–29). He became prime minister in 1937 and is the British politician most associated with the policy of appeasement. He believed Hitler's demands were reasonable and at first totally rejected any idea of an alliance with the Soviet Union. Hitler's continued aggression persuaded him to begin rearmament and he declared war on Germany after the invasion of Poland. The Axis Powers' early successes after the invasion of Poland in September 1939 led to much criticism of appeasement and Chamberlain resigned in May 1940 (following the British failure to prevent Germany gaining control of Norway).

ineffective Non-Intervention Committee. The following month, Hitler signed the **Anti-Comintern Pact** with Japan, designed to confront the Soviet Union.

Japan

At the same time, Japan was greatly increasing its armaments expenditure – by 1936 it was 47 per cent of GDP, up from a level of 31 per cent in 1931. As the military began to dominate in Japan, the Asian–Pacific region came to be seen as Japan's natural 'sphere of influence' in which it had a right to expand. In 1936, this was formalised by a government policy statement (known as the 'Fundamentals of future national policy') which made it clear that Japanese interests in south-east Asia would continue to expand in the immediate future.

Japan then refused to renew the Washington Naval Treaty of 1922 and the more recent Treaty of London of 1930, in which Britain, Japan, Italy and the USA had agreed to set limits on submarines and to scrap some warships. In July 1937, in clear defiance of the League – and clearly in line with the 'Fundamentals' policy, Japan began its invasion of China. As a League member, China appealed for help – the League's response was to call an international conference. Though Britain and France did give some financial assistance to China, they made no offer of military help.

Why was the policy of appeasement followed?

By 1937, with war in China, civil war in Spain and growing threats from Germany and Italy, it was clear the League of Nations was in practice defunct. It was in this tense period of decline in international co-operation that **Neville Chamberlain** became prime minister of Britain. He hoped that a policy of appeasement would calm international relations and bring about a lasting peace.

For many years, this policy has been criticised for being short-sighted. Many believed that it encouraged Hitler to continue his aggressive policies and was therefore a significant contributory factor to the outbreak of the Second World War. Yet many contemporaries saw it as the only practical policy for averting another war – though some, such as Churchill, advocated an alternative policy of forming a grand anti-fascist alliance.

The only significant European power capable of resisting Nazi Germany was the Soviet Union. Many western politicians rejected Stalin's Russia as a potential ally, partly because it was going through the turmoil of the Great Purges, which seriously affected the Soviet Red Army (see Chapter 8), and partly because of its stated commitment to communism and world revolution. Chamberlain was not alone in being extremely anti-communist.

The alternative of reviving the collective security role of the League of

Nations seemed totally unrealistic, given Germany's, Italy's and Japan's non-membership and the League's failure to act effectively in the years since 1929. By 1937, the League was weak and extremely discredited.

Many British politicians saw France as their only possible ally, yet this was not very feasible either. The Stresa Front had collapsed, Germany was openly ignoring the Treaties of Versailles and Locarno and it seemed likely that, because of German and Italian help, a pro-Axis state would soon be in existence in Spain on France's southern borders.

More importantly, in 1937 Chamberlain was informed by military advisers that the British armed forces were in no state to give effective military support to France or even to defend British cities from air raids. In addition, he was told that the British navy could not effectively protect British colonies in the Far East, in view of Japan's expanding military strength. Furthermore, the majority of British citizens were opposed to Britain rearming and many believed that some revision of the peace settlements was legitimate. Those who, like Chamberlain, had lived through the horrors of the First World War did not want to risk another war.

Consequently, most British government ministers supported Chamberlain's policy of appeasement which was intended to avoid war by negotiating a mutually acceptable revision of the Treaty of Versailles. In November 1937, Lord Halifax was sent to Germany to meet Nazi officials and to tell them that Britain would support legitimate German claims in Europe, provided they were negotiated peacefully. Eden, the foreign secretary, objected to this and later resigned.

Anschluss with Austria, March 1938

Despite the failure of his attempted *Anschluss* with Austria in 1934, it remained one of Hitler's objectives. In July 1936, he had persuaded the Austrian government to accept German supervision of its foreign policy in return for German promises to guarantee Austria's sovereignty. In February 1938, Hitler summoned the Austrian chancellor, Schuschnigg, to Germany and bullied him into accepting two Austrian Nazis into his cabinet, and into giving the Austrian Nazi Party full freedom in Austria (despite the fact that in January 1938 Austrian police had found evidence of its plans to seize power).

However, when Schuschnigg returned to Austria, he decided to call a referendum on Austrian independence. When it looked as if the voters might reject union with Germany, Hitler forced Schuschnigg to resign. A new government took over, dominated by Austrian Nazis and led by Seyss-Inquart, leader of the Austrian Nazi Party. This government then requested German troops to enter Austria to help deal with disorder – which was being caused by the Austrian Nazis.

On 12 March 1938, German troops crossed into Austria and *Anschluss* was finally achieved, in clear violation of the Treaty of Versailles. France later denounced this action, but did not threaten any military response. Britain was not deflected from its policy of appeasement: the British ambassador in Berlin informed Chamberlain that Schuschnigg was largely to blame for having called a 'provocative' referendum.

Crisis over Czechoslovakia

As well as breaching Versailles, the *Anschluss* also strengthened Nazi Germany's ability to threaten Czechoslovakia. By 1938 Czechoslovakia was the only democracy left in central Europe and had a significant industrial base, a small but modern military force and good border defences.

Its prime minister, Edvard Beneš, had been an active supporter of the League of Nations and the enforcement of the peace treaties. However, Czechoslovakia was facing problems with the 3.5 million German-speakers who lived in the **Sudetenland**, along its borders with Austria. These former citizens of the Austro-Hungarian empire were unhappy about their position in the new state of Czechoslovakia. Many supported the pro-Nazi Sudeten German Party, funded by Nazi Germany since 1933.

In May 1938, the Czech government claimed Hitler was planning to invade in support of the 'oppressed' minority of Sudeten Germans. Hitler denied this and Chamberlain sent Lord Runciman to mediate between the Czech government and the Sudeten Germans. Runciman concluded that the Sudeten Germans were an oppressed minority and that they should be allowed to become part of Germany. The situation continued to deteriorate towards possible war; in September 1938, Chamberlain decided to negotiate with Hitler in person. On 15 September, they met at Berchtesgaden and on 22 September at Bad Godesberg and at both meetings Hitler increased his demands.

Even though the French were not directly involved, both Britain and France informed the Czech government that they should hand the Sudetenland over to Germany or risk fighting a war on their own. The Soviet Union, which in 1935 had signed a treaty with France to protect Czechoslovakia, was not even consulted.

Munich

Chamberlain met Hitler for the third time on 29 September in Munich. At this meeting, Germany, Britain, France and Italy finally agreed that the Sudetenland should be handed over to Germany, on the basis that self-determination had been denied to these German-speakers in 1919. Once again, neither Czechoslovakia nor the Soviet Union was consulted.

On 10 October, the Sudetenland became part of Germany: without firing a

The **Sudetenland** was part of the old Austro-Hungarian empire which was given to the newly created state of Czechoslovakia in 1919. It contained a large number of German-speakers who began to demand the right to become part of Germany, especially after the *Anschluss* between Germany and Austria in March 1938.

A Soviet cartoon about the Munich Agreement of 1938. The signpost says 'Western Europe' and 'USSR' – Britain and France are shown directing the Nazis to the USSR.

shot, Hitler obtained the part of Czechoslovakia which contained their border defences and the important Skoda armaments works. In return, he made vague promises to leave the rest of Czechoslovakia alone and signed a document with Chamberlain stating that Germany and Britain would never go to war against each other – the infamous 'peace in our time' pledge.

At the time, however, many believed Chamberlain's policy of appeasement had peacefully revised an injustice of the 1919–20 peace settlements, to the extent that Chamberlain was nominated for the 1938 Nobel Peace Prize.

By November 1938, however, the anti-Jewish violence of the event known as *Kristallnacht*, as well as intelligence reports that revealed a possible invasion of the Netherlands, added to growing concern over Hitler's real intentions. Consequently, in February 1939, Britain promised to support France and began to create a large British expeditionary force to do so and discussions began between British and French military leaders.

Why was the Sudetenland considered so important?

Invasion of Czechoslovakia

Meanwhile Hitler's foreign policy now centred on destroying the rest of Czechoslovakia. The Slovaks were bullied into declaring their independence and Poland and Hungary were encouraged to make their own territorial demands. On 15 March 1939, Nazi Germany finally invaded Czechoslovakia. Though **Daladier** did put France on a war footing, no further action was taken by Britain or France. Hitler then turned his attention to the Lithuanian port of Memel, where its German inhabitants had been demanding to be returned to Germany. The result of this was that Memel became a free port zone, effectively under Nazi control.

Born in 1884, Edouard **Daladier** was a Radical and served as prime minister of France in 1933, 1934 and from 1938 to 1940. He also signed the Munich Agreement in 1938 and declared war on Germany in September 1939. He was interned by the Vichy government in France (which, with German permission, ruled part of the country following France's defeat in 1940) and deported to Germany, where he remained a prisoner until the end of the war in Europe in 1945.

Poland

Soon after the Munich Conference, Germany had begun to request the return of Danzig (run by the League of Nations as an International free city) and the building of road and rail links across the Polish Corridor to East Prussia. Once Czechoslovakia and Memel had been taken, it became clear to most people that Poland was Hitler's next target. By the end of March, both Britain and France had made a significant policy change and guaranteed to protect Polish independence. Similar promises were made to Greece, following Italy's invasion of Albania in April 1939.

Hitler was not convinced these promises would be acted on – even after the USA moved a battle fleet from the Atlantic to the Pacific (allowing British and French fleets to move to the North Sea) or when Britain announced conscription for all men aged 20–21.

The Nazi–Soviet Non-Aggression Pact

The Soviet Union had been offering Britain an anti-Nazi alliance for some time but Chamberlain, a strong anti-communist, was opposed to the idea – in part because it might provoke Germany and also because Poland opposed such an agreement. However, by mid 1939, there was strong public support in both Britain and France for such an alliance. Chamberlain reluctantly agreed to open negotiations, but only at a low level. Eden, who had offered to conduct them, was excluded from the initial negotiations.

Since the Munich Conference, however, Stalin had come to suspect that Britain and France were prepared to accept German conquests in the east. Britain's slow responses to these low-level negotiations in the summer of 1939 seemed to confirm this fear, so Stalin also began to respond to German requests for negotiations on a non-aggression pact.

Hitler, who had already set a date for the invasion of Poland, believed that such a pact was necessary because of the Soviet Union's military capacity – he calculated that, with no Soviet ally, Britain and France would not honour their pledges to Poland. Stalin saw such a pact, in the event of no firm alliance with Britain and France, as giving the Soviet Union more time to prepare defences against a German invasion. Thus the Molotov–Ribbentrop Non-Aggression Pact was concluded on 23 August 1939.

On 29 August, Hitler 'offered' Poland the choice of peaceful dismemberment by negotiation – allowing the country to be broken up to prevent a German invasion – or war. Following Poland's refusal, Germany invaded Poland on 1 September. Two days later Britain and France declared war on Germany, although throughout the '**phoney war**' there was essentially only conflict between Germany and Poland.

The '**phoney war**' was the period from September 1939 to April 1940, when there was no fighting in western Europe. Fighting only began when Germany occupied Denmark and began its invasion of Norway.

Soviet foreign policy

The crucial turning point in the **Nazi–Soviet Pact** seems to have been the Munich Conference; up until then Litvinov, the Soviet commissar for foreign affairs, believed that Britain and France could be persuaded to defend collective security by joining with the USSR. However, Stalin also considered that another way of at least postponing a war with Germany would be to sign an agreement with Hitler. When in May 1939 Molotov replaced Litvinov, he was instructed to pursue a new diplomatic policy.

Evidence released since the collapse of the Soviet Union in 1991 suggests that a military alliance with Britain and France was Stalin's favoured option, but historians remain divided as to the real aims and motives of Soviet foreign policy in the 1930s. Beginning with A. J. P. Taylor's *The origins of the Second World War*, many have argued that Stalin's policy, as pursued by Litvinov, was genuine. Opposed to this view are those historians who argue that Stalin's approach to the West was a screen behind which the Soviet Union followed its main policy of maintaining the close links with Germany established in the 1920s by the Treaty of Rapallo. These 'Germanist' historians believe negotiations with the West were just ploys to put pressure on Nazi Germany to sign an agreement with the USSR. A third group of historians, however, stress the importance of 'internal politics' in understanding the two different strands of foreign policy pursued by Stalin from 1933 to 1939. They have pointed out the genuine policy differences which existed between the pro-western Litvinov (his wife was English) and Molotov, who placed his faith in the independent strength of the Soviet Union, and the fact that Stalin wavered between these two options.

The **Nazi–Soviet Pact** was, officially, a 20-year non-aggression pact between Germany and the USSR. However, it contained secret clauses which divided Poland and large parts of eastern Europe between the two powers. Germany was to have western Poland, while the USSR got eastern Poland, the three Baltic republics and part of Romania, all of which had belonged to tsarist Russia.

What were the main points of the Nazi–Soviet Non-Aggression Pact?

The Asian–Pacific War

The Second World War also saw protracted and bitter conflict in the Asian–Pacific region. Japan had been involved in conflict with China since 1931 and especially since 1937. Japan's attack on the USA naval base Pearl Harbor in December 1941 brought the USA into what then became a truly worldwide war. Of particular interest and historical debate are the motives behind the foreign policies of the USA and Japan.

At the Tokyo war tribunal which took place at the end of the Second World War, Japanese leaders were blamed for planning a deliberate campaign of expansion through war and for attacking the USA without any provocation. Since then, however, revisionist historians have raised many questions about the role of the USA in contributing to the conflict in the region. Such historians argue that in the 1930s Japan had no real plan for military expansion in the region and that its attack on China was a response to fears that, in the context of the Depression, the nationalist government of China was threatening important Japanese investments there. The high cost of this war is thus seen as a factor driving Japan to seek expansion in south-east Asia, in order to obtain vital supplies of oil and other raw materials. According to such revisionist views, Japan believed it would be possible to expand in the region without provoking war with the USA. All this indicates that Japan's foreign policy was more opportunistic than pre-planned.

According to the revisionists, the USA is no longer seen as totally innocent concerning the outbreak of this conflict. Under Roosevelt, the USA followed a policy of isolationism and neutrality towards both Europe and Asia in the 1930s, despite the growing signs of tension and crisis, and only decided to become involved after Nazi Germany's early successes in Europe. Yet, during the 1930s, relations between the USA and Japan steadily worsened. Some historians have even suggested that in order to justify US intervention in the Second World War Roosevelt deliberately provoked Japan by freezing all Japanese investments in the USA and imposing an oil embargo, which had serious implications for the Japanese military campaign in China. It is clear that the USA and Britain decided that they should take firm measures to block Japanese plans for expansion in the region and were advised by their respective military experts that Japan would not be difficult to defeat.

Did Hitler plan the Second World War?

One of the assumptions behind the **Nuremberg Trials** that followed the end of the Second World War was that Hitler had deliberately planned for such a war even before he came to power (his comments on foreign policy in *Mein Kampf*, written in 1924, seem to support this theory). Certainly, there was the belief that after 1933 he followed a master plan which he consistently pursued up to and beyond the start of the war. Initially, most historians shared this view, pointing to how, as early as 1934, Hitler began attempts to drive wedges between Poland and France, and between Italy and its other Stresa Front partners, Britain and France.

This belief is given credence by the evidence of Hitler's 1936 four-year war plan. It was intended to make Germany more self-sufficient, especially in war-related products.

The Hossbach Memorandum, 1937

Of even greater interest than the four-year plan is the **Hossbach Memorandum**. On 5 November 1937, Hitler summoned the foreign minister, the war minister and other leading military chiefs to a meeting. They were told to get Germany ready for conquests in the east (to be completed by 1943–45) while Germany was still militarily superior to Britain for, although Britain had begun rearmament, it was at the time behind German levels, especially as

The **Nuremberg Trials** were tribunals which tried captured leading Nazis for war crimes; most committed suicide before or after sentencing. Many were never captured.

The **Hossbach Memorandum** refers to notes made by Colonel Hossbach after a meeting called by Hitler on 5 November 1937 which involved political and military chiefs. According to the notes, Hitler outlined his plans for 'conquest in the east' which would require the seizure of Austria and Czechoslovakia, even if this provoked war with Britain and France. However, Hossbach did not make these notes during the meeting and only wrote them out five days later, from memory. Though it was never an official document, most historians accept it as reliable.

regards air power. The Hossbach Memorandum also included plans to seize Austria and Czechoslovakia, even though this might provoke war with Britain and France. Later in November, Schacht, the economics minister, who opposed rapid rearmament, was sacked and in January 1938 the moderate war minister van Blomberg was also dismissed. Hitler himself took over this post and filled other leading positions with convinced Nazis. Later, another leading Nazi, von Ribbentrop, replaced von Neurath as foreign minister.

The examination of specific crises tends to confirm that Hitler had planned for war – for example, during the Czech crisis in 1938, Hitler set a date for the invasion of Czechoslovakia (1 October) as early as May 1938. Similarly, once the whole of Czechoslovakia had been invaded and Memel had been taken from Lithuania, Hitler then set 1 September 1939 as the date for the invasion of Poland – before he had secured the Non-Aggression Pact with the Soviet Union.

This orthodox view (the Intentionalist school) was first strongly criticised by the historian A. J. P. Taylor in *The origins of the Second World War*, published in 1961. It provoked heated historical debate, as Taylor claimed Hitler had not followed a pre-determined master plan for war and questioned the reliability of the Hossbach Memorandum as historical evidence. Instead he argued that Hitler's foreign policy was essentially improvised and based on simply making the most of opportunities when they arose. He also stressed how Hitler's desire to overturn the Treaty of Versailles, and also to restore German greatness, was an aim 'shared by all German politicians, by the Social Democrats who ended the war in 1918 as much as by Stresemann'. Taylor claimed that German rearmament after 1936 was not as great as claimed by Hitler, so that by 1939 Germany's armed forces were not strong enough to sustain a world, or even a European, war.

Since then the debate has continued, with historians divided into two camps. The first of these camps, the Orthodox-Intentionalists, argue that Hitler's expansionist policy was more the result of preconception than opportunism. The other school, the Revisionist-Opportunists, argue that Hitler's policies were a response to internal problems and external opportunities rather than part of a preconceived plan.

> Why do some historians dispute the reliability of the Hossbach Memorandum?

Continuity or discontinuity?

Historians are also divided over whether German foreign policy after 1933 was merely a more aggressive continuation of previous policies of expansion or whether it was a distinctive break arising from Hitler's personal priorities. Most historians stress the continuity in policy, even though the addition of anti-Semitism and the policy of extermination of ethnic minorities can be seen as stemming from Hitler's personal prejudices and his Austrian (rather than German) roots.

Historical sources

1 Hitler's early thoughts on foreign policy, as set out in his book, *Mein Kampf*

We take up where we broke off 600 years ago. We stop the endless German movement to the south and west, and turn our gaze towards the land of the east. At long last we break off the colonial and commercial policy of the pre-war period and shift to the soil policy of the future. If we speak of soil in Europe today, we can primarily have in mind only Russia and her vassal border states.

A. Hitler, *Mein Kampf*, translated by R. Mannheim, London, 1969, pp. 597–98

2 Extract from the statement made on 22 November 1945 before the Nuremberg war crimes tribunal by Franz Halder, the German army's chief of staff, 1938–42

I, furthermore, state and affirm that in March 1941, before the start of the Russia campaign which happened in June of that year, Hitler called the chiefs of command of the three parts of the armed forces and also high commanders to a conference . . . In that conference Hitler said as follows: 'The war against Russia will be such that it cannot be conducted in a knightly fashion. This struggle is a struggle of ideologies and racial differences and will have to be conducted with unprecedented, unmerciful and unrelenting harshness.'

F. McDonough, *The origins of the First and Second World Wars*, Cambridge, 1997, p. 87

Historical-source questions

1   What was the significance of the references in Source 1 to 'the land of the east'?
2   What name is usually given to the 'soil policy' mentioned in Source 1?
3   What were the 'ideologies and racial differences' mentioned in Source 2?
4   To what extent do the two sources support each other and what happened after 1939? Use the sources and your own knowledge.

Summary questions

1   Identify and explain any *two* reasons why the USSR finally signed the Non-Aggression Pact with Germany in 1939.

2   Compare the importance of at least *three* factors which led the British government to follow a policy of appeasement towards Nazi Germany in the late 1930s.

The USSR, 1924–53

6 The rise of Stalin, 1924–29

Focus questions

◆ Why was there a power struggle?

◆ What were the key stages of the power struggle?

◆ Why did Stalin emerge as leader?

Significant dates

1921 *March* Tenth Party Congress; Kronstadt Rising; NEP

1922 *April* Stalin becomes general secretary of the Communist Party
May Lenin's first stroke
December Lenin offers Trotsky a joint bloc for democracy; Lenin's second stroke; his Testament; triumvirate formed against Trotsky

1923 *January* Lenin's Postscript recommends Stalin's dismissal
February Triumvirs begin campaign against Trotsky
March Lenin's third stroke
October Statement of the 46

1924 *January* Lenin dies; Thirteenth Party Conference condemns the views of Trotsky and the 46
May Central Committee keep Lenin's Testament secret and decide not to dismiss Stalin; Thirteenth Congress confirms condemnation of Trotsky
June Congress of Comintern also votes against Trotsky
November Trotsky's 'Lessons of October'

1925 *January* Trotsky dismissed as commissar for war; Zinoviev and Kamenev unsuccessfully attempt to persuade Stalin to replace Trotsky
April Party debate over 'socialism in one country' versus permanent revolution
May Trotsky appointed to the Supreme Council of the National Economy; start of the Leningrad Opposition
October Zinoviev and Kamenev joined by Sokolnikov and Krupskaya
December Fourteenth Party Congress

1926 *April* Trotsky, Zinoviev and Kamenev hold talks for joint opposition
July United Opposition formally announced; Zinoviev dismissed from Politburo

1927 *October* Stalin persuades Central Committee to expel Trotsky and Zinoviev
November Trotsky and Zinoviev expelled from the Communist Party and Kamenev from the Central Committee

1927	**December**	Fifteenth Party Congress; Zinoviev and Kamenev end the United Opposition
1928	**January**	Trotsky deported to Alma Ata in Turkestan
	July	Stalin and Bukharin clash over collectivisation
	August	Bukharin tries to form alliance with Trotsky
1929	**January**	Trotsky deported to Constantinople
	April	Bukharin removed as editor of *Pravda*
	November	Bukharin removed from Politburo

Overview

In the two years before he died in 1924, **Lenin**, the leader of the Communist Party and prime minister of Russia, suffered a series of increasingly serious strokes. Policy differences and personal rivalries between other leading communists, which existed before 1922, now came to the fore. **Trotsky**, Zinoviev and Kamenev were the most important Communists after Lenin.

Lenin was worried by these developments and in December 1922 he wrote a Testament outlining the strengths and weaknesses of the main leaders and warning about the dangers of a split. Stalin's activities as commissar for nationalities and as general secretary of the Communist Party worried him, so he wrote a Postscript in January 1923 recommending that Stalin be dismissed. At the same time, he tried to persuade Trotsky to take the necessary steps to defeat Stalin.

However, Trotsky's main rivals, Zinoviev and Kamenev, formed an alliance with Stalin (known as the triumvirate) in order to prevent Trotsky replacing Lenin. The triumvirs then began a campaign against 'Trotskyism'. Using his position as general secretary, Stalin was able to control meetings and elections to congresses and conferences. Trotsky was soon isolated.

With Trotsky defeated, Stalin then turned on Zinoviev and Kamenev, with the support of Bukharin and the right. In response Zinoviev and Kamenev united with Trotsky, but Stalin was able to defeat this United Opposition.

In 1928, Stalin turned on Bukharin and by 1929 he had also defeated the right of the party. His main rival, Trotsky, was then exiled from the Soviet Union, leaving Stalin the sole ruler of the Communist Party.

Why was there a power struggle?

Political and economic problems 1921–24

After the Bolshevik Revolution of November 1917 (see marginal note on page 65), Russia underwent a civil war between the Reds (communists) and Whites (non-communists), which was further complicated by the intervention of

Vladimir **Lenin** was born in 1870; his real name was Vladimir Ilyich Ulyanov. He joined the RSDLP (see p. 58) in 1898; at its Second Congress in 1903, he argued for a small party made up of committed revolutionaries, with strong central control after democratic debate (democratic centralism). This provoked a split – Lenin's faction became known as the Bolsheviks (meaning 'majority') as they had won a majority at the congress, although there were more Mensheviks (meaning 'minority') in the party as a whole. He remained in exile until April 1917, returning after the March Revolution. He soon began to urge the Bolsheviks to organise a second revolution. He acted as Soviet prime minister from 1917 to 1924. He was married to another Bolshevik revolutionary, Nadezhda Krupskaya.

Leon **Trotsky** was born in 1879; his real name was Leon Bronstein. He joined the RSDLP in 1899; at its Second Congress in 1903 he sided with the Mensheviks against Lenin. However, he split from them in 1904. In May 1917, he returned to Russia and joined the Bolsheviks in August, as both he and Lenin had by then developed very similar outlooks. He was the main organiser of the November Revolution and later formed and led the Red Army during the civil war.

Emergency measures taken by the Bolshevik government at the start of the civil war were known as **war communism**. Grain was requisitioned from the peasants to ensure adequate supplies for the Red Army and the industrial centres, all private trade was banned, all factories, mines and banks were nationalised and money was allowed to lose value. It was replaced by the NEP in 1921.

The **Kronstadt Rising** took place in March 1921 when sailors and workers at the Kronstadt naval base organised an insurrection against war communism and the political restrictions imposed by the Bolsheviks during the civil war. It was crushed with great loss of life on both sides.

The **soviets** were workers' councils. They had originally acted as strike committees and involved all workers regardless of politics. These spread throughout Russia in 1917, with each town or rural soviet sending delegates to an All-Russian Congress of Soviets. After 1917, they became the main political authority, in theory controlling the government.

Why was the Kronstadt Rising so important for later political developments in the Soviet Union?

What was the significance of the 1921 ban on factions?

14 foreign armies supporting the Whites. Though the Reds finally won in 1921, the civil war had thrown up many sharp policy differences between the leading Bolsheviks.

The most important difference concerned economic policy: during the civil war, a policy known as **war communism** was adopted as an emergency measure, but the combination of the damage suffered during the civil war and the **Kronstadt Rising** led Lenin to persuade the party to adopt the New Economic Policy (NEP) at the Tenth Party Congress, held in March 1921.

The NEP not only ended war communism, it also introduced a partial step back towards capitalism. Though the major banks and industries remained nationalised, small firms and retail businesses were returned to private control and peasants were allowed to sell part of their surplus produce for profit. Soon, though the economy began to improve, wealthy businessmen (known as Nepmen) and rich peasants (called kulaks) emerged. This angered and worried many communists: the Workers' Opposition called NEP the 'new exploitation of the proletariat'.

The 1921 ban

The combination of the Kronstadt Rising (which revealed the growing isolation of the Bolsheviks) and the divisive NEP proposals led Lenin at the Tenth Congress to introduce a ban on factions within the Communist Party and a ban on opposition parties in the **soviets**.

Up until then (even during the civil war), strong disagreements within the Communist Party had been normal and several parties (such as the Mensheviks and Social Revolutionaries) had continued to operate, despite temporary restrictions, within the soviets. Several communists were opposed to this ban and later Lenin stated it was a temporary measure, intended to cope with the acute political and economic crisis. It was not a ban on opposition within the party or on dissent in general.

Lenin's illness

In May 1922, Lenin had the first of a series of strokes, which increasingly restricted his ability to take an active part in politics. The arguments over economic policy continued and, at the same time, there emerged significant political differences over internal political democracy, the policy towards the nationalities that made up the Russian Federation and what attitude to adopt towards furthering world revolution.

The contenders for succession

These economic and political arguments became bound up in personal rivalries between leading communists who began to consider what would happen

A Soviet photo-montage, made in 1920, of the leaders of the revolution. Lenin and Trotsky appear together in the centre of the picture. Stalin's photograph has not been included because he was not widely known as an important Bolshevik leader.

if Lenin died. The most important communists after Lenin were the other members of the Politburo: Trotsky, Zinoviev, Kamenev, **Bukharin**, Rykov, Stalin and Tomsky. Of these, Trotsky seemed the most likely to replace Lenin: he had been the main organiser of the November Revolution, had built up the Red Army that defeated the Whites and was **commissar** for war.

After him, Zinoviev and Kamenev were strong political leaders (of Petrograd and Moscow respectively) and had long been associated with Lenin. Their weakness was that they had been opposed to the November Revolution at first and had leaked early plans to the opposition's press. Bukharin, too, was a well-known and popular revolutionary leader. Stalin was not well known and seemed unlikely to emerge as a major leader. However, he had been appointed commissar for nationalities after the Revolution and, in April 1922, was appointed general secretary of the Communist Party, where one of his duties was to appoint and dismiss communist officials.

Many of these leading communists resented Trotsky's rapid rise to the top of the party, partly because they had supported Lenin in 1903 when Russia's Social Democratic Labour Party (RSDLP) had split into Bolshevik and Menshevik factions, while Trotsky had sided with the Mensheviks from 1903 to 1904. He had then formed an independent grouping, comprising mainly intellectuals, until he joined the Bolsheviks in August 1917. Zinoviev and

Nikolai **Bukharin** was born in 1888. He joined the Bolsheviks and, at first, was on the left of the party. From 1924, he moved increasingly to the right and was the main defender of the NEP until 1928, when he was defeated by Stalin. Allowed back into the party in the 1930s, he helped draft the 1936 constitution. He was executed in 1938.

Commissar was the name selected by Trotsky immediately after the November Revolution to replace 'minister', e.g. commissar for war.

What important position did Stalin take on in 1922? How did this help him become the ruler of the USSR?

The Russian Social Democratic Labour Party (RSDLP) was a Marxist party set up in 1898. It split into two factions which, by 1912, had developed into two separate parties – the Bolsheviks (led by Lenin) and the Mensheviks. The Bolshevik Party changed its name to the **Communist Party** in 1918.

Why did Lenin write a Postscript to his Testament in January 1923?

'Triumvir' is the Latin for a ruler acting together with two others.

The **Central Committee** was, in theory, the Communist Party's ruling body between congresses and was elected by congress delegates. The Central Committee then elected the Politburo.

The party **congresses** were, in theory, the Communist Party's supreme decision-making body, made up of delegates elected by local party branches.

Kamenev, in particular, believed they should take over from Lenin and in December 1922 they turned to Stalin for help (via his control of party appointments and organisation) to stop Trotsky from obtaining majority support.

Lenin's Testament

Although Lenin's strokes kept him from active involvement in politics, his awareness of these political and personal tensions caused him growing concern. He proposed to Trotsky that they should form a joint bloc for democracy against growing signs of bureaucracy in the party and the state.

He was prevented from doing this by his second stroke which he suffered at the end of December. Concerned about what might happen after his death, he dictated his initial thoughts for what he believed would be his last Testament in December 1922, outlining the strengths and weaknesses of all the leading members of the **Communist Party**. Growing concern over Stalin's power led him to add a Postscript in January 1923, recommending Stalin's removal. From then until his death the following year, Lenin urged Trotsky on several occasions to launch a campaign against bureaucracy and for the restoration of party and soviet democracy.

What were the key stages of the power struggle?

Early campaign against Trotsky

By January 1923, the alliance between Stalin, Zinoviev and Kamenev was finalised and the **triumvirs** decided to open up party records to all **Central Committee** members as this would make available the letters in which Lenin had expressed early disagreement with Trotsky before they joined forces in August 1917. Soon a whispering campaign concerning Trotsky's non-Bolshevik past, his earlier disagreements with Lenin and his 'ambitions' was underway.

However, in March 1923 Stalin appeared to be in serious trouble – his rudeness to Lenin's wife, Krupskaya, had caused Lenin to send him a harsh letter. Kamenev was aware of this and also of Lenin's intention to politically crush Stalin. But then Lenin suffered a third stroke, which left him paralysed and speechless for most of the time until his death in January 1924.

The Twelfth Congress, April 1923

This **congress** opened with the customary greetings from party cells (branches): all mentioned Lenin and Trotsky, several mentioned Zinoviev and Kamenev as well, but hardly any referred to Stalin. As far as the party's rank and file were concerned, it was obvious who Lenin's successor was going to be. Nonetheless, with Lenin absent, the triumvirs were able to isolate Trotsky.

The congress then re-elected Stalin as general secretary and elected a new enlarged Central Committee – of its 40 members, only 3 were strong supporters of Trotsky.

A new control commission was set up to examine the qualities of party members and to dismiss any 'careerists, politically immature people and corrupt officials'. As general secretary, Stalin supervised this commission and he began to replace Trotsky's supporters with supporters of the triumvirs, especially those who were loyal to him. By the end of 1923, Stalin already had enough control of the party machine at local level to ensure that most of his nominees were elected as delegates to future congresses.

The statement of the 46

In July and August 1923, a wave of unofficial strikes broke out in Moscow and Petrograd. The triumvirs immediately blamed the Workers' Opposition (a left faction within the Communist Party) and called for the expulsion of all party members who broke the 1921 ban on factions.

In October, 46 leading members of the Communist Party issued a statement criticising the leadership over economic policy and the lack of full party democracy. Though Trotsky himself was not involved with this statement, several of his supporters were among the 46, as were members of the Workers' Opposition and the Democratic Centralists (another left faction in the Communist Party). The extent of the opposition shocked the triumvirate; they refused to publish the statement or to call a conference. Instead, they persuaded the Central Committee to censure Trotsky and the 46 for their actions and to threaten expulsion if they circulated the statement.

Who were the Workers' Opposition and the Democratic Centralists?

The Left Opposition

It was at this point that Trotsky and the 46 joined forces to form what became known as the Left Opposition. Stalin now began to use his power to stifle criticism and to isolate the Left Opposition, in preparation for the January 1924 Thirteenth Party Conference at which these economic and political issues were to be debated. Despite much party support for Trotsky's views, the secretaries (who were Stalin's nominees) 'lost' most of the resolutions that supported Trotsky's position.

Stalin also used his growing power over the party machine – and the fact that the preparations for the conference were in the hands of his nominees – to ensure that as many supporters of the Left Opposition as possible were removed by the process of indirect election of delegates to the conference. (Regional party conferences decided which delegates elected by smaller branches should go to the national party conference.)

Because Trotsky was ill, he was unable to attend the conference. In the event his views and those of the 46 were denounced as a 'petty bourgeois deviation

Short for Political Bureau, the **Politburo** was the Communist Party's body responsible for making political decisions which could then be approved or rejected by the Central Committee and the party congress. In practice, this small group soon came to dominate the other two bodies.

from Leninism' and he was accused of disloyalty to the **Politburo** and the Old Guard (the party leaders). Only three delegates supported Trotsky. The conference also voted that the Old Guard needed to maintain their control as the party now had over 400,000 members, not all of whom were true communists.

The Thirteenth Party Congress, May 1924

At this point, Trotsky was on his way to convalesce at the Black Sea, as advised by his doctors. While on this journey, he received a telegram from Stalin, informing him of Lenin's death. When Trotsky spoke of returning, Stalin told him to continue his journey as he would not be able to get back in time for the funeral and that it was now even more important that Trotsky recover from his illness. In fact, Stalin had deliberately given him the wrong date; at Lenin's funeral, the triumvirs put themselves forward as Lenin's successors and raised doubts about Trotsky's absence. Meanwhile, more and more Oppositionists were demoted or dismissed from posts of responsibility.

Grigori **Zinoviev** was born in 1883. He joined the Bolsheviks and worked closely with Lenin during the latter's exile in the years 1908–17. He became the powerful leader of the Petrograd (Leningrad) party and president of Comintern. He was executed in 1936.

Leo **Kamenev** was born in 1883. He joined the Bolsheviks and was elected to their Politburo in 1917. Like Zinoviev, he had opposed Lenin's call for a second revolution in November. He became the leader of the Moscow party organisation. He was executed in 1936.

Comintern was the Communist International (or Third International) set up in 1919, to which all communist parties belonged. It was set up to help revolution in other countries.

Before the congress met, Lenin's widow revealed Lenin's Testament to the Central Committee and senior congress delegates. Its clear recommendation for Stalin's dismissal seemed guaranteed to prevent him ever succeeding Lenin as leader of the Communist Party. He was saved by **Zinoviev** and **Kamenev** who, thinking he was now seriously weakened, argued that he had changed his policies and that the party needed to stick together. Trotsky, who had only just returned from his convalescence, said nothing and, despite Krupskaya's protests, the Central Committee decided not to remove Stalin as general secretary and not to publish Lenin's Testament (its existence was kept a secret in the USSR until 1956).

The congress voted to accept the condemnation of Trotsky made by the previous conference. Trotsky accepted the verdict of the party. The triumvirs – using Zinoviev's position as president of **Comintern** – also began to manipulate the Communist International into supporting the criticisms of Trotsky. By then, hopes of revolution in Germany, Poland and Bulgaria had been dashed – this accelerated the drift of the Russian Communist Party to the right.

In June 1924, Comintern's Fifth Congress confirmed the condemnation of Trotsky, who was not re-elected as a full member of its executive, and elected Stalin in his place. Trotsky was then threatened with expulsion if he engaged in any further political controversy. His Left Opposition had been defeated, thus ending what turned out to be the first stage of the power struggle.

Socialism in one country

The next stage in the power struggle lasted from 1924 to 1926 and was relatively quiet. Almost immediately after the end of the Thirteenth Congress, the triumvirs began a campaign against 'Trotskyism' (said to be opposed to

'Leninism') and started to present an 'official', distorted history of the Revolution and the civil war.

At first, Trotsky remained silent but, in November 1924, the publication of his speeches and writings of 1917, prefaced by his new 'Lessons of October', sparked off another dispute. This preface exploded the myth of him being a Menshevik from 1903 to 1917 and showed how he had been opposed to them since 1904. It also showed how close his views were to those of Lenin and disclosed that Zinoviev and Kamenev had opposed Lenin on several important issues. Only Stalin seemed not guilty of any offences against Lenin – inadvertently Trotsky actually strengthened Stalin's position. This caused the triumvirs to launch a counter-attack, once again dragging up all Trotsky's disagreements with Lenin before and after 1917 and attacking his theory of permanent revolution (developed from Marx by Trotsky in 1906 and, by 1917, shared by most of the leading Bolsheviks).

In the autumn of 1924, Stalin first revealed his alternative to permanent revolution: 'socialism in one country'. This stressed the need for peace and stability and stated that, despite its backwardness and isolation, the new Soviet state could construct socialism on its own. It rejected Trotsky's continued call for world revolution and was supported by Bukharin who, during 1924–25, completed his shift to the right of the Communist Party. Stalin (for the centre) and Bukharin (for the right) thus argued that, with the failure of revolution in the rest of Europe, it was even more important to maintain the alliance (known as the **smychka**) with the peasantry, who still comprised about 70 per cent of the population. They also accused Trotsky of lack of faith in Russia and its people.

In January 1925, the triumvirs used their control of party and state bodies to deprive Trotsky of an important political base – his position as commissar of war. Trotsky was then warned that any renewed controversy would result in his expulsion from the Politburo and the Central Committee. Trotsky, who had in practice disbanded his Left Opposition (though informal discussions with other Oppositionist leaders such as Radek, Pyatakov and Preobrazhensky continued), gave up his positions without a fight.

In May, he was given a new economic post on the Supreme Council of the National Economy (Vesenkha). Soon he began pointing out the threat posed by US capitalism and argued for more socialist planning to strengthen the NEP and for Comintern to adopt a more revolutionary line. Once again, he was perceived to be stirring up controversy.

Divisions within the triumvirate

These economic differences coincided with a number of developments. By 1925, many communists were becoming aware that, although the NEP had

What did Stalin mean by 'socialism in one country'?

Smychka refers to the political and economic 'alliance' between the industrial workers and the peasants – this link between town and country was the foundation of the NEP and it was seen as vital to keep the peasants happy, given that they formed the vast majority of the population.

What was the *smychka*?

achieved some economic improvement, the recovery was uneven. It was also becoming clear that some peasants were beginning to oppose the Soviet regime's attempts at centralisation – in some areas, soviet officials were actually murdered. In addition, many had come to enjoy the relative peace and prosperity of the NEP and feared Trotsky's proposals and his theory of permanent revolution would threaten both internal and external peace. Stalin and Bukharin thus seemed to offer a more attractive future.

At first, the main arguments were not between Stalin and Trotsky, but between Bukharin and Preobrazhensky. Unrest among the peasants, however, soon resulted in a serious controversy which led to a split between the triumvirs and another realignment in the Communist Party. By 1925 the party was clearly split into a left, centre and right. The left consisted of Zinoviev and Kamenev, along with Preobrazhensky. As early as January, they tried to ease Stalin out of his post as general secretary by proposing he take Trotsky's place as commissar for war. By April, Zinoviev and Kamenev were opposing socialism in one country as anti-Leninist. The right, consisting of Bukharin, Rykov and Tomsky, supported Stalin and the centre (which included Molotov, Kaganovich and Andreev) and their aim of socialism in one country.

The Leningrad Opposition

By the summer of 1925, the disagreements between the triumvirs came into the open when Zinoviev's supporters in Leningrad (as Petrograd had been renamed in 1924) attacked the growing dominance of Bukharin's rightist views. In September, Zinoviev and Kamenev began to voice their concerns about developments in the party and called for a renewal of the struggle for equality and a revival of Leninist internationalism. This was a direct attack on the theory of socialism in one country, which was seen to be at odds with orthodox Marxism that said this could only be achieved after world revolution. In October, at a Central Committee meeting which was making preparations for the Fourteenth Party Congress, Zinoviev and Kamenev were joined by Krupskaya and Sokolnikov in presenting a joint statement that called for a free debate on all these issues. With the support of the right, Stalin was able to defeat this call and the left were warned not to make any public criticisms of official policy.

Stalin then began to remove Kamenev's supporters from their positions in the Moscow party; however, he had little success with the Leningrad party where Zinoviev was still strong. All this time, Trotsky remained silent in order not to be accused of factionalism. In fact, in September, he even agreed to deny that Lenin's Testament existed. By now Zinoviev and Kamenev were advocating views very similar to those held by the Left Opposition of 1923–24. In addition, Zinoviev was still in a strong position – as well as controlling the Leningrad party, he was also president of Comintern and had the support of Krupskaya.

The congress met in December 1925 and there was a fierce debate between the differing groups. Trotsky still remained silent – even when Zinoviev referred to Lenin's Testament and his warnings about Stalin's abuse of power and when Krupskaya expressed her opposition to the campaign against Trotskyism. However, apart from a setback over the Leningrad delegates, Stalin had been able to ensure that the majority of those present supported him and Bukharin. Zinoviev and his supporters were defeated by 559 votes to 65; the congress then elected a new Central Committee with a Stalinist–Bukharinist majority. This then elected a new Politburo which also had a centre–right majority. The Central Committee also demoted Kamenev to a candidate (probationary) member and three of Stalin's supporters were promoted from candidate to full membership.

Despite this defeat, Zinoviev continued his campaign in Leningrad. When the new Central Committee proposed disciplinary measures against him, Trotsky opposed them. As a result, Stalin began a new campaign against Trotsky in which he accused Zinoviev of Trotskyism. In early 1926, Zinoviev was forced to hand over the leadership of the Leningrad party to Kirov, one of Stalin's supporters; at the same time, Zinovievists were removed from their positions.

The United Opposition

So far, Trotsky had not joined forces with Zinoviev and Kamenev. In April 1926, he at last offered them support. In secret talks, they revealed how they had fabricated the anti-Trotskyist campaign and their fears regarding Stalin's methods and policies. With some support from a few prominent party members, Trotsky, Zinoviev and Kamenev formed a United (Joint Left) Opposition. This began the next stage in the power struggle.

In June Stalin launched his attack on Trotsky, criticising his views. Trotsky in turn wrote to the Politburo, warning them of the possibility of autocratic rule if the party was not reformed. A decisive contest then took place over the next 18 months.

The United Opposition formally declared its existence in July 1926 and described its position as the 'Bolshevik left'. It argued for greater party democracy, more industrial planning, moves towards extensive (but not compulsory) collectivisation of agriculture and, above all, the rejection of socialism in one country as being incompatible with Marxism–Leninism. They called instead for a more revolutionary policy to be adopted by Comintern. The remnants of the Workers Opposition joined the Oppositionists, giving the United Opposition just over 6,000 supporters out of a total party membership of about 750,000 (though only about 20,000 members were actively involved in this inner-party conflict). However, in the summer, their campaign began to falter, as Stalin's control of the party enabled him to ban meetings and dismiss Oppositionists.

Why did the Leningrad Opposition join up with Trotsky's Left Opposition in 1926?

Stalin then accused them of breaking the 1921 ban on factions and made an attack on Zinoviev, who was still president of Comintern. The Central Committee voted to remove him from the Politburo. As Kamenev had been a non-voting member since the Fourteenth Congress, only Trotsky remained to oppose Stalin in the Politburo. The United Opposition then decided to appeal directly to the party rank and file, but again Stalin's control of the party machine and his appeal to national pride (he accused Trotsky of believing Russians were incapable of building socialism) meant they had little success. At the same time, Zinoviev and especially Kamenev became alarmed at calls from some Oppositionists to declare themselves as an independent party. These more radical views, and their growing isolation, led Zinoviev and Kamenev to fear expulsion from the only legal party with the result that they began to move away from Trotsky. In October 1926, in an effort to keep the United Opposition together, Trotsky agreed that they should offer the Politburo a truce; this was accepted by Stalin and his supporters.

However, while plans were being made for the Fifteenth Party Conference, one of Trotsky's supporters published the full text of Lenin's Testament in the *New York Times*. The Politburo angrily ended the truce and a Central Committee meeting expelled Trotsky from the Politburo and removed Zinoviev from his position as president of Comintern. During the conference itself, the leaders of the Opposition remained silent until attacks by Stalin and Bukharin provoked them into defending their views. Though Trotsky and Kamenev stuck to their guns, Zinoviev tried to back-peddle. The conference confirmed the expulsion of the three Opposition leaders from the Politburo and threatened them with further actions if they reopened the controversies. Their obvious isolation led Krupskaya (who feared the Communist Party was in danger of splitting) and leaders of the Workers Opposition to break away and make their peace with Stalin.

Defeat of the United Opposition

The newspapers continued their attacks on the United Opposition and its lesser members lost their jobs. Though Zinoviev and Kamenev decided to keep quiet, Trotsky decided to fight on.

In April 1927 controversy flared up again over the leadership's policy towards events in China, following Jiang Jieshi's massacre of Chinese communists. At the end of May, Trotsky was able to force a debate on this issue at the Comintern's executive. Stalin was able to side-step this by accusing of factionalism the 84 prominent communists (excluding Trotsky) who had drafted an appeal which was signed by over 300 others. Consequently, Oppositionists continued to be demoted, sent to isolated parts of the Soviet Union or dismissed from their jobs. In June, Stalin asked the Central Committee and the

Control Commission to expel Trotsky and Zinoviev from the Central Committee because he did not want them to speak at the Fifteenth Party Congress, planned for November 1927. At first, Stalin was unable to persuade the Central Committee to do this and he postponed the congress until he finally got his way.

In the meantime, the Opposition had prepared their platform (policy programme), thinking it would be discussed at the congress. Even though the Central Committee refused to publish it, the Opposition printed it themselves and began to collect signatures from those who agreed with their suggestions. In the end, because of attacks and other actions, they collected only 6,000 signatures rather than the 20,000–30,000 they had hoped for.

Attempts by the Oppositionists to address the crowds at the tenth anniversary celebrations of the **November Revolution** were thwarted by Stalin's supporters and the police. These actions were seen as attacking the leadership and were thus in breach of the rules regarding factionalism. Stalin then demanded that Trotsky and Zinoviev be expelled from the party and, on 14 November, this was agreed; at the same time, Kamenev and Rakovsky were expelled from the Central Committee. Hundreds of expulsions of lesser Oppositionists also took place.

When the congress finally met in December 1927, the United Opposition issued a statement signed by 121 of their leading members, asking for the expulsions to be annulled, but this was overwhelmingly rejected. By then, Trotsky was beginning to believe that it might be necessary to form a new party. This alarmed Zinoviev and Kamenev, who were encouraged by signs that Stalin was about to abandon the NEP in favour of a programme of industrialisation and collectivisation of agriculture. For this reason, Kamenev announced during the congress that he and Zinoviev would surrender and make no more criticisms in order to stop the expulsions and to prevent the formation of a second party. Trotsky's supporters, however, would have no part of this, with the result that by 10 December 1927 the United Opposition was over.

Immediately after the congress, another 1,500 Oppositionists were expelled, and 2,500 signed statements of recantation. On 18 December, in front of congress, Zinoviev and Kamenev announced that their ideas had been 'wrong' and 'anti-Leninist'. Despite Bukharin's willingness, Stalin refused to readmit them until they had served at least six months' probation.

Meanwhile, Stalin was making plans to deport Trotsky and his unrepentant supporters. First attempts to persuade them to accept minor posts in remote places broke down in January 1928. Instead, Trotsky was forcibly deported to Alma Ata in Turkestan, near the Chinese border. It was also decided that the state publishers would no longer print Trotsky's works; those already in existence were removed from bookshops and libraries. Other Oppositionists

The **November Revolution** was the second revolution in Russia in 1917 (the first had been in March and resulted in the abdication of the tsar and Russia becoming a republic). The November Revolution, pushed for by Lenin, was planned by Trotsky and carried out by the Bolshevik Red Guards (militia) and their supporters. After the unelected provisional government was overthrown, power was handed over to the All-Russian Congress of Soviets.

were deported elsewhere, in an attempt to isolate them and prevent them from communicating with each other, though this was not very successful.

The defeat of the right

The final stage of the power struggle began almost immediately. As early as the autumn of 1927, a crisis had been brewing in rural Russia. Despite three good harvests, there were bread shortages and high food prices all over Russia as peasants refused to sell their produce at the prices fixed by the state. They thought that the prices being offered were too low and, in addition, there were not enough tools or other industrial goods for the peasants to spend their money on. In many places, there had been riots and forced grain collections by the state. Such events – and Stalin's consequent decision to adopt a new 'left' course as regards industry and agriculture – began to cause a rift between the Bukharinists (who wanted to make concessions to the peasants) and the Stalinists (who preferred more forceful methods). On 6 January 1928, the Politburo issued secret instructions to party organisations to be severe with those who obstructed grain collections and *Pravda* began publishing articles attacking the kulaks.

In April, the Central Committee began to use the arguments of the Left Opposition against the kulaks (as capitalists, they were enemies of the workers'/ socialist state) and introduced emergency measures such as imposing compulsory loans on the kulaks (which forced them to produce and sell surplus food in order to pay them) and grain requisitioning. Those who were seen as having been too lenient with the kulaks (mainly Bukharinists) were removed from positions of power – this, of course, strengthened Stalin's position.

At first, Trotsky's supporters were pleased to see some of their policies being adopted and expected to be readmitted to the party. Some even thought they had been wrong about Stalin and should now join forces with him against Bukharin and the right and the forces of re-emerging capitalism. Trotsky himself believed that Stalin and the centre should be encouraged to break with the right. In fact, since early 1927, Trotsky had seen Bukharin's faction (which included Rykov and Tomsky) as more of a danger to the gains of the November Revolution than Stalin's, as it was bigger and more right wing.

Stalin, however, was determined to do without Trotsky or Zinoviev, although he did try to win over their supporters. By May 1928, it was clear that Stalin was planning a second revolution and Trotsky's supporters began to split into 'conciliators' and 'irreconcilables'. In particular, Preobrazhensky, Radek and Pyatakov called for an offer of support to be made to Stalin; Trotsky, however, argued that the first move must be made by Stalin, when he really needed their help. Nonetheless, in June, Zinoviev and Kamenev (and about 3,000 other Oppositionists) successfully applied to be reinstated in the party.

Why did Stalin and Bukharin fall out in the late 1920s?

The Bolshevik/Communist Party newspaper *Pravda* (its name is Russian for truth) was first edited by Stalin and later by Bukharin.

During July, the food crisis became worse. Temporarily, it seemed that Bukharin's faction was gaining the upper hand when he surprisingly won a vote in the Central Committee to stop emergency measures and when a 20 per cent increase in the price of bread was announced. However, these divisions emerged again at the Sixth Congress of Comintern later in the month. By August, Stalin (having secured a majority in the Politburo) renewed his left-ward course and the breach with Bukharin was confirmed. Both factions then turned to the defeated Left Oppositionists for support.

Bukharin used Kamenev as a go-between for an approach to Trotsky, saying he feared Stalin was the 'new Genghis Khan' and that he 'will strangle us'. Bukharin argued that the main issue was not economic policy but the freedom of the party and the state, claiming that Stalin was preparing to create a police state and take total power. Stalin, however, refused any direct contact with the Left Oppositionists, though he dropped many hints of a possible alliance.

By September 1928, Trotsky had become alarmed at Stalin's increasing use of violence against the peasants and was attracted by the idea of an alliance with Bukharin to restore full inner-party and soviet democracy. However, the two leaders' respective supporters were extremely reluctant to co-operate with their former enemies. The left, in particular, objected to an alliance with the right just when Stalin seemed about to implement some of their own economic policies. As a result, Stalin was able to defeat the right without the formal support of the left – Bukharin and the right, now in panic, surrendered while the left remained divided. Thus there was no need for Stalin to recall the exiled Left Oppositionists – he had managed to defeat both factions by relying solely on his own supporters.

Stalin calculated, on the basis of **GPU** reports, that his plans for agriculture and industry might initially create conditions for the growth of opposition. Support for Trotsky had started to grow in some party cells as Stalin adopted some of his ideas. Consequently, Stalin decided that Trotsky needed to be expelled entirely from Soviet Russia – partly because he feared a left–right alliance in the future and partly because he suspected that some of his own faction still had some sympathy with the Opposition.

On 16 December 1928, Trotsky was warned to stop all 'counter-revolution-ary' activity. When he refused, the Politburo voted to **expel** him from Russia, despite Bukharin, Rykov and Tomsky opposing it. In February 1929, Trotsky was deported to Constantinople. During the same period, Stalin moved against the right. Bukharin, Rykov and Tomsky were charged with factional-ism. In April 1929, Bukharin was removed as editor of *Pravda* and political secretary of Comintern, while Tomsky was dismissed from the Central Council of Trade Unions. The right were warned that further violations of party discipline would result in their expulsion from the Politburo. Finally, in

GPU (State Political Administration) were the secret police from 1922 to 1923 (from 1917 to 1922, the Cheka had been the secret police and from 1923 to 1934, it was the OGPU).

After his **expulsion** from the Soviet Union in 1929, Trotsky set up the Trotskyist Fourth International in 1938, as he was convinced by then that the Communist International and its parties had become unreformably Stalinist and conservative. He was assassinated in Mexico in 1940 by one of Stalin's agents.

A photograph of Stalin with other communist leaders at the Sixteenth Party Congress in July 1930. By then Trotsky had been exiled and Bukharin had been expelled from the Central Committee. Having defeated both the left and the right, Stalin and his supporters now controlled the Communist Party.

November 1929, Bukharin was removed from the Politburo for leading the 'right deviation'. Stalin now appeared to have almost complete control of the Communist Party, though Tomsky still had a seat on the Politburo and Rykov continued as a member of the Central Committee.

Why did Stalin emerge as leader?

Historians are not agreed on the reasons for Stalin's rise to power. While their ideas often overlap, different schools of thought can be identified.

One school argues that Stalin's rise was the result of the deliberate manipulation of differences among the Bolshevik leaders. His success also depended, however, on the errors and weaknesses of his rivals. Bukharin was too focused on the NEP, Kamenev too weak willed, Zinoviev too careerist and Trotsky too isolated to be able to react to the dangers Stalin posed, while Lenin was too ill from 1922 onwards to be politically active.

For the structuralists, however, Stalin was a natural product of Russian history and of the administration set up after 1917. As the administrative apparatus grew, so did Stalin's power to appoint people to positions at both local and national level. By this method Stalin gained control of party congresses, the Central Committee and the Politburo itself. As elected soviets were increasingly ignored, central control increased. The Stalinist bureaucratic state was, therefore, a logical outcome.

Sociocultural explanations of Stalin's rise emphasise the impact of the social structure on the politics and development of the Communist Party and the Soviet state. The politically mature working class was lost either by death in the civil war or by appointment to government bureaucracy afterwards which removed them from the working-class community and created a vacuum in communist support which was often filled by ex-peasants with no real understanding of Marxism or Bolshevik history. They were much more easily manipulated by the party leadership.

Some historians also give ideological explanations for Stalin's rise to power. According to this school Stalin's policies provided a middle road between two opposed groups within the party leadership. The left were concerned that the NEP would lead to the restoration of capitalism and the right envisaged a long period with a mixed economy, with the NEP and the *smychka* seen as essential to the survival of the economy. Stalin's rise can thus be seen as a genuine political response to steer a middle course. In the beginning the centre believed the NEP was essential for recovery and so opposed the left, who seemed to endanger it. But, later, once the peasants began to defend their interests against the workers' state, they came to see a change was necessary. Hence it became necessary to attack the policies of the right, who wished the NEP to continue virtually unchanged.

One explanation of Stalin's rise, which combines elements of the sociocultural explanation, was developed by Trotsky himself. Pointing to the failure of international revolution and the consequent isolation of the new Soviet state, he argued that Russian backwardness and the growing political apathy of the working class undermined the early Soviet democracy. This allowed conservative and reactionary elements to come to the fore and eventually resulted in what he called 'bureaucratic degeneration'. Trotsky argued that a new social and political elite with increasing privileges emerged which, at first, supported the right but, once the problems of the NEP exploded in 1927–28, shifted to Stalin and the centre as their best bet for maintaining their positions. Thus Stalin's victory was the result of unforeseen historical and cultural developments after 1917 rather than because of the mistakes of his opponents.

Historical sources

1 Extracts from Lenin's Testament (25 December 1922) and Postscript (4 January 1923)

Since he became general secretary, Comrade Stalin has concentrated in his hands immeasurable power, and I am not sure that he will always know how to use that power with sufficient caution. On the other hand Comrade Trotsky . . . is distinguished not only by his outstanding qualities (personally he is the most capable man in the present Central Committee) but also by his excess of self-confidence and a readiness to be carried away by the purely administrative side of affairs . . .

Stalin is too rude, and this fault, entirely supportable in relations amongst us communists, becomes insupportable in the office of general secretary. Therefore, I propose to the comrades to find a way of removing Stalin from that position and to appoint another man who in all respects differs from Stalin only in superiority; namely, more patient, more loyal, more polite, less capricious, and more attentive to comrades.

M. Lynch, *Stalin and Khrushchev: the USSR 1924–64*, London, 1990, pp. 15–16

2 From Stalin's 'Political report of the Central Committee to the Fifteenth Congress of the Communist Party', 3 December 1927 (commenting on the expulsion of the United Opposition)

Have we the dictatorship of the proletariat or not? Rather a strange question . . . Nevertheless, the opposition raise it in every one of their statements. The opposition say that we are in a state of Thermidorian degeneration. What does that mean? It means that we do not have the dictatorship of the proletariat, that our economics and our policies are a failure, are going backwards, that we are not going towards socialism, but towards capitalism . . . Why did the Party expel Trotsky and Zinoviev? Because they are the *organisers* of the entire anti-party opposition . . . If the opposition want to be in the Party, let them submit to the will of the Party, to its laws, to its instructions, without reservations.

J. Laver, *Russia 1914–1941*, London, 1991, p. 54

Historical-source questions

1 How did Stalin use the power he had as general secretary, referred to by Lenin in Source 1?

2 What was the United Opposition, the subject of Stalin's comments in Source 2?

3 To what extent was Stalin in control of the Communist Party by the Fifteenth Congress in December 1927?

Summary questions

1 Identify and explain any *two* reasons for the power struggle which emerged in the Communist Party in the early 1920s.

2 Identify and explain any *two* factors which made Stalin determined to strengthen his position in the 1920s.

3 Compare the importance of *three* factors which enabled Stalin to defeat all opposition by 1929.

7 Stalin's revolution

Focus questions

◆ Why did Stalin make a 'turn to the left' in 1928?

◆ What were the main features of collectivisation and the five-year plans?

◆ How successful were Stalin's economic policies?

Significant dates

1925	*December*	Fourteenth Party Congress
1927	*December*	Fifteenth Party Congress
1928	*July*	Bukharin wins Central Committee vote to slow down collectivisation
	October	First Five-Year Plan starts
1929	*April*	Sixteenth Party Conference
	December	Kulaks to be 'liquidated as a class'
1930	*January*	Start of mass collectivisation
	June	Sixteenth Party Congress
1932–33		Crisis in industry; forced collectivisation causes famine
1934	*January*	Seventeenth Party Congress approves Second Five-Year Plan
1935	*August*	Start of the Stakhanovite movement
1939	*March*	Eighteenth Party Congress approves Third Five-Year Plan

Overview

By 1926, agricultural production under the NEP was producing insufficient grain. These problems continued into 1927, despite the adoption of emergency measures in some areas. By 1928, the situation led Stalin to consider collectivising agriculture and pushing for more rapid industrialisation. This led to a clash with Bukharin and the right who wanted to continue the *smychka* and the NEP.

In 1928, the First Five Year Plan for industrialisation was drawn up by **Gosplan** – it concentrated on heavy industry (iron, coal, steel, electricity, oil and machinery) and set high targets for increased productivity for each industry. In 1929, Stalin announced the forced collectivisation of agriculture by which

The State General Planning Commission or **Gosplan** had its HQ in Moscow. Each soviet republic also had its own Gosplan which was subordinate to the central one in Moscow.

A **kulak** was a rich peasant (named from the Russian word for a fist, i.e. a grasping fist). There were two other categories of peasants: *seredniak* (a middle peasant) and *bedniak* (a poor peasant).

several privately owned farms would be grouped into one state-run farm or collective. This met with great opposition from the **kulaks** (who often destroyed their animals, crops and tools rather than hand them over to the collectives).

In late 1929, Stalin determined to destroy the kulaks as a class – 1.5 million (out of 5 million) were forcibly deported to poorer parts of the Soviet Union; many died on the journey and many more once they reached the new areas.

By 1932, as food production slumped, this disruption of agriculture led to famine in some parts of the USSR. Results in industry were better – a Second Five-Year Plan was drawn up in 1933 which continued the emphasis on heavy industry. 'Shock brigades' of super-workers (known as the Stakhanovites) were set up to encourage workers to break their production targets. In 1938, a Third Five-Year Plan began, which was to concentrate on light industry and consumer goods but, in 1940, this was shifted to armaments production as fears of a Nazi invasion increased. Despite unrealistic targets and practical problems, industrial production did increase and many new railways, canals, dams and industrial centres were built.

Why did Stalin make a 'turn to the left' in 1928?

Problems with the NEP, 1926–27

Born in 1886, Evgeny **Preobrazhensky** joined the Bolsheviks in 1903 and became prominent in 1917. He was a supporter of Trotsky for many years and was one of those behind the statement of the 46. His views on the need to speed up industrialisation led him to criticise the NEP, causing clashes with Lenin and Bukharin. He also supported the restoration of party democracy and was active in the United Opposition. As a result, he was expelled from the party; later, he was a defendant in the 1936 Show Trial and was executed in 1937 (see Chapter 8).

In August 1924, **Preobrazhensky** published *The fundamental law of socialist accumulation*, arguing that in order to fund industrialisation the state should obtain food cheaply from the peasants and then sell it at a higher price to consumers. This method of 'primitive socialist accumulation' would create the surplus funds necessary to finance industrialisation. During 1923 Trotsky had come to similar conclusions. This marked the start of an industrialisation debate within the party, which was a feature of the struggle for power over the next five years. Initially, Stalin and the right rejected Preobrazhensky's argument, partly because it threatened the NEP and the *smychka* – in 1925, Bukharin actually encouraged peasants to 'enrich' themselves.

Industry

In the mid 1920s, when Trotsky and the Left Opposition were already arguing for a shift towards industrialisation, Stalin and his supporters defended the maintenance of the NEP, stating that it was a Leninist policy. Bukharin's reaction to Preobrazhensky's ideas was also dismissive, though in 1924 he also opposed the call from Lev Shanin from the State Bank for free market forces to be allowed to operate with no controls. However, by April 1925, he had moved further to the right and closer to Shanin's views. He dismissed the left's arguments that the NEP was generating class forces (in the form of a developing capitalist class of kulaks and Nepmen) which were threatening the socialist nature of the Soviet state and warned against the dangers of creating 'a state of war with the peasantry'.

There is evidence, however, that as early as November 1925 Stalin was beginning to contemplate a new revolutionary shift, in order to make a transition from the NEP to a socialist economy. He continued to work with Bukharin, however, as Zinoviev and Kamenev had joined forces with Trotsky. At the Fourteenth Party Congress in December 1925 (later called the 'Industrialisation Congress'), Zinoviev's and Kamenev's continuing criticisms of the NEP were rejected, but the principle of economic modernisation was also supported. At the Fifteenth Party Conference in the autumn of 1926, Stalin called for the Soviet Union to catch up with and overtake the West as regards industrialisation; nonetheless, he still insisted that this had to be achieved by maintaining the worker–peasant alliance.

Meanwhile, Gosplan (set up in 1921) was involved in economic planning, producing its first economic plan in August 1925. Its second plan, in 1926, included an outline five-year plan, with specific plans for each year. At the same time, **Vesenkha** was also drafting schemes for the development of the Soviet economy. However, there were divisions in these organisations between non-party specialists, who were more conservative about short-term possibilities, and the party specialists, who believed rapid industrialisation was possible and that the NEP was now hindering this. In particular, with existing industry mostly restored to pre-1914 levels of production, they began to look forward to a period of 'socialist construction'.

In addition, by 1927, there were fears of **imminent war** and many came to believe that rapid industrialisation was necessary if the Soviet Union was to be in a position to meet any invasion. Furthermore, by 1927 the United Opposition had been defeated, so Stalin felt able to adopt (albeit in a crude and distorted form) some of the economic policies advocated by Trotsky and Preobrazhensky. To prepare the way for this a Hero of Socialist Labour medal was introduced in the summer of 1927 to encourage increased productivity and labour discipline, while cuts in administrative costs were ordered so that more funds would be available for industrial expansion.

At the Fifteenth Party Congress in December 1927, however, there was still talk of maintaining the basic elements of the NEP, though Stalin did stress the foreign threats and the need to develop heavy industry. Despite the Politburo's approval of several railway, canal and hydroelectric developments, there were no general agreements on growth targets; in fact, Vesenkha and Gosplan produced rival plans.

The grain crisis in agriculture, which developed in 1927–28, persuaded Stalin that the NEP should be abandoned in favour of rapid industrialisation. This led to a serious split between Stalin and Bukharin at the Central

The **Vesenkha** was the Supreme Council of the National Economy. It existed from 1917 to 1932 and was responsible for state industry. There was great rivalry between Vesenkha and Gosplan.

What were the roles of Gosplan and Vesenkha?

Imminent war seemed likely: Britain broke off diplomatic relations in 1927, relations with France and Poland were poor and Japan seemed threatening.

Committee meeting in July 1928. As the conflict with the right developed during 1928, Stalin and his supporters accused their opponents of lacking faith in the Soviet people and of betraying the socialist ideals of Lenin and the Bolsheviks. By the end of 1928, with the right virtually defeated, Stalin pushed for higher production targets from Vesenkha and Gosplan and purged non-party specialists. By April 1929, two draft five-year plans, developed by Vesenkha and Gosplan together, were presented to the Sixteenth Party Conference. The Politburo, under Stalin's leadership, recommended adopting the plan which forecast the doubling of Soviet industry by 1932 – a much bigger increase than the left had called for or believed possible.

Agriculture

From 1924 to 1926, the NEP led to a gradual increase in agricultural production. However, despite a good harvest in 1926, state collections were 50 per cent of what had been expected. This was mainly because, as peasants prospered, they consumed more of their produce; in addition, there was less incentive to sell their surplus as there were insufficient consumer goods being

A photograph taken in 1923 of Soviet peasants working. In many areas, little had changed by 1928.

produced by industry. As a consequence, only about 13 per cent of the grain harvest found its way into the towns.

Fearing another 'scissors crisis' like that of 1923 (when low food prices and high industrial prices had led peasants to reduce food production), emergency measures were taken in some areas against kulak 'speculators' and Nepmen, including the seizure of grain and increasing the taxes on kulaks to force them to sell more grain. At this stage, although heavy industrial production figures had virtually returned to pre-war levels, there was still unemployment and many in the party began to think the state sector needed to be developed.

In 1927, the government reduced prices of industrial goods but grain deliveries declined further. Although this was due in part to poor weather, many communists believed it was because the kulaks were deliberately withholding grain (in fact, because of a scare over a possible Polish attack, hoarding did take place). State purchases of grain in 1927 were considerably down on what was required – this not only threatened hunger in the expanding towns, it also undermined the possibility of stepping up industrialisation.

Thus, by the time of the Fifteenth Party Congress in December 1927 (later known as the 'Collectivisation Congress'), many communists were beginning to see that the continuation of the NEP was blocking both agricultural and industrial development. Stalin argued that these problems could be overcome by strengthening co-operative farms, increasing mechanisation and supporting the voluntary collectivisation of farms (**kolkhozes**) which would result in bigger farms and higher yields. At this stage, there was no mention of forced collectivisation or of destroying the kulaks as a class.

In 1928, however, the problem of insufficient grain purchases continued – in Siberia, Stalin instructed local officials to increase state grain procurements. Their response was to seize more grain, to close markets and to arrest those who resisted as kulaks under Article 107 of the Criminal Code (passed in 1927 to deal with speculation). After the 1928 harvest, these actions (which became known as the Ural-Siberian method) began to result in serious unrest in rural areas and led to bread shortages, as grain was hidden to avoid requisitioning or to await higher prices.

In July 1928, at a Central Committee meeting, Bukharin was able to ensure an increase in the price of grain and an end to the forcible measures, as he argued that the *smychka* must be maintained. Stalin was determined that industrial development should not be disrupted by any diversion of money to the kulaks and after the meeting he ordered that emergency actions should continue. This provoked Bukharin, in September 1928, into publishing a defence of the NEP, which was also an implicit criticism of Stalin's actions.

The crisis in agriculture, however, continued. By the end of 1928, a combination of a fall in sales of grain to the state and a crop failure in the central and

A **kolkhoz** was a voluntary co-operative or collective farm made up of peasants' land that had become state-owned. They were allowed to use it rent free, in return for fulfilling the state grain procurement quotas. Any surplus was divided among the members, according to how much work they had done for the *kolkhoz*. Each peasant family was also allowed access to a small area of plotland and to keep some animals. A *kolkhoz* should not be confused with a *sovkhoz*, which was a state farm on which the workers were paid a regular wage. These were much larger and much more mechanised.

Why did Stalin decide that the collectivisation of agriculture was necessary?

What was the Ural-Siberian method?

Why were Bukharin and the right opposed to Stalin's policy of forced collectivisation?

south-eastern regions of the USSR led to dramatic increases in free-market prices, a further slump in grain deliveries to the state and the introduction of rationing during the winter of 1928–29. During 1929, the forcible seizing of grain was carried out in most of the Soviet Union, and the NEP and the *smychka* were destroyed in all but name. In November and December 1929, Stalin (having defeated the right at the Sixteenth Party Conference in April) launched a programme of collectivisation and called for the kulaks to be 'liquidated as a class'.

What were the main features of collectivisation and the five-year plans?

Collectivisation of agriculture

By the end of 1929, motivated by the fear of war and armed with an extremely ambitious five-year plan, Stalin was determined that the crisis in agriculture would be resolved before the spring sowing for the 1930 harvest. As a first emergency measure, a massive grain procurement campaign was launched, with extremely high quotas. Officials, determined to avoid punishment for failure (as had happened in 1928), used their power to arrest, deport and confiscate the property of any peasant who failed to hand over their quota. In all, some 16 million tons of grain were collected – in some areas, over 30 per cent of the entire crop was taken, causing serious food shortages in some rural areas.

Campaign against the kulaks

The grain procurement campaign of 1929–30 was a short-term emergency measure, similar in principle, if not in degree, to earlier ones in 1927 and 1928. To bring about lasting changes to safeguard industrialisation plans, Stalin decided the kulaks needed to be 'liquidated as a class' and called for this in December 1929. Action was first taken against kulaks who resisted the grain collections, though 'identification' of kulaks often went beyond Stalin's definition of a kulak as a peasant with two horses and four cows.

The Young Communist League or **Komsomol** was set up in 1918 for young people aged 18–28. It provided many volunteers for various party programmes and policies, and also assisted the police and the Red Army. Many went on to join the Communist Party as full members once they had reached the age of 28.

Mass collectivisation, 1930

Action against kulaks was stepped up after January 1930 when urban brigades of workers and **Komsomol** members, with the support of police and soldiers, went into the countryside to organise the setting-up of collectives. Initially, persuasion was the main method, but Stalin pressed for rapid results and violence was increasingly used. This was especially true after a decree in February which gave local committees power to apply 'necessary measures' against the kulaks, who were then divided into three categories. Two groups, 'counter-revolutionaries' and 'exploiters', were to be given harsh punishments – execution or deportation, respectively.

Richer peasants often destroyed their crops and livestock rather than hand them over to the local *kolkhoz* or raided the *kolkhozes* to reclaim their property. Local parties were given targets of how many households should be collectivised – officials (either ambitious for promotion or fearful of being denounced as 'rightists') often resorted to force. Official figures said about 4 per cent of households were kulaks, but in the end some 15 per cent of households were affected by forcible collectivisation. Many were imprisoned or executed for their resistance and around 150,000 were forcibly moved to poorer land in the north and east.

By March 1930, it was reported that 58 per cent of peasant households had been collectivised, but the process had provoked serious resistance, including arson, riots and armed rebellions (often killing communist officials). This was especially serious in the Ukraine, North Caucasus and Kazakhstan. This chaos and violence worried the Politburo – apart from the political dangers of rebellion, the spring sowing was jeopardised. So, in March 1930, Stalin was pressurised by other communist leaders into calling a halt. Official policy returned to voluntary collectivisation and many peasants, wrongly classified as kulaks, had their property restored. By October 1930, only about 20 per cent of households were still collectivised (the figure in October 1929 had been 40 per cent).

Collectivisation, 1930–37

Stalin's retreat in 1930 was only temporary; once the 1930 harvest had been secured, collectivisation resumed in earnest. By 1931, 50 per cent of households were in collective farms; by 1934, it was 70 per cent, by 1935, 75 per cent, and by 1937, the official figure was 90 per cent. Each collective (normally about 70 households) was headed by a farm manager who took control of the harvest and ensured all taxes (in kind or money) were paid to the government. Machine Tractor Stations (MTS) were established to supply seed and to hire out machinery to local *kolkhozes* (payment was made in grain). Between 1929 and 1932, over 2,500 of these were built.

These statistics hide the great upheaval and confusion that resulted in a dreadful famine in 1932–33. The first sign of problems came in October 1931, when it was revealed that many agricultural areas had been affected by drought. Famine first appeared in the Ukraine in the spring of 1932. With occasional slight improvements, it spread to several more areas, especially parts of the North Caucasus. It went on to become the worst famine in Russia's history. Though the worst was over by 1933, some areas were still affected by serious food shortages in 1934.

Despite the warning signs of this rural catastrophe, Stalin had persisted with forced collectivisation and high state grain procurements. In all, millions died; however, historians are still not agreed on the total figures – in part,

> What happened in several important agricultural areas of the Soviet Union in the years 1932–33?

because the Great Purge and the Great Terror in the second half of the 1930s have confused matters (see page 83).

After 1933, agriculture did revive, though grain production increased slowly. In 1935, it finally exceeded pre-collectivisation figures (75 million tonnes); there was a drop in 1936 to 56 million tonnes, then another increase in 1937 to 97 million tonnes. Livestock numbers increased even more slowly and in fact did not exceed pre-collectivisation levels until 1953. However, the drive to collectivise continued and state procurement quotas were constantly raised. As a result, life on the collectives remained very hard for most of the 1930s.

Industrialisation

The First Five-Year Plan, 1928–32

The First Five-Year Plan began on 1 October 1928; encouraged by the successful completion of the early targets, higher ones were set almost as soon as the plan began. It concentrated mainly on heavy industry – coal, iron, steel, oil and machine production; overall, production was planned to increase by 300 per cent. Light industry, too, was to double its output and, in order to ensure sufficient energy was available, electricity production was to increase by 600 per cent. Many workers were enthused by the vision of creating a planned

A Soviet poster, 1933. The top half shows a copy of the First Five-Year Plan of 1928 with a foreign capitalist saying: 'Fantasy, Lies, Utopia'. The bottom half shows the capitalist proved wrong, silenced by the plan's success after only four years.

socialist economy and worked hard to fulfil each year's targets – soon, reports (mostly unreliable) began to arrive in Moscow of how targets were being exceeded. Talk then began in 1929 of fulfilling the plan in four years, not five. Stalin officially backed this in June 1930 and posters appeared proclaiming '2+2=5'. Stalin urged Communist Party and Komsomol members to form 'shock work' and 'socialist emulation' brigades (made up of especially productive workers) to encourage other workers and set the right example.

Under the plan, there were significant achievements that fundamentally transformed the Soviet economy. In particular, hundreds of new factories and mines were set up in many regions, some of which had had no industrial development before 1928. New industrial complexes, such as Magnitogorsk, were built, as were new rail links and hydroelectric schemes. Part of the reason behind Stalin's push for rapid industrialisation was the uncertainty of the international situation. In 1931, he pointed out the USSR's relative economic backwardness (50 or 100 years behind western countries) and said that the Soviet Union had to make this up in 10 years: 'Either we do it, or they crush us.' Stalin's announcement in December 1932 that the First Five-Year Plan had been fulfilled was an exaggeration – despite tremendous growth, no major targets had actually been met.

The crisis year, 1932–33

Ironically, the real achievements and too rapid implementation of the First Five-Year Plan created problems in the period 1932–33, which delayed the drafting and implementation of the next plan. Implementation costs had been much greater than allowed for by Gosplan and the great increases in the volume of coal, iron and industrial goods proved too much for the railway system to cope with. At the same time, rapidly expanding urban populations led to housing shortages, while the effects of forced collectivisation led to food shortages and rationing. In this situation, many workers frequently changed jobs, and managers, desperate to retain skilled workers so they could complete their plan targets, were forced to increase wages and offer additional, unofficial, perks. This move away from egalitarianism towards increasing wage differentials and introducing piece-rates and bonuses added to the problem of workers moving and changing jobs as they could exploit the situation by playing off one manager against another for higher pay and better perks.

The Second Five-Year Plan, 1933–37

Nonetheless, Gosplan drew up the Second Five-Year Plan which was at first intended to create a fully socialist economy by removing money from the economy. However, nothing was finally approved until the Seventeenth Party Congress in January 1934 – the delay was the result of the economic crisis which forced Gosplan to continually modify cost calculations and targets. The final draft simply called for increased production and improved living standards, and the need to build on the achievements of the first plan.

From 1934 to 1936, there were many successes – in particular, machine production and iron and steel output grew rapidly, making the Soviet Union practically self-sufficient in these areas. Many of the new industrial plants began producing, while the number of new enterprises opened was nearly 5,000 (compared with almost 2,000 under the first plan).

The Stakhanovite movement

Part of the reason for the success of the Second Five-Year Plan was the big increase in labour productivity. The Stakhanovite movement was set up to encourage workers to follow the example of Stakhanov, a miner in the Donbas mining region. He dug out a massive 102 tonnes of coal in one shift (the usual figure was 7 tonnes) in August 1935 and was held up as an heroic example which workers were urged to follow. Most industries had their own model workers, who received higher bonuses and other material advantages (such as new flats) as well as being given medals for being 'Heroes of Socialist Labour'. By now, the worst effects of forced collectivisation were over, allowing rationing to be abandoned in 1935.

Who was Stakhanov and what was his significance for Stalin's industrialisation programme?

The Third Five-Year Plan, 1938–42

Once again, despite significant achievements and successes under the second plan, the industrialisation programme was hit by problems in 1937. The winter of 1937–38 was severe and caused serious fuel shortages which, in turn, affected factory production and the transportation of goods and raw materials by rail. Industrial planning was also affected by the growing impact of the Purges, which saw thousands of managers and experts either imprisoned or executed (see Chapter 8), and by the worsening international situation, which meant that increasingly funds were diverted to defence (see Chapter 9).

Planning began in February 1936, but the purging of Gosplan specialists created confusion and delays and the Third Five-Year Plan was not formally approved until the Eighteenth Party Congress in March 1939. By then, earlier proposals to develop light industry and to increase the production of consumer goods were already being undermined by a new emphasis on heavy industry and defence.

Vyacheslav **Molotov** was born in 1890. He was a great supporter of Stalin, becoming a member of the Politburo in 1926. He backed Stalin's economic policies as well as the Great Purge. From 1939 to 1949, he was commissar for foreign affairs. He continued to hold high office after Stalin's death, but was removed from the Central Committee in 1957.

Nonetheless, huge increases in production were planned (92 per cent) and **Molotov** claimed that, because the first two plans had laid the foundation for a socialist economy, this third plan would complete the process and enable the Soviet Union to begin the transition to communism. The Third Five-Year Plan, however, was totally disrupted in June 1941, when Nazi Germany launched its invasion.

How successful were Stalin's economic policies?

Did Stalin plan his 'revolution from above'?

Many historians have suggested that Stalin did not have a master plan for the measures he implemented in 1928, once he had defeated his opponents on the left and right of the Communist Party. They point to the fact that changes came about in both agriculture and industry because of unforeseen problems arising from the NEP. In particular, Stalin's initial response to the grain crisis is seen as an emergency short-term measure which triggered off a sequence of developments that led to more and more radical decisions being taken. It can also be argued that Stalin's constant interference – especially by increasing the targets – prevented the plans from being coherently and successfully implemented. These historians argue that Stalin did not really know where his policies might take the Soviet Union.

Others argue that Stalin clearly intended to modernise the Soviet Union and adopted deliberate agricultural and industrial policies to do so, once he considered that political factors enabled him to begin. Others go on to argue that Stalin was deliberately attempting to complete the Bolshevik Revolution of 1917; this revolution was considered incomplete because the peasants had been allowed to own land privately and the NEP involved a partial return to capitalism (compared to the total nationalisation under the earlier policy of war communism). Once he felt politically secure, he consciously launched his own 'second revolution, from above' which, unlike that of 1917, was the result of a government decision and not because of a spontaneous grassroots movement.

How reliable are the statistics?

Official statistics, produced during and after Stalin's rule, about the increases in productivity achieved by the five-year plans are highly suspect: for the period 1928–40, the official figure for increased industrial production is 852 per cent. Similar doubts apply to figures relating to specific industries. However, by applying stricter criteria, most historians, such as A. Nove, accept that there were tremendous increases in production, especially in heavy industry.

One problem with these official statistics is that many factory managers, fearful of being punished for non-fulfilment of targets, either deliberately underestimated production capacity or claimed production figures higher than those actually achieved. An associated problem was the lack of skills of many of the industrial workers in state enterprises, who expanded in numbers from 1.4 million in 1928, to 6.4 million in 1932, to 7.9 million in 1937 and 8.3 million in 1940. Many were ex-peasants: 9 million alone joined the ranks of industrial workers under the First Five-Year Plan. They had little basic training and no experience of factory discipline; most were under the age of 29 and fewer than 20 per cent had 5 years' experience of factory work. Such workers, used to seasonal working, found factory discipline hard to accept.

Impact on workers

In order to meet the high production targets, new work practices were introduced. In 1929, the 'uninterrupted' week was introduced, with shift work organised so that factories were not idle at the weekend. Absenteeism and late arrival for work were punished, either by the loss of the job and factory housing or, after 1931 when such offences were criminalised, by imprisonment or sentence to a labour camp such as the Gulag. This strict discipline led many to change jobs frequently, especially once the plans had ended unemployment and created extra employment.

Overall, most historians agree that the rushed pace of industrialisation – especially during the first plan – drastically reduced living standards, particularly through food shortages and rising prices as well as continued housing shortages. Even recovery during the mid 1930s did not, according to some historians, restore living standards to pre-1928 levels. However, the plans did end the high unemployment of the 1920s, while the huge increase in the numbers of workers (including many women) enabled joint family incomes to increase. Those peasants who became industrial workers also experienced improvements in living standards, while many younger women, who under the old tsarist system might have become domestic servants, were able to find employment in offices. Many workers also benefited from the opening-up and expansion of education (especially technical colleges and universities) from 1929 which were designed to increase the skills and hence the productivity of the workforce.

The Gulag

In 1929, OGPU (see page 67) were instructed to establish forced labour camps in the remoter regions. In 1930, OGPU set up the Chief Administration of Camps (Gulag) to run these camps. Previously, some historians estimated that the numbers in forced labour camps grew from about 30,000 prisoners in 1928 to about 2 million in 1932 and to an estimated 8 million by 1938. These prisoners (*zeks*) were increasingly used to undertake huge construction projects, such as canals and railways. Many of the prisoners were deported ex-kulaks or workers who had committed labour discipline offences and many more came from those purged during the 1930s. Conditions were hard and food often scarce, particularly in the Kolyma camps where prisoners worked the goldfields under extremely primitive conditions.

However, since **glasnost** and the subsequent collapse of the Soviet Union, historians have used newly released evidence to estimate that by 1939 the total number of prisoners detained in such camps was just under 3 million. A similar debate surrounds the numbers who perished in the Gulag.

How did the setting-up of the Gulag in the 1930s contribute to the industrialisation of the Soviet Union?

Glasnost refers to the policy of 'openness' in the Soviet Union, begun after Gorbachev became general secretary of the Communist Party in 1985. As a result, many secret documents became available for research by both Soviet and western historians.

Collectivisation

The move towards collectivisation was intended to solve a serious shortfall in the amount of grain needed to feed the urban population. However, the destructive resistance by kulaks and the disruption caused by deporting about 2.5 million people to the Gulag in the years 1930–31 led to a serious and sudden drop in food production generally by 1931. As we have seen, this led to the famine of 1932–33 in which millions died.

Historians are not agreed on the total number of people who died in the famine, with estimates varying from 3.5 million to 7 million. However, these deaths are only some of the deaths that can be attributed to the process of collectivisation in general. Again, historians are divided, with total estimates (including the famine) of people who died as a result of collectivisation ranging from 6 million to 20 million.

The economic results of collectivisation are also an area of controversy, though historians agree that, after 1928, grain deliveries to the state did increase, despite total agricultural production suffering a serious decline in the 1930s. One group of historians supports the orthodox view, which argues that, despite the decline in agricultural output, collectivisation did shift resources and funds from rural to urban areas and so allowed rapid industrialisation to succeed. Others argue that if the NEP had continued, industrial growth rates would have been much lower than those achieved by the five-year plans. However, historians taking the revisionist line claim that collectivisation was an economic disaster which consequently made little contribution to the industrialisation programme.

Historical sources

1 Extract from an article written by Stalin in 1931, on the need to industrialise as quickly as possible

It is sometimes asked whether it is not possible to slow down the tempo a bit, to put a check on the movement. No, comrades, it is not possible! The tempo must not be reduced! On the contrary, we must increase it as much as is within our powers and possibilities . . .

To slacken the tempo would mean falling behind. And those who fall behind are beaten . . . Do you want our socialist fatherland to be beaten and to lose its independence? If you do not want this you must put an end to its backwardness in the shortest possible time and develop a genuine Bolshevik tempo in building up its socialist system of economy. There is no other way. That is why Lenin said during the October Revolution: 'Either perish, or overtake and outstrip the advanced capitalist countries.'

We are 50 or 100 years behind the advanced countries. We must make good this distance in ten years. Either we do it, or they crush us.

J. Laver, *Russia 1914–1941*, London, 1991, pp. 60–61

2 A western historian's view on the impact of Stalin's economic policies

The proper assessment of living standards at this time is rendered almost impossible not only by the existence of rationing, price differences and shortages, but also of queues, decline in quality, neglect of consumer requirements . . . Therefore, any figures comparing wages and prices are bound greatly to understate the decline in living standards . . . 1933 was the culmination of the most precipitous peacetime decline in living standards known in recorded history.

A. Nove, *An economic history of the USSR*, London, 1980

Historical-source questions

1 Which were the advanced countries referred to by Stalin in Source 1?

2 What events in the period 1918–21 made Stalin fear the USSR might be invaded?

3 How can the comments by Stalin in Source 1 help explain the view offered in Source 2 about the decline in living standards in the USSR in the early 1930s?

Summary questions

1 Identify and explain any *two* of Stalin's methods to modernise the Soviet economy in the 1930s.

2 Identify and explain any *two* problems associated with Stalin's economic policies.

8 Show trials and purges

Significant dates

1928–30 Party purge expels thousands of lower-ranking party members

1930 *June* Sixteenth Party Congress

December Syrtsov's 'bloc' expelled from Central Committee

1932 *September* The Ryutin Affair

December Party purge ordered

1933 *January* Smirnov's 'anti-party group' charged with attempting to replace Stalin

1934 *January* Seventeenth Party Congress

December Kirov murdered; thousands arrested

1935 *January* Mass arrests continue; Zinoviev, Kamenev and 17 other members of a 'Moscow Centre' faced a secret trial

1936 *August* First show trial (Trial of the Sixteen); Great Purge begins

September The Stalin–Zhdanov telegram; Yezhov replaces Yagoda as head of NKVD

December The Stalin Constitution adopted by special party congress

1937 *January* Second show trial (Trial of the Seventeen)

February Bukharin and Rykov expelled from the party

May Purge of the Red Army begins

1938 *March* Third show trial (Trial of the Twenty-one)

December Beria replaces Yezhov as head of the NKVD

1939 *March* Eighteenth Party Congress; the Great Purge officially ends

Overview

Although Stalin had defeated the Left, the United and the Right Oppositions by 1929, dissent still existed within the Communist Party. The early problems of forced collectivisation and the First Five-Year Plan caused further criticism of Stalin to emerge at the Sixteenth Party Congress in June 1930. In 1932, the Ryutin Affair revealed that this dissent was ongoing. Stalin was further troubled when a majority of the Politburo refused to support his call for Ryutin to be executed.

The Seventeenth Party Congress, held in January 1934, revealed both continuing criticism of Stalin and the growing popularity of **Kirov**. On 1 December, Kirov was assassinated under suspicious circumstances. Stalin then ordered a series of arrests and executions. After a secret trial, Zinoviev, Kamenev and other leading communists were given prison sentences. Then in August 1936, the Great Purge was launched by the first of the show trials; more took place in 1937 and 1938.

The Great Purge was undertaken by the **NKVD**, led by Yagoda. He was replaced later in 1936 by Yezhov whose more extreme methods began the Great Terror. In 1937, this spread to include the officer corps of the armed forces as well as Communist Party officials. As a result of the Great Purge, several million people were arrested in the period 1936–39, large numbers of whom were either executed or sent to the Gulag where many perished because of the harsh conditions and inadequate diet.

In 1938, Beria replaced Yezhov as head of the NKVD and the Great Terror began to diminish. In 1939, at the Eighteenth Party Congress, the Great Purge was officially ended. By then, virtually all the 'Old Guard' Bolsheviks (those who had worked with Lenin) had either been executed or had committed suicide.

What were the immediate causes of the Great Purge, 1936–39?

Purges before 1930

Purges had taken place in the Communist Party before Stalin's rise to power. During the power struggle of the 1920s, many of Stalin's opponents to the left and right lost senior posts or were expelled from the party. However, even these purges were not violent, nor were they as extensive as those of the 1930s. Up until this time, the majority of Gulag prisoners were ex-kulaks or workers who had breached labour discipline; from the mid 1930s, the vast majority of Gulag inmates were the victims of Stalin's purges.

Though Stalin had defeated his main opponents by 1929, he was not totally dominant. In the late 1920s, his calls for stricter action against defeated

Sergei **Kirov** was born in 1888 and joined the Bolsheviks in 1904. He was elected to the Politburo in 1930. As head of the Leningrad Communist Party, he was a popular moderate. He opposed some of Stalin's more extreme economic and repressive measures.

The **NKVD** are the initials of the People's Commissariat for Internal Affairs, set up in 1917. In July 1934, it took over the secret police (OGPU) and kept this responsibility until 1943.

In the Russian Communist Party, '**purge**' initially referred to checking the personal qualities and behaviour (e.g. drunkenness, political inactivity) of party members. In such purges or 'cleansings' (*chistki*), those found wanting had their party cards taken away. Violence was not used and those involved were later allowed to rejoin if their behaviour improved. Such purges took place in 1919, 1921, 1929 and 1933. The Great Purge in the 1930s, with mass imprisonment and executions, was a very different phenomenon.

opponents were not always supported by members of the Politburo and his lack of complete control meant he had to accept compromises. Furthermore, though removed from high office, Bukharin, Rykov and Tomsky (leaders of the defeated Right Opposition) still had sympathisers and supporters in the party, with the result that at the Sixteenth Party Congress in June 1930 these three were re-elected to the Central Committee. In addition, the early problems arising from mass collectivisation and rapid industrialisation began to create doubts and political division even within the Politburo, where only Molotov and Kaganovitch were uncritical supporters of Stalin. In December 1930, Syrtsov and others were expelled from the Central Committee for criticising the excesses being committed in the name of collectivisation – significantly, they had previously supported Stalin in the struggle against Bukharin and the right.

Why were the criticisms made by Syrtsov of the methods used in collectivisation of significance to Stalin's position in the party?

The Ryutin Affair, 1932

A more serious indication of the extent of opposition to aspects of Stalin's policies came in 1932 when Ryutin, a Rightist who became important in the early 1930s, wrote a document calling for the end of forced collectivisation, the rehabilitation of the defeated Oppositionists (including Trotsky) and the dismissal of Stalin. Ryutin's document also accused Stalin of destroying the communist revolution and was signed by several prominent communists. They were put on trial in September and Ryutin, Zinoviev, Kamenev and 17 others were then expelled from the Central Committee. Stalin had wanted Ryutin executed, but the Politburo refused to go that far, thus underlining the fact that Stalin did not yet have complete control. During the next two years, nearly 1 million members were expelled from the party for being 'Ryutinites'.

What was the Ryutin Affair? How did it show that Stalin was not in complete control of the Communist Party in 1932?

The Seventeenth Party Congress, 1934

Despite these expulsions, however, opposition to Stalin continued after the Ryutin Affair. In January 1933, Smirnov (another leading communist) was expelled for forming an 'anti-party group' in order to remove Stalin.

A major turning point seems to have been the Seventeenth Party Congress (which became known as the 'Congress of Victors') which took place in January 1934. (The economic chaos and the unrest generated by collectivisation and industrialisation meant that no congress was called between 1930 and 1934.)

This congress abolished the post of general secretary – this meant that, in principle, Stalin was now no more important than the three other newly elected secretaries of the Communist Party – Kirov, Kaganovitch and Zhdanov. Although it is possible that Stalin himself desired this, in order to share responsibility for the economic crisis, the Central Committee elected by the congress indicates that not all in the Communist Party approved of Stalin's leadership – it appears that Kirov received votes from almost all the 1,225 delegates who voted for seats on the Central Committee, while about 300 did not vote for Stalin at all.

The Kirov Affair, 1934

Why did Stalin possibly see Kirov as a threat?

There is evidence to suggest that Kirov, who was a Politburo member and the party leader in Leningrad, might have been asked by some leading local officials before the Seventeenth Party Congress to replace Stalin, but he refused. He was known to have doubts about the pace of industrialisation and Stalin's methods of disciplining the party. When he was assassinated in December 1934, under suspicious circumstances, Stalin immediately claimed this was part of a plot to overthrow him and the rule of the Communist Party, supposedly by a 'Leningrad Opposition Centre' which had links with Trotsky's Left Opposition and the United Opposition. The recently reorganised NKVD, headed by Yagoda, was given sweeping powers of arrest, trial and execution under a special terrorist decree passed the day after Kirov's assassination.

How did Stalin use Kirov's assassination in 1934 to extend his control over the Communist Party?

In the next few weeks, over 100 party members were shot and thousands of Trotskyists and Zinovievists were arrested, including Zinoviev and Kamenev. Trotsky himself was abroad, having been deported in 1929. In January 1935, Zinoviev and Kamenev and 17 others were tried and imprisoned for 5 to 10 years. A few days later, 12 important NKVD members in Leningrad were also tried and imprisoned and several thousand 'bourgeois elements' were then rounded up and imprisoned.

What was the Great Purge?

By mid 1935, the purges described above had begun to come to a halt, in part because of the improving economic situation. In this relatively calm period, the drafting of a new constitution, taking into account the Soviet Union's advance to socialism, went ahead. Known as the 'Stalin Constitution', it was approved and came into effect in 1936. After this period of relative calm, a new purge began in the summer of 1936, involving the first show trial and signalling the start of what became known as the Great Purge.

The Trial of the Sixteen, August 1936

In early 1936, the NKVD claimed to have uncovered a Trotskyist–Zinovievist counter-revolutionary conspiracy, in league with capitalist states, White Guards and kulaks. Although in prison, Zinoviev and Kamenev as well as Smirnov, Syrtsov and 12 others were accused of organising this conspiracy and plotting to kill Stalin and other Politburo members. NKVD interrogations

A photograph of Vyshinsky, the prosecutor-general in the first show trial (against Zinoviev and Kamenev) in August 1936.

Karl **Radek** was born in 1885 and joined the Bolsheviks after the 1917 Revolution. He was a leading member of the Comintern and was a supporter of Trotsky for a time.

Born in 1895, Nikolay **Yezhov** joined the Bolsheviks in 1917 and played an active part in the November Revolution and the civil war. He helped organise the collectivisation of agriculture as well as developing the idea of a Trotskyist–Zinovievist conspiracy. As head of the NKVD from 1936 to 1938, he organised the show trials against the Old Bolsheviks and the purge of the armed forces.

Born in 1883, Andrei **Vyshinsky** at first supported the Mensheviks, but joined the Bolsheviks during the civil war. He acted as deputy state prosecutor during the show trials. In 1940, he became deputy commissar for foreign affairs.

(based on the 'conveyor system' of sleep deprivation, continued questioning and beatings) resulted in 14 of them admitting their 'guilt'. All 16 were found guilty and then executed. At the same time, 43 other leading communists disappeared.

Some of the 'confessions' made to the NKVD implicated the former Right Opposition leaders, Bukharin, Rykov and Tomsky. They and others (including **Radek** and Piatakov) were questioned, but were not arrested, although Tomsky committed suicide. Eventually Yagoda dropped the investigations, possibly because Bukharin and Rykov refused to confess or possibly because of disagreements within the Politburo. As a result, Stalin had Yagoda replaced by **Yezhov**, on the grounds that Yagoda had not been active enough in exposing the full scale of the 'conspiracy'.

The Trial of the Seventeen, January 1937

In January 1937 a second show trial of 17 communist leaders took place. They were accused of plotting with Trotsky (said to be in league with Nazi Germany and Japan) to carry out assassinations, terrorist activities, sabotage of industry and spying. Those accused again included Radek and Piatakov and once again NKVD interrogations produced 'confessions' which provided **Vyshinsky**'s main 'evidence'. This time, 13 – including Piatakov (who was deputy commissar for heavy industry) – were sentenced to death.

Following this second show trial and the subsequent executions, the Central Committee met during February and March 1937. Its main business was to consider stepping up the exposure and destruction of the 'Trotskyist

Conspiracy', as revealed by Stalin and Molotov. Yezhov, recently appointed general commissar for state security, took his cue from Stalin and accused Bukharin of having known of Trotsky's plans. Bukharin refused to confess to this and a special sub-committee expelled both him and Rykov from the party. They were immediately arrested and taken to the Lubianka, the NKVD headquarters, where they were held for interrogation. At the last Central Committee meeting, in early March, Bukharin, Rykov and Tomsky (already dead) as well as Yagoda were charged with having links with Trotsky and his supporters.

The Trial of the Twenty-one, March 1938

This, the last and biggest of the show trials, focused on Bukharin, Rykov and 19 others. They were accused of membership of a Trotskyist–Rightist bloc which was supposedly responsible for industrial sabotage, weakening the Red Army, spying for foreign enemies and attempting to restore capitalism, among other things. Once again, most of the accused 'confessed' to their 'crimes', though Bukharin refused to admit his guilt. Vyshinsky called for them to be found guilty and shot. The court returned the desired verdict and Bukharin and Rykov, along with 16 others, were shot.

The Great Terror

Yezhovshchina (literally 'the time of Yezhov') refers to the height of the Great Purge, from 1937 to 1938, when Yezhov was head of the NKVD.

Why was the Great Terror known as the Yezhovshchina?

By this time the Great Purge had begun to transform into the Great Terror – or **Yezhovshchina** – as the number of denunciations, expulsions, trials, imprisonments and executions multiplied. Initially, the purges had mainly affected party members; by mid 1937, they had widened to include large numbers of administrators and specialists, including engineers and railway workers. In the years 1937–38, many important officials were arrested and shot, all of the Leningrad party's central committee were removed and almost the entire party structure in the Ukraine, from the Politburo downwards, was purged. In most of the other republics, high-ranking party officials were purged. Moscow even set each region quotas to fulfil. Many ended up in the Gulag, while others were simply executed by the NKVD.

This purge also spread to the Red Army. Some officers or former officers had been implicated in the first or second show trials in 1936–37. In May 1937, Marshal Tukhachevsky (chief of general staff and a deputy commissar for defence) and Gamarnik (head of the Red Army's political commissars and also a deputy commissar for defence) were arrested and accused of plotting with Trotsky and foreign enemies to assassinate Soviet leaders. On 12 June 1937, Tukhachevsky and some other leading commanders were executed. Gamarnik, like Tomsky, committed suicide once sentence had been passed. The Great Terror then spread down to the lower ranks of the Red Army so that, by the end of 1938, the list of those executed included 3 out of the 5 Red

An anti-Soviet cartoon commenting on Stalin's purges on the leadership of the Communist Party.

Army marshals, 14 out of the 16 top commanders, all 8 admirals, 60 of the 67 corps commanders, 136 out of the 199 divisional commanders and 221 out of the 397 brigade commanders. Also badly hit were the airforce officers and the military intelligence service. In all, about 35,000 of the entire officer corps (about 50 per cent) were either executed or imprisoned; all 11 deputy commissars for defence and 75 of the 80 members of the Supreme Military Council were also executed.

The Great Terror also began to affect large numbers of ordinary people – many, keen to avoid suspicion falling on themselves, tried to prove their loyalty to Stalin by denouncing others. Some also saw it as a way of settling scores or securing for themselves the jobs of those purged. By the end of 1938, most Russians were in a state of terror, reluctant to talk openly to anyone. It was at that point, however, that the Great Terror began to diminish.

How did the Great Purge affect the Red Army?

The end of the Great Terror

As early as October 1937, Stalin raised doubts about purging industrial workers and in January 1938 the Central Committee decided a party recruitment

Born in 1899, Lavrenti **Beria** was an early supporter of Stalin. In 1938, he replaced Yezhov as head of the NKVD and was responsible for the elimination of Yezhov and several other NKVD officials at the end of the Great Terror. When Zhdanov died in 1948, it was thought Beria would succeed Stalin as ruler of the Soviet Union; but when Stalin died in 1953, Beria was quickly arrested and executed.

drive was necessary to replace those purged as a result of false denunciations. In December 1938, **Beria** replaced Yezhov as general commissar for state security and at the Eighteenth Party Congress in March 1939 Stalin and Zhdanov announced that 'mass cleansings' were no longer needed and even admitted 'mistakes' had been made. Later in 1939, Yezhov was accused of being a British agent and was executed. As a result, mass arrests ended, several thousand Gulag prisoners were released and many more who had been expelled from the party and had lost their jobs were rehabilitated – this time is sometimes referred to as the 'spring of liberalism'. However, it is important to note that people continued to be arrested and imprisoned or executed, albeit on a much smaller scale.

How can the Great Purge and the Great Terror be explained?

Totalitarian theories

The orthodox or traditional views on the causes of the Great Purge centre on the role of Stalin and are based on his position as dictator of the Soviet Union, which was clearly established by the time it ended. Some historians have argued that Stalin launched the purges because he was suffering from some form of mental illness, or at least paranoia, that led to irrational and extreme action. Others, while accepting his responsibility for and planning of the Great Terror, argue that it should be seen, at least in part, as a 'rational' response to the circumstances of the 1930s, serving Stalin's determination to remain as leader.

Revisionist theories

More recently, several historians have turned their attention away from Stalin himself and on to other factors, such as the existence of genuine opposition that posed a potential threat to Stalin's position. Echoing the structuralist debate over the nature and distribution of power in Nazi Germany, some historians, such as G. Rittersporn, have argued that although Stalin made crucial appointments (especially replacing Yagoda with Yezhov as head of the NKVD) the NKVD and local party bosses were often out of control in the chaos of the 1930s and frequently took matters well beyond Stalin's intentions: at times, the Great Terror was an opportunity for rival local leaders to settle old scores.

Others, such as J. Arch Getty, have also suggested that there is evidence that Stalin's belief in a Trotskyist–Zinovievist plot was based, at least in part, on fact. There is evidence to suggest that, between 1930 and 1932, middle-ranking communist officials contacted Trotsky about forming a new opposition bloc and that proposals for a Trotsky–Zinoviev alliance were being made.

However, the number of victims of the Great Purge was far greater than the number of likely Oppositionists by the mid 1930s.

Stalin and Leninism

Although Trotsky joined Lenin's Bolshevik Party in August 1917, this was only after almost 14 years of intermittent differences about party organisation and the likely course of the revolution when it came to Russia. By 1917, both Lenin and Trotsky had moved closer to the other's positions. Trotsky's reasons for not joining the Bolshevik faction when the RSDLP split in 1903 were mainly based on his fears concerning Lenin's insistence that the party be run on the basis of democratic centralism. Given the lack of democracy in Tsarist Russia, Trotsky believed this would lead to 'substitutism', with the party organisation substituting for the party as a whole, then the Central Committee for the party organisation, until 'finally a single dictator substitutes himself for the Central Committee'.

However, Trotsky always rejected the argument that Stalin and Stalinism were the logical outcome of Lenin's ideas and methods of rule. Historians such as Isaac Deutscher and R. Medvedev have also portrayed Stalinism as being quite distinct from Leninism, pointing to the fact that terror was not used against Communist Party members before Stalin. In addition, at several points in the 1930s the Communist Party leadership tried to limit actions taken against various opponents. They point out that Lenin never tried to force defeated political opponents to recant their views or to make preposterous 'confessions' – such methods were only used by Stalin. Several historians also point out that the early purges had much more to do with expelling the many careerists and politically immature (who had begun to join the Bolsheviks in large numbers when it became clear that they were winning the civil war) for personal deficiencies than with attempting to create an ideologically 'pure' and monolithic party. Thus Stalin's Great Purge, which cost so many lives, appears to have been uniquely violent and a clear break with Leninist traditions.

Historical sources

1 Zinoviev to Stalin in December 1934, following his arrest after the assassination of Kirov

I am guilty of nothing, nothing, nothing before the party, before the central committee and before you personally. I swear to you by everything that is sacred to a Bolshevik. I swear to you on Lenin's memory. I cannot even imagine what could have aroused suspicion against me. I beg you to believe my word of honour. I am shaken to the depths of my soul.

D. Volkogonov, *Stalin: triumph and tragedy*, translated by H. Shukman, London, 1991, p. 277

2 Stalin reporting to the Eighteenth Party Congress in March 1939 on the purges from 1933 to 1936

It cannot be said that the cleansings were not accompanied by grave mistakes. There were, unfortunately, more mistakes than might have been expected. Undoubtedly, we shall have no further need to resort to the method of mass cleansings. Nevertheless, the cleansings of 1933–36 were unavoidable and their results, on the whole, were beneficial.

C. Ward, *Stalin's Russia*, London, 1993, p. 119

Historical-source questions

1 What position had Kirov held in the Communist Party before his assassination in 1934 as mentioned in Source 1?

2 To what extent might Stalin's comments in Source 2 be seen as supporting the confusion displayed by Zinoviev in Source 1?

3 How reliable are Stalin's references in Source 2 to the 'cleansings of 1933–36' being 'unavoidable' though being 'accompanied by grave mistakes'?

Summary questions

1 Identify and explain any *two* reasons Stalin used to justify the purges of the 1930s.

2 Compare the importance of at least *three* of the effects of the Great Purge on the Soviet Union.

9 Foreign policy in the 1930s and the Great Patriotic War, 1941–45

9

Focus questions

◆ What were the motives behind Soviet foreign policy in the 1930s?

◆ How was the Soviet Union able to win the Great Patriotic War, 1941–45?

◆ What were the immediate consequences of the Great Patriotic War?

Significant dates

1932   *November*   Franco-Soviet Non-Aggression Pact

1933   *January*   Hitler becomes chancellor of Germany

1934   *September*   Soviet Union joins League of Nations

1935   *May*   Franco-Soviet Alliance

1936   *November*   Anti-Comintern Pact between Germany and Japan

1937   *July*   Japan invades China
       August   Soviet Union signs treaty with nationalist China

1938   *September*   Sudetenland Crisis

1939   *March*   Germany invades rest of Czechoslovakia
       May   Molotov replaces Litvinov as commissar for foreign affairs
       August   Nazi–Soviet Non-Aggression Pact
       September   Start of Second World War; Poland divided up by Germany and the USSR
       November   Winter War between the USSR and Finland begins

1940   *July*   The Baltic states are made part of the USSR

1941   *June*   German invasion of the Soviet Union begins; Stavka and GKO formed
       September   The Siege of Leningrad begins
       October   Moscow under threat
       December   Zhukov's counteroffensive

1942   *January–February*   Germans push south to Stalingrad
       September   The Siege of Stalingrad by the German Sixth Army begins
       November   Red Army encircles the Sixth Army

1943   *February*   Sixth Army surrenders
       July   Battle of Kursk

1944   *January*   Siege of Leningrad ends
       June   D-Day

Overview

In the 1920s, the new workers' state of Soviet Russia was totally isolated. Gradually, however, diplomatic links were established with most European countries, particularly with Germany. After 1933, when Hitler came to power in Germany, Soviet foreign policy centred on strengthening the League of Nations (the Soviet Union became a member in 1934) and on trying to achieve an anti-fascist alliance with Britain and France. Such attempts failed and, in August 1939, the USSR concluded a non-aggression pact with Nazi Germany, sometimes known as the Molotov–Ribbentrop agreement (respectively the Soviet and German foreign ministers). This pact included secret clauses for the partition of Poland between the two countries and for the USSR to take over the **Baltic republics**.

The **Baltic republics** were Estonia, Latvia and Lithuania. They had been part of the Tsarist Russian empire, but had become independent after the Bolshevik Revolution.

From 1939 to 1941, the Soviet Union stayed neutral in the Second World War, despite continuing to send raw materials to Germany. During this time it concentrated on building up its defences. When, by 1940, Germany had failed to defeat Britain, Stalin decided an attack from Germany was now unlikely and defensive measures were scaled down. The massive German invasion of the Soviet Union (known as Operation Barbarossa) which began on 22 June 1941 took Stalin completely by surprise. Within months, the Germans had pushed deep into the USSR, threatening Leningrad and Moscow. The Soviet Union was saved mainly by its determined resistance and by the onset of a harsh winter, both of which slowed down and then stopped the German advance (though US aid via the lend–lease agreement also played a part).

The **Great Patriotic War** was first described as such by Stalin in 1943.

Soviet counteroffensives in late 1941 and in 1942 began to push the Germans back. By 1943, the Germans were in retreat and in 1945 the Red Army crossed into Germany. However, during this **Great Patriotic War**, over 25 million Soviet citizens perished and many of the industrial achievements of the five-year plans were destroyed.

What were the motives behind Soviet foreign policy in the 1930s?

Isolation of the Soviet republic

The Bolshevik Revolution in November 1917 alarmed most European states and consequently communist Russia was increasingly boycotted. After the Treaty of Brest–Litovsk in March 1918, which formally ended Russian involvement in the First World War, the remaining Allied powers decided to intervene in the civil war that had just broken out in Russia. By the end of this foreign involvement in 1920, 14 states (including Britain, France, Poland, Japan and the USA) had sent armies to help the Whites against the Reds.

In addition, communist Russia was not invited to help negotiate the peace treaties of 1919–20 and was not allowed to join the League of Nations. After most foreign troops were withdrawn from Russia in 1920 (the last Japanese troops did not leave until 1925), many European states placed restrictions on trade and economic relations with the new workers' state. It was hoped that this would bring down the communist government or at least encircle communist Russia in a *cordon sanitaire* made up by the successor states.

Why was communist Russia isolated before the mid 1920s?

To begin with, the communists were neither too bothered nor too surprised and hoped that the Comintern (set up in 1919) would help assist existing (in Germany, Hungary and Italy) and future revolutionary movements to succeed in their aim of achieving socialist states. Russian isolation would then be ended by the appearance of other workers' states, which would help economic recovery and growth in Russia. However, these revolutionary movements were repressed and by the end of 1923 it was clear that the communist state would have to survive on its own.

Relations with Germany

With hopes of immediate revolution in Europe dashed, Lenin's government was desperate for foreign financial and technical assistance. Shunned by the USA, the western European democracies and the increasingly authoritarian regimes in central and eastern Europe, communist Russia turned to the other outcast in Europe: Germany. In 1922, they signed the Treaty of Rapallo: in return for allowing secret German military training and arms manufacture in Russia, Germany provided Russia with economic assistance and established trade links. The 1930 Treaty of Berlin continued and developed these arrangements.

The approach of war, 1933–41

Diplomatic tensions in the 1920s

By the end of 1924, as the economic and political situation in Europe improved, the intense hostility of the post-war years declined and the Soviet Union was able to establish diplomatic links with all major states except the USA, which remained extremely anti-communist. However, diplomatic developments such as the Treaty of Locarno in 1925 and the admission of Germany to the League of Nations in 1926 led Stalin to believe that Britain and France were moving towards the creation of a new west European alliance against the Soviet Union.

In 1926, the USSR signed a five-year neutrality pact with Germany which led to a deterioration in its relationship with France. Then in 1927, the British Conservative government broke off diplomatic relations with the USSR mainly as a result of the contact between the Soviet Union and British trade unions during the General Strike of 1926. These events led to a 'war scare' in the Soviet Union in 1927, based on fears that Britain was encouraging a Franco-Polish invasion of the USSR. Worryingly for Stalin, Soviet attempts to sign neutrality pacts with France – in 1927 and in 1928 – were totally rejected.

The Great Depression

However, when the Depression began to hit the USA in 1929 and the rest of the world by the early 1930s, even American firms began to show an interest in doing business with the USSR which, with its non-capitalist planned economy, was the only major country to remain unaffected. Nonetheless, Stalin remained deeply suspicious of all capitalist countries. This was in part due to his fear of imminent war, which led to the belief that the USSR needed to catch up quickly and which in turn motivated the five-year plans and the drive for rapid industrialisation.

By 1932, with Germany moving increasingly to the right, France started to see that the Soviet Union's Red Army might be a powerful deterrent in the east to rising German militarism. Consequently, in November 1932, the Franco-Soviet Non-Aggression Pact was finally signed. By then, Soviet Russia had already signed similar pacts with Poland, Finland and the three Baltic republics in an attempt to safeguard its western borders from German expansionism.

> Why did the Great Depression and its impact in the years 1929–33 lead Stalin to have growing concerns for the security of the USSR?

The Nazi threat

When Hitler and the Nazis came to power in Germany in 1933, Stalin's fears were rekindled. He and his supporters had believed that the Nazis would be swept away by a communist-led revolution – in the November 1932 elections in Germany, the Nazis had lost a large number of seats while the German Communist Party had continued its steady rise. However, after the suppression of the German Communist and Social Democratic Parties in the summer of 1933 and then the Night of the Long Knives in June 1934 (see page 41), it soon became clear that the Nazis would be secure for some time to come.

Nazi ideology was violently anti-communist; in addition, one of Hitler's stated aims was to claim 'living space' in the east, especially from the USSR and its 'inferior' Slavic population. Once Nazi Germany left the World Disarmament Conference and withdrew from the League of Nations, Germany's relations with the Soviet Union began to deteriorate. Stalin cancelled all military co-operation with Germany and took up French offers of joint military discussions and assistance. In November 1933, the USA – which, like the Soviet Union, was becoming alarmed at Japanese aggression (see pages 49–50)

– finally asked the Soviet Union to establish diplomatic relations. Soviet fears also led Stalin to apply for League membership, which was finally granted in 1934.

The Soviet Union and 'collective security'

As early as December 1933, **Litvinov**, the Soviet commissar for foreign affairs, began to argue that, because of the threats from Japan and especially Germany, the Soviet Union's best defence lay in approaching Britain, France and the USA to seek an alliance to uphold the peace settlements of 1919–20 against threats from Nazi Germany.

In 1934, the Soviet Union and France began to draft a treaty by which the Soviet Union would help guarantee France's borders with Germany in return for French military help if Germany attacked the Soviet Union. They also discussed the possibility of involving Nazi Germany in an agreement to guarantee the security and independence of the successor states (see note on page 6) and the three Baltic republics. However, the proposals to guarantee Germany's eastern frontiers foundered: the eastern European states distrusted the motives of the USSR, Nazi Germany was totally opposed to the idea and Britain (and, later, France) was not really interested. Despite these disappointments, when the Soviet Union attended its first League of Nations meeting in September 1934, it began to make real efforts to strengthen the League's 'collective security' role. However, events in 1935 and 1936 soon led Stalin to return to direct diplomacy.

The search for an anti-fascist alliance

By 1935, Stalin had ordered the Comintern to pursue a new policy of seeking to form alliances with any party prepared to join in the anti-fascist struggle. Also in 1935, France signed a new treaty with the Soviet Union which agreed to the protection of Czechoslovakia from any attack by Nazi Germany. However, France specifically avoided making any definite military commitment because they were afraid to commit themselves irrevocably without British support.

When, in October 1935, Italy invaded Abyssinia, Stalin was disturbed by the lack of any effective response from the League. He was further unsettled by the League's weakness over Hitler's reoccupation of the Rhineland in March 1936 and, later in the year, over German and Italian involvement in the Spanish civil war.

Despite keeping his options open by attempting, periodically, to achieve some kind of non-aggression agreement with both Germany and Japan, the main thrust of Stalin's foreign policy in 1936 was towards achieving an anti-Nazi alliance between the USSR, Britain and France. However, Britain's **National government** was strongly anti-communist and saw Nazi Germany

Born in 1876, Maxim **Litvinov** joined the RSDLP at its foundation in 1898. From 1908 to 1918, he lived in England, where he married an Englishwoman. He worked hard to persuade the League to adopt complete disarmament during the 1920s. In July 1930, he became Soviet commissar for foreign affairs.

With which countries did Stalin sign a series of pacts in the early 1930s?

The **National government** was a coalition mainly made up of Conservatives, but also had a few renegade MPs who had been expelled from the Labour Party.

Foreign policy in the 1930s and the Great Patriotic War, 1941–45   **99**

as a useful block against the spread of communism; in addition, many members of the government believed that aspects of the Versailles settlement should be revised to take account of Germany's 'legitimate' grievances. Thus, Britain saw 'appeasement' of Nazi Germany as preferable to strengthening the League or forming an alliance with the USSR. Britain's attitude played a large part in France's 1935 decision to avoid making specific military promises in the Franco-Soviet treaty to protect Czechoslovakia.

Meanwhile, events in Asia continued to worry Stalin. Jiang Jieshi, the leader of nationalist China, still refused to launch an attack on the Japanese invaders in Manchuria (see page 34), preferring instead to try and wipe out the Chinese Communist Party. Stalin tried to reach an accommodation with the Japanese, by agreeing to the sale of the Eastern Railway to **Manchukuo**. Japan's foreign policy was still undecided regarding expansion at the expense of the Soviet Union – one faction favoured this option, while the other wanted to expand in the Pacific and south-east Asia.

Then in November 1936, Japan signed the Anti-Comintern Pact with Germany and, in 1937, so did **Fascist** Italy. This was followed in July 1937 by a full-scale Japanese invasion of China. These events led Stalin to fear that the USSR might have to face a combined two-pronged attack from Nazi Germany and Japan. Consequently, in a new treaty with China, signed in August 1937, the Soviet Union sent military aid to the Guomindang and, in August 1939, the Red Army inflicted a serious defeat on Manchukuo forces at the Battle of Khalkin-Gol.

The Nazi–Soviet Non-Aggression Pact, August 1939

While events were unfolding in Asia, the Soviet Union's diplomatic approach to western European states was beginning to falter. Litvinov still believed an agreement with Britain and France was possible, in view of Germany's ongoing breaches of the Versailles settlement. However, in March 1938, neither Britain nor France opposed Hitler's *Anschluss* with Austria. More worrying for the USSR was the growing crisis over the Sudetenland in Czechoslovakia.

As Hitler's demands for land increased during September 1938, the Soviet Union offered to act on the Franco-Soviet Pact of 1935, designed to protect Czechoslovakia. France, however, was not prepared to act without Britain – and Britain refused to become involved. Poland also refused to give permission for the Red Army to cross Polish territory. Soviet offers of further talks were also ignored and, instead, Britain, France and Italy agreed in Munich on 29 September 1938 that Czechoslovakia should hand over the Sudetenland to Germany.

Then, in March 1939, Nazi Germany invaded the rest of Czechoslovakia, with Britain and France once again refusing to take any action. However,

Manchukuo was the new name given to Manchuria by Japan.

The **Fascists** (the name is derived from the Italian word 'fascio' meaning group, band, league or union) were founded by Mussolini in 1919 to fight against socialists and communists. Mussolini merged all the groups to form the far-right ultra-nationalist Fascist Party. After a march on Rome by armed Fascist members in October 1922, he was invited by the Italian king to form a government. Once in power, he began to turn Italy into a one-party Fascist dictatorship.

Britain finally decided that Poland, Hitler's next likely target, should be protected and in April it initiated talks with the Soviet Union about the possibility of joint action between Britain, France and the USSR to 'guarantee' Poland against Nazi aggression. At this point France's Popular Front government collapsed and was replaced by a right-of-centre government which was more hostile to the Soviet Union. At the same time, the majority of the British cabinet began to have second thoughts about allying with communist Russia, so the talks faltered.

Stalin had become increasingly suspicious of the real motives behind British and French foreign policy. In 1939, he decided that, in order to avoid war, more serious approaches should be made to Germany and Japan to sign non-aggression pacts. Consequently, in May 1939, Litvinov was replaced as commissar for foreign affairs by Molotov, who was instructed to pursue a new diplomatic policy.

Britain was still continuing to drag out the negotiations in a half-hearted way when, on 23 August 1939, it was announced that Molotov and von Ribbentrop (the German foreign minister) had signed a non-aggression pact. Secret clauses in this pact divided Poland and large parts of eastern Europe between the two signatories – Germany was to have western Poland, while the USSR would get eastern Poland, Finland, the three Baltic republics and the part of Romania (Bessarabia) that, like the other territories, had been part of Tsarist Russia. Shortly afterwards, on 1 September 1939, Germany invaded 'its' part of Poland and on 3 September – to both Hitler's and Stalin's surprise – Britain and France declared war on Germany.

> Why did Stalin come to the conclusion that Britain would never sign an anti-German alliance with the Soviet Union?

> What were the terms of the Nazi–Soviet Non-Aggression Pact of 1939?

Soviet motives and the historical debate

Historians are divided as to the real aims and motives of Soviet foreign policy in the 1930s. Many have argued that Stalin's policy, as pursued by Litvinov, was genuine and that Stalin hoped for an alliance with France and Britain even after the Munich agreement of 1938. Evidence released since the collapse of the Soviet Union in 1991 suggests that a military alliance with Britain and France remained Stalin's favoured option. Others claim that Stalin's approach to the West was a screen behind which he followed his main policy of maintaining the close links with Germany established in the 1920s by the Treaty of Rapallo. Recently released Soviet archives, however, reveal that Soviet contacts with Nazi Germany were infrequent from 1935 to 1939 and were only in response to German approaches. It was rather the reluctance of France and Britain to negotiate seriously with the USSR which left Stalin little choice but to opt for an isolationist policy and make a deal with Nazi Germany in order to buy time for the Red Army to prepare itself for a fight with the **Wehrmacht**.

> The **Wehrmacht** was the German army, not to be confused with the Waffen SS or the other SS organisations which operated during the German invasion of the USSR. All SS units were separate from the ordinary German army, although the latter was frequently ordered to assist the SS in their 'special actions'.

How was the Soviet Union able to win the Great Patriotic War, 1941–45?

The 'peaceful' interlude, 1939–41

After Britain and France declared war on Germany in September 1939, Stalin believed the danger of an imminent German attack had passed. He did not believe Hitler would attack (and so risk a two-front war) until Britain and France had been defeated in the west. In this interval before the Nazi attack on the Soviet Union, however, Russian military action did take place:

- The Red Army had been involved in military actions in Manchukuo since 1937. This was seen as essential if the Soviet Union was to prevent a clearly aggressive **Japan** from invading Siberia for the fourth time in 50 years.

- Despite declaring war on Germany over its invasion of Poland, Britain and France at first did nothing (the so-called 'phoney war') confirming Stalin's suspicions about their real intentions. He therefore decided to invade the 'Soviet half' of Poland on 17 September.

- At the end of November, the Soviet Union attacked Finland in what became known as the Winter War. In earlier attempts to obtain better protection for Leningrad (where there were important armaments factories) and Murmansk (the USSR's only northern ice-free port), Stalin had tried to negotiate exchanges of territory and the lease of some strategic islands from Finland. When Finland refused, he ordered an invasion even though he was concerned about Finland's good relationship with Nazi Germany. The Red Army, still adversely affected by the Great Purge and not prepared for a winter offensive, did badly against Finnish troops, even though technically the USSR won the war. As an inducement to the Finns to make peace quickly, before Britain became involved, Stalin did not push for agreement to all his original demands. The Red Army's poor performance persuaded many – especially Hitler – that it was a poor fighting machine.

- While the fighting in Finland was taking place, Stalin was also taking over the Baltic states. In 1939, military agreements were signed, allowing Soviet troops to be stationed in their territories. In June 1940, Lithuania was taken over as well as Bessarabia and northern Bukovina from Romania. In July 1940, all three Baltic states became republics of the USSR.

By the summer of 1940, therefore, the Soviet Union had, via a mixture of border wars and diplomacy based on the threat of military aggression, extended its frontiers in the west and south. As a result, any German attack could now be resisted by the Red Army on non-Russian territory. Also by then the 'phoney war' had ended – in fact, France had already been defeated in May 1940. However, Britain remained undefeated, which allowed Stalin to feel

Japan had invaded Siberia in the Sino-Japanese War of 1894–95, the Russo-Japanese War of 1904–05 and the civil war of 1918–20.

Why did the Soviet Union launch the Winter War against Finland in 1939?

reasonably confident that Germany would not be able to attack in the near future.

Some historians see these conflicts and occupations as being a continuation of Tsarist imperialism or proof of Soviet intentions to 'export' revolution by conquest. Many others, however, see these as essentially defensive steps, given the West's inaction over the open aggression displayed by the Nazi Third Reich and Japan.

Why did Stalin slow down the USSR's military preparations in 1940?

Operation Barbarossa, June 1941

Despite the signing of the Nazi–Soviet Non-Aggression Pact in August 1939, Stalin still expected a German attack. As a result, measures were rushed through to improve the Soviet Union's military defences. The tremendous success of German campaigns, based on **Blitzkrieg** methods, confirmed the necessity of these Soviet military preparations (Denmark, Norway, the Netherlands, Belgium and France were all defeated in brief campaigns by 1940). However, when the Battle of Britain prevented a further German victory, Stalin began to think that Britain and Germany might exhaust each other in war. Consequently, military preparations in the Soviet Union were slowed down, despite warnings from Soviet spies in Germany and from British intelligence that Hitler was planning an attack. Stalin believed the latter was a trick designed to make him break the non-aggression pact.

In fact, Hitler had been preparing for an invasion of the USSR since December 1940. Britain's continuing resistance, Italy's poor performance in Greece, bad weather and delays in building airfields near the post-1939 Soviet border postponed the start of the offensive (known as Operation Barbarossa or Operation Red Beard) until 22 June 1941. Immediately prior to this, there had been open and massive German military preparations along its eastern frontiers as well as several Luftwaffe incursions over the Soviet borders. Stalin and several senior NKVD officials dismissed reports from NKVD agents that an invasion was imminent; instead, they believed these actions were just manoeuvres to extract some concessions. Even warnings by Schulenberg, the non-Nazi German ambassador in Moscow, two weeks earlier, were dismissed as attempts to provoke war. As a result, Stalin issued orders against mobilisation and for all provocations to be ignored where possible. Though many units quietly ignored these orders, many others did not and Stalin's belated signal to expect imminent attack came too late for them.

The German invasion was massive and swift – over 5 million **Axis** troops (over 3 million Germans initially, plus later, units from Italy, Hungary, Finland, Bulgaria, Romania, Slovakia and Spain) were involved, along with over 3,000 tanks, 50,000 pieces of artillery and 5,000 war planes.

Using the tried-and-tested Blitzkrieg methods, the Wehrmacht invasion

Blitzkrieg is German for 'lightning war' (i.e. a rapid attack involving massive forces, with extensive use of tanks and the airforce, in order to defeat an enemy as quickly as possible). In 1940, the Germans successfully used this method to occupy much of northern and western Europe.

The **Axis** powers were Germany, Italy and Japan. In 1936, Germany and Italy signed the Rome–Berlin Axis. They were later joined by Japan to form the Rome–Berlin–Tokyo Axis, on the basis of which the three Axis powers would rule the world.

forces advanced quickly and deeply into western Russia. The German forces were divided into three: Army Group North was directed against the Baltic states and Leningrad; Army Group Centre against Belorussia and Moscow, and Army Group South against the Ukraine and Kiev. Although the Soviet troops outnumbered the Axis forces in men and equipment in places, the Soviet Union lacked the economic strength of Germany, which also had the resources of occupied Europe at its disposal. Within a week, the Red Army's defences had been smashed, vast quantities of equipment and supplies had been destroyed or captured and a third of the airforce had been destroyed before it could even take off, and over 500,000 were taken prisoner.

Stalin lost his nerve and, for the first few days of the invasion, Molotov took effective charge of the country. The system of military command was altered. **Stavka** was set up to take charge of all land, air and sea operations and the State Committee of Defence (GKO) was set up a few days later to oversee not just the military but also the political and economic aspects of the war.

On 3 July, Stalin announced that, because of the tremendous German advances, a **'scorched earth' policy** was to be adopted. At the same time, partisan and sabotage units, mainly controlled by the NKVD, were set up to operate behind enemy lines.

By August, the Baltic republics had been lost and much of the important agricultural areas of Belarussia and the Ukraine were occupied. At this stage, the Soviet Union was helped by the fact that Hitler ignored the advice of his military commanders; in August he ordered that the Ukraine's cornfields and the oilfields of Baku should be the main targets of the offensive. Initially successful, the German army was soon bogged down by heavy rain and mud.

Then in September, just as German forces were encircling Leningrad, Hitler diverted forces for a massive attack on Moscow (Operation Typhoon) which took Stavka by surprise. The Soviet Red Army suffered heavy losses and was forced to retreat. Initially deeply shocked, Stalin moved many government offices from Moscow to Kuibyshev in the east, while considering the possibility of seeking peace terms. However, in the end, he decided to stay and fight.

Moscow – and the Soviet Union – were saved by a combination of factors. First, the serious defeats suffered by the Red Army led to **Marshal Zhukov** taking command of all Soviet forces facing the German advance on 19 October 1941. His forces for the defence of Moscow were strengthened by Siberian troops moved from the Far East. This move was possible because Soviet spies had discovered that the debate within the Japanese army about whether to attack the Soviet Union or to expand in the Pacific had been won by the latter group. Even before the Japanese launched their attack on Pearl Harbor in December 1941, about half the troops protecting Siberia had been moved west.

Stavka, the special Soviet High Command chaired by Stalin, was set up to oversee the Great Patriotic War – it took its name from a similar body which had existed in Tsarist Russia.

The **'scorched earth' policy** was implemented by the Soviet army and Soviet citizens when forced to retreat. They were ordered to remove everything (machinery, food, livestock) to the east. What could not be moved had to be destroyed (e.g. unharvested crops, houses) in order to leave nothing for the advancing enemy. This had harsh consequences for Soviet civilians left behind, as well as for German troops.

Born in 1896, Georgii **Zhukov** fought in the First World War and the Russian civil war, having joined the Communist Party in 1919. In the late 1930s, he commanded Soviet troops along the Manchurian border and was responsible for the victory at Khalkin-Gol in August 1939. In 1941, he became a member of the Central Committee and was made chief of the general staff.

Second, the Russian weather began to affect German troops and equipment, neither of which were prepared for a winter war. Frostbite affected large numbers of troops at a time when anti-freeze was virtually non-existent, while the 600,000 horses which pulled carts and much artillery were suffering from lack of food owing to the 'scorched earth' policy.

The original plan of Operation Barbarossa was that all objectives would have been achieved before winter began. As the German advance slowed down, Zhukov began to plan a counteroffensive. This was launched in December 1941, initially to save Moscow. Early success here led to further counter-offensives in the north, the Ukraine and the Crimea. Although these were not as successful as the Moscow offensive, the Germans suffered high casualties and were pushed back several hundred kilometres in places. Soviet tanks proved superior to German ones and the **Katyusha** rocket launcher proved effective – none of this military equipment had been used in the Winter War against Finland.

Despite its successes, by the end of 1941 the Soviet Union's position seemed desperate: about 4 million soldiers were either dead or captured, and the Red Army had lost huge amounts of equipment. This was due, in part, to low morale following the Great Purge and Stalin's orders that Red Army units should not retreat, which led to heavy losses and many being surrounded and taken prisoner.

In early 1942, Stalin planned a new offensive, as the Red Army had been strengthened by equipment (mostly jeeps and lorries) from the USA under the terms of a lend–lease agreement it had made with the Soviet Union in November 1941. Prior to that, in July 1941, Britain and the Soviet Union had signed a mutual assistance pact for equipment and supplies with the possibility of troops being supplied later. Soviet requests for troops, however, were ignored, although after the USA declared war on Germany in December 1941, the flow of equipment increased. Another important factor was Japan's decision, in December 1941, to concentrate on opposing the USA in the Pacific; this meant that the fresh Siberian divisions could now be transferred to face the Germans.

Stalingrad

The Wehrmacht, now under Hitler's personal command, launched another massive and successful offensive in the south, towards the Caucasus and Stalingrad in June 1942. In August, the Germans began their attempt to take Stalingrad – heavy bombing was followed by a fresh offensive. At times, the Germans held most of Stalingrad, but there was strong Soviet resistance for over a month of bitter close-quarter fighting over every street and building (by this time, Nazi cruelty had caused great national resentment and a determination

The **Katyusha** was the Soviet rocket launcher that fired barrages of explosive missiles. It was nicknamed 'Stalin's organ'.

A Red Army sniper. The Siberian Divisions played a big part in the battle for Stalingrad.

The **second front** refers to the plan to invade German-occupied western Europe. As early as July 1941, Stalin had urgently requested that Britain open up a second front in France, to take pressure off the Soviet forces fighting on the eastern front. Though the USA and Britain agreed it was necessary, there were differences over timing. In May 1942 Roosevelt promised to open up a second front in Europe later that year – but was persuaded by US military advisers and Churchill to postpone it till 1943. Then the USA and Britain decided to invade Italy first – it was not until June 1944 that France was finally invaded.

Why was the battle for Stalingrad so important?

Ostfront is German for the eastern front (the war against the Soviet Union). This saw the heaviest and most bitter fighting of the war.

to fight them). Stalin's request for the USA and Britain to open up a **second front** in Europe was rejected. While Soviet defenders held on, Stalin and Zhukov clashed over what to do. Finally, Stalin agreed to Zhukov's plan for a counteroffensive. Known as Operation Uranus, it began in September and, by November, the German Sixth Army was surrounded. However, the savage fighting continued until February 1943, when the remnants of von Paulus's Sixth Army finally surrendered, much to Hitler's fury.

The battle for Stalingrad was an important turning point in the war – according to Churchill, the Soviet victory there 'tore the guts out of the German army'. With the exception of the Allied bombing of Germany and the North African and Italian campaigns in 1942 and 1943, the Soviet Union faced the bulk of the German forces on their own. At least 75 per cent of all German troops and military equipment was sent to the Russian front (*Ostfront*). By June 1944, when the Allies finally opened up a second front (via the D-Day landings in Normandy), there were 228 German and Axis divisions fighting the Russians, compared to 61 divisions in western Europe.

The final stages, 1943–45

During 1943, the Red Army slowly pushed the Wehrmacht westwards, but Russian losses continued to be heavy. In July 1943, Hitler ordered another offensive, intended to surround the Soviet armies in the Ukraine. The fighting centred on Kursk, in what was to be the biggest tank battle in history, involving over 6,000 tanks, 5,000 aircraft, 30,000 pieces of artillery and over 2 mil-

The devastated remains of Stalingrad at the end of the war – all that is left of the houses are their stone chimneys. The Soviet Union suffered far more destruction (human and material) than any other country during the Second World War.

lion soldiers. It was the Germans who found themselves surrounded; once again, they suffered heavy losses.

From September 1943, the Soviet offensive was stepped up – by the end of the year, over 60 per cent of the territory lost since 1941 had been recaptured. During 1944, the victories continued: in January, the long **Siege of Leningrad** was ended and Smolensk and Kiev were retaken; in May and June, the Crimea and Belorussia were recaptured; and, by August 1944, all German forces had been expelled from the Soviet Union. The Red Army then began to invade Germany's Axis partners in eastern Europe; by early January 1945, the Red Army crossed into Germany, reached the River Elbe in April and entered Berlin in May.

The **Siege of Leningrad** lasted 900 days, beginning in September 1941, during which 900,000 people died from starvation, exposure and bombing. Most of these deaths occurred during the winter of 1941–42.

Conclusion

Ever since the end of the war, historians have argued about the reasons behind the final victory of the Soviet Union, focusing on the various military, political and economic factors. Overall, however, as noted by C. Ward, these differing viewpoints can be divided into negative and positive interpretations.

The negative argument essentially explains the Soviet victory by pointing to Nazi Germany's weaknesses and mistakes, and tends to reject the idea of Soviet strengths. What saved the USSR, according to this view, was a combination of Axis errors and Soviet luck. The errors include Hitler's refusal to put Germany on a total war footing until 1944, which was really too late as the USSR was out-producing Germany in the replacement of destroyed military equipment. In addition, Nazi ideology – and the barbarism it produced – lost Germany the support of many Soviet citizens who, in the beginning, had been willing to aid the German invaders. Some historians estimate that over 2 million Russians (the willing and the unwilling) fought with the Axis powers. However, Nazi racial theories meant Hitler was reluctant to make full use of these Slavic *Untermenschen* (they had to be redefined as Cossacks). Hitler also ignored German army intelligence advice which, from the autumn of 1941, was saying that in order to defeat the USSR a civil war should be encouraged.

The USSR was also saved by the weather – first the autumn rains which turned Soviet roads into quagmires and then the winter frosts and snow. The Wehrmacht was not well prepared for this, as Hitler had predicted that the Soviet Union would collapse in a few months – many of the troops rushed from the Balkans to the *Ostfront* were still in summer uniforms. Thus, the German army got bogged down outside Moscow, which finally gave the Soviet forces the chance to counter-attack.

Other historians, however, emphasise the positive features of the Soviet Union's ability to respond to the German invasion. These include the expertise of its military leaders and the underlying strengths of the Soviet system. On the military side, Stavka soon began to operate on the principles of 'superior force' and 'defence in depth'. This approach led to the many victories in 1943. There was also an intelligent use of guerrilla warfare.

Military successes – and the heroic survival of Leningrad and Stalingrad – appear to have genuinely raised Soviet morale, over and above the efforts of official propaganda. Popular patriotism and heroism were widespread and went beyond the ranks of party members and officials, who wished to emulate the heroes of the Revolution and the civil war. Many ordinary industrial workers and members of collective farms took pride in the achievements of socialist construction in the 1930s, while others were determined to defend the USSR from the hated invaders.

In addition, the Soviet administrative and economic systems proved resilient. Despite early setbacks, collective farms kept military personnel and industrial workers from starvation. Also, many new factories had been built in and behind the Ural Mountains, as part of the pre-war five-year plans: this allowed Soviet production to recover rapidly from the initial destructive impact of the Nazi invasion.

What were the immediate consequences of the Great Patriotic War?

The human cost

Overall, the Second World War resulted in some 50–60 million deaths – of these, about 25 million were Soviet citizens. Some estimates of Soviet deaths put the figure as high as 28 million, but it is impossible to be exact as there were no published censuses in the twenty years from 1939 to 1959. Of these deaths, about 9 million were Soviet military personnel – approximately half of these died after being captured, from various causes, including starvation, exposure, disease, forced labour and execution. This figure of 9 million also includes those killed or executed by the Soviet authorities; at critical times (for instance, at Stalingrad), units of the NKVD's special department operated on the frontlines to prevent desertion, either by shooting deserters in battle or executing them later. Axis military losses were also high on the *Ostfront* – approximately 8 million soldiers died in all.

Civilians, however, suffered even more – at least 15 million Soviet civilians also died, from bombing, hunger, exposure, forced labour, reprisals for partisan actions and from 'special actions' carried out by SS units. At first, in some areas (such as the Ukraine, which had particularly suffered under Stalin's collectivisation policy) many Soviet citizens had welcomed German troops as 'liberators' and many had volunteered to fight for the Germans. The Soviet authorities generally took a very severe line with such 'former Russians', both during and immediately after the war.

A photograph showing German soldiers executing two Soviet partisan resistance fighters.

However, Hitler and the Nazis believed Slavs were racially inferior and, like Jewish people, should be exterminated. As early as 1941 the Wehrmacht's senior officers had been informed of the 'special orders' and 'special tasks' to be carried out in captured Soviet territory. As well as 'collective measures of force' against villages where partisans were active and the 'commissar order', which stated the army was to hand over all communist officials, partisans and Jews to the SS or Secret Field Police, army officers were told of the need to co-operate with the SS Sonderkommando and security police.

A 'jurisdiction order' effectively gave German soldiers *carte blanche* to loot, rape and murder. This was justified on the grounds that, for Hitler and the Nazis, this was no ordinary war, but a war of annihilation between Nazi ideology and communism and, at the same time, a *Rassenkampf* (race war). Not all Wehrmacht officers agreed with this and some were clearly disgusted. However, very few protested and many did co-operate.

Economic devastation

The Great Patriotic War was immensely destructive to the Russian economy. Between what was destroyed by the Germans or looted and sent back to Germany and what the Russians themselves destroyed by their 'scorched earth' policy, many of the gains of the five-year plans were wiped out. In all, about 25 per cent of all factories, mines and transport facilities were lost – in some of the occupied areas, the percentage was more than double this. By 1942, almost 80 per cent of productive capacity was devoted solely to the war effort. Though the Soviet armaments industry managed to produce more than was destroyed, so enabling final victory, it was a tremendous waste of resources.

Historical sources

1 Message from Litvinov, the commissar for foreign affairs, to his London representative, March 1939

For five years, we have been making suggestions and proposals for the organisation of peace and collective security, but the Powers have been ignoring them. If England and France are really changing their line, let them either make known their views on our previously advanced proposals or else make their own proposals. The initiative must be left to them.

J. Hallam, *The Soviet Union and the struggle for collective security in Europe, 1933–39*, London, 1984, p. 206

2 V. Grossman's notes on an engagement during the Battle of Stalingrad, as reported to him by Lieutenant Skakun, one of the defenders

Cut off from its regiment . . . this ack-ack battery fought alone . . . repulsing attacks from the air and ground . . . There were girls in his battery . . . they fought side by side with their fellow gunners . . . This terrible battle lasted for twenty-four hours. Only in the evening of the next day did the four men who were left . . . and the wounded commander get to the regiment. They said that during the fighting the girls had never once gone off to the shelter.

V. Grossman, *The years of war, 1941–1945*, Moscow, 1946, p. 187

Historical-source questions

1   What did Litvinov mean in Source 1 when he referred to 'collective security'?
2   What was the main proposal made by the USSR to Britain and France?
3   What does Source 2 tell us about the nature of Soviet resistance and morale during the Great Patriotic War?

Summary questions

1   Identify and explain any *two* factors which led Stalin to sign a non-aggression pact with Nazi Germany.
2   Compare the importance of *three* factors which contributed to the victory of the USSR in the Great Patriotic War.

10 The USSR in Europe, 1945–53

Focus questions

◆ What was Stalin's position after the war?

◆ How did the Soviet Union recover from the war?

◆ What motivated the Soviet Union's takeover of eastern Europe?

Significant dates

1945   *February*   Yalta Conference
       July   Potsdam Conference
       August   USA drops nuclear bombs on Japan

1946   *January*   Beria loses control of secret police
       March   Fourth Five-Year Plan

1947   *September*   Cominform formed

1949   *May*   Comecon formed
       July   Leningrad Affair

1951   *March*   Fifth Five-Year Plan
       November   Mingrelian Case

1952   *October*   Nineteenth Party Congress

1953   *January*   Doctors' Plot
       March   Death of Stalin

Overview

After the war, Stalin remained deeply suspicious of potential rivals. The army commanders were very popular by 1945 and many hoped for a relaxation of Stalinist rule. At first, Stalin used the party machine to reassert control over the military – Stavka and GKO were abolished and several top commanders (including Zhukov) were demoted. Once he had achieved this, Stalin then virtually ignored leading party bodies such as the Politburo and the Central Committee. Instead, he preferred to work with a small group of advisers, whose composition varied over the years.

During the years 1945–53, occasional purges took place, but not on the scale of the 1930s. While reasserting his political control, Stalin also launched the reconstruction of the Soviet Union through the Fourth and Fifth Five-Year Plans. While industry soon revived, agriculture continued to under-produce. In foreign affairs, relations between the Soviet Union, the USA and Britain (the Grand Alliance partners) began to deteriorate in what was soon called the Cold War. The Soviet Union's chief aim was to secure control of all eastern European states – by 1948, this had largely been achieved.

What was Stalin's position after the war?

Victory

Against all expectations, Stalin – and the Soviet Union – had survived the Great Patriotic War. The Generalissimo (Stalin promoted himself to this position in June 1945), whose policies of forced collectivisation and the Great Terror had rendered both himself and his Stalinist state hugely unpopular with large numbers of Soviet citizens, was now seen by many as a national hero. While final victory owed much to the determination and ruthlessness of the Soviet state, millions of Soviet citizens and soldiers had shown genuine bravery and patriotism, without the need for any NKVD intimidation.

After the war, those who survived felt proud of their system which they believed had saved not only the Soviet Union but also the rest of Europe from Nazi domination. This pride was increased by the fact that most of this had been achieved by their own efforts, with little help from the western Allies in the years 1941–44 (beyond the material help provided by lend–lease aid).

However, many of these same people hoped for some political relaxation now that the war was over. Such hopes were quickly dashed as Stalin, fearing the growing antagonism building up between the Soviet Union and the western powers, was determined to maintain tight control.

The armed forces

Stalin was determined to reassert political control over the armed forces after the war. He became increasingly suspicious of the Red Army's generals, whose prestige had been tremendously increased by their recent victories. Stavka and the GKO were abolished in September 1945 and the system of political commissars in the army was reintroduced in August 1946 – these were communist officials who supervised the military officers and had to approve commands. In March 1947, **Bulganin** took Stalin's place as minister of defence and, from 1946 to 1948, also sat on the Politburo. At the same time, Marshal Zhukov lost his place on the Central Committee and other high-ranking officers also lost their influence and positions. From 1945 to 1953, there were virtually no

Bulganin was a political general who replaced Voroshilov as the chief armed forces' representative on the GKO as early as November 1944.

How did Stalin reassert control over the military immediately after 1945?

During the leadership struggle, Stalin initiated a **cult of personality**, presenting himself as the true disciple of Lenin and branding his opponents as anti-Leninists. During the 1930s he was portrayed as the 'father of the nation'. Posters, paintings and statues appeared everywhere and the media began referring to him as a 'universal genius' and 'shining sun of humanity'. He was credited with having made the Soviet Union the envy of the world through the achievements of the five-year plans.

What did Stalin do about the Politburo and the Central Committee? Why was this significant?

Born in 1896, Andrei **Zhdanov** joined the Bolsheviks in 1915. He was active during the Revolution and the civil war, and was elected to the Central Committee in 1925 and to the Politburo in 1935. He became one of Stalin's closest advisers. From 1934 to 1945, he headed the Leningrad party. In 1946, he launched a campaign to achieve ideological 'purity'.

promotions to the higher ranks in the armed forces. In this period, Stalin also continued with his **cult of personality**.

The party

In order to reassert political control the Politburo met fortnightly from December 1945. However, Stalin was also suspicious of potential rivals within the Communist Party. Once the military had been brought sufficiently under control, Stalin decided to exclude leading party members from the decision-making processes. He thus by-passed both the Politburo and the Central Committee – the full Central Committee did not meet again until the Nineteenth Party Congress in October 1952. Instead, he met with small sub-committees composed of those he trusted at any particular time. Party affairs were now supervised by a new Orgburo which, along with a new Politburo and Secretariat, had been elected by the Central Committee in March 1946 (although the Politburo and Central Committee continued to exist, Stalin simply refused to convene meetings).

Beria, who was made a marshal in 1945, still headed the NKVD and aided Stalin in his efforts to remain in total control. Soon Stalin resorted to his old methods of retaining power, including purges. He became increasingly suspicious of everyone, even his old allies: in January 1946, for example, Beria lost control of the secret police (NKGB), which was handed over to a new ministry of state security (MGB).

The Zhdanovshchina

Between 1946 and 1948, the Soviet Union went through another period of repression, mostly affecting the sectors of science and culture. As this was supervised by **Zhdanov** (who, along with Molotov and Malenkov, was one of Stalin's main advisers), this period is known as the **Zhdanovshchina**, even though it actually peaked after his death.

The Communist Party also suffered during this period. When Tito, the communist leader of Yugoslavia, was expelled from Cominform in June 1948 (see pages 143–44) and Zhdanov died in August, Stalin decided to purge the Leningrad party organisation, partly because Zhdanov had once invited Tito, before his expulsion, to visit Leningrad and partly because the Leningrad party had often tried to assert its independence. In July 1949, over a thousand leading party and administrative officials were arrested and many were executed in what became known as the Leningrad Affair.

From then on, there were frequent personnel changes at the top as Stalin, increasingly ill, attempted to confuse and weaken those who might be considered his successors. In 1951, the Mingrelian Case erupted in the Georgian Republic. A group of Georgian communists were accused of attempting to 'liquidate Soviet power' by urging Mingrelian tribesmen to break away from the USSR. This far-fetched claim was almost certainly an attempt to weaken Beria, who was from Mingrelia (which was a part of Georgia). Though he survived, many leading Georgian party officials were purged.

The Nineteenth Party Congress, 1952

This congress, delayed for five years until October 1952, was significant for several reasons. (The delay was the result of Stalin ignoring the Comminist Party.) As Stalin was too ill to make his usual Central Committee report, two leading communists – **Malenkov** and Khrushchev – began to emerge as potential successors. While Malenkov gave the Central Committee report, Khrushchev announced that the Politburo and Orgburo were being disbanded, as were party conferences. Instead, a new top body, called the Praesidium (twice the size of the old Politburo), was to be set up, while the Secretariat and the Central Committee were also going to be expanded. These administrative announcements clearly indicated further changes and the expansion of the number of staff. This congress also voted to change the name of the party from the All-Russian Communist Party (Bolsheviks) to the Communist Party of the Soviet Union, the title it retained until the collapse of the Soviet Union in 1991.

Stalin's death

In early 1953, the medical profession narrowly avoided being purged: a group of 'saboteur-doctors' were accused of plotting with the USA and Britain to murder 'the leading cadres of the USSR'; they apparently 'confessed' to having poisoned Zhdanov. The campaign ended shortly before Stalin's death on 5 March 1953.

How did the Soviet Union recover from the war?

Economic reconstruction

Not surprisingly, the economy was a top priority for the Soviet government after the war: nearly 100,000 *kolkhozes* and 2,000 *sovkhozes* had been partially or completely destroyed, along with over 17 million cattle lost and almost 5 million homes destroyed. In addition, large numbers of railways, roads and bridges were destroyed and the retreating German armies had systematically stripped the occupied areas of all the industrial equipment and agricultural produce they could and had destroyed the rest. To make matters worse, the lend–lease aid was stopped immediately the fighting in Europe ended in May 1945. With the USA and Britain refusing to agree to massive reparations from Germany as a whole, it was clear that the Soviet Union would have to rely on its own resources (see pages 122–23).

Zhdanovshchina means 'the time of Zhdanov' and refers to the period from the mid 1940s when there was a push for 'ideological purity' in all parts of Soviet life, including science, literature, the arts and the media. This was in part based on Zhdanov's idea that all literature, the arts and the media should 'serve the masses' (known as 'socialist realism') which he developed in the 1930s.

Georgi **Malenkov** was born in 1902. He became one of Stalin's close advisers and, on Stalin's death in 1953, he became prime minister of the Soviet Union. In 1955, he was ousted by Khrushchev and, in 1957, lost his seat on the Politburo.

The Fourth Five-Year Plan

To deal with these problems, Stalin outlined a 15-year programme for long-term recovery and announced the Fourth Five-Year Plan in March 1946. Though hopes were dashed that the pre-war drive for industrialisation and collectivisation might be eased, the harsh labour laws and methods of implementing them did not reappear. As with the earlier plans, most emphasis was placed on rebuilding heavy industry and on reviving agriculture. However, civilian needs were also given priority – within nine months of the end of the war in Europe, over 2.5 million homeless people had been rehoused.

Though the first year of the plan was not very successful (in part because of a drought in 1946), as the surviving mines and factories were reopened and the war industries were switched back to industrial production, industrial revival took off in subsequent years. By 1950, Stalin was claiming that the targets set had already been exceeded and that production levels were equal to or higher than those for 1940. While these were exaggerations, a surprisingly rapid and extensive recovery was made.

Agriculture

The revival of agriculture was less successful. Even before 1941, agricultural production had been insufficient to meet the needs of consumers, but the effects of war (destruction of livestock and machinery, the lack of male agricultural workers) were disastrous. In many areas, the collective farming system had totally collapsed and many peasants had seized land to farm as private plots and had sold produce on the black market.

In September 1946, Stalin announced that all previously collectivised land would be reclaimed; even so, the drought which hit many areas together with the genuine lack of labour resulted in a poor harvest (about 40 per cent of the 1940 total). The reduced number of farm animals – and the relative lack of grain to feed them – also led to a drop in meat production.

However, after 1946, matters did begin to improve. State meat procurements were just about back to 1940 levels by 1950, though the 1950 harvest was still about 15 per cent below the figure for 1940. Significantly, by 1950, almost half of agricultural production was still in the hands of the private sector, despite the existence of over 250,000 *kolkhozes*.

The Fifth Five-Year Plan

This plan, which ran from 1951 to 1955 and was approved by the Nineteenth Party Congress in 1952, set relatively lower targets than the previous plan. Despite the fact that the Cold War meant that increasing amounts of state funds were diverted to the defence industry, tremendous improvements were made by the time of Stalin's death in 1953. Rationing ended in 1947 and real wages (which in 1947 were only about 60 per cent of 1940 levels) began to rise steadily from 1948; by 1952, they had surpassed the 1940 levels. Much had also been done to deal with the housing shortage.

What motivated the Soviet Union's takeover of eastern Europe?

Tensions in the Grand Alliance

Although the Soviet Union emerged from the Second World War as one of the victorious great powers, it was much weaker – both militarily and economically – than either Britain or the USA realised. As a consequence, Soviet foreign policy during Stalin's last years – despite being opportunistic and expansionist at times – remained largely defensive and conservative, as it had been prior to 1941.

Soviet foreign policy post-1945 was also coloured by the fact that, even before the Second World War ended, tensions between the 'Big Three' Grand Alliance partners had begun to emerge. This was not surprising, given the mutual suspicion and hostility that had existed between the Soviet Union and the western powers during the 1920s and the 1930s. Even the Grand Alliance itself had only come about because the three countries were facing a common enemy. The USSR did not help Britain in the years 1939–41, and the USA did little to assist the USSR until, as a result of Pearl Harbor in December 1941, the USA found itself at war with both Japan and Germany.

After 1944 tensions between the Grand Alliance partners centred around growing differences over what to do about Germany. At the Yalta Conference in February 1945, with the war still continuing, disagreements over the questions of German reparations and Poland's borders and government were largely papered over. By then, however, it was becoming increasingly clear that Stalin wanted the eastern European states to act as a buffer zone against any future **German invasion**.

By the time of the Potsdam Conference in July 1945 (by then, Roosevelt had died and been replaced by Truman), these differences had become greater. Tensions increased even more after August 1945, when the USA refused to share the technology of its nuclear weapons with the USSR, which it had shown it was prepared to use (some USA statesmen had recommended sharing this technology to avoid the possibility of a destructive arms race developing). Stalin condemned the US stance and rapidly gave top priority to the development of a Soviet **atomic bomb** and, at the same time, to the exploration of other uses of atomic energy. Within four years, despite the economic devastation in the Soviet Union, the USSR had developed its own A-bomb – this was the start of a nuclear arms race between the two superpowers.

German invasion: Stalin needed no reminding of the fact that Russia had already been invaded twice since 1900 by German armies advancing through Poland (in 1914 and again in 1941).

The race to develop an **atomic bomb** began during the Second World War, when it was discovered that Nazi Germany was already carrying out experiments. Both the USA and the USSR were aware of this, but the USA – with its much greater resources – was the first to develop one. However, the USA refused to share the technology with its ally, the USSR, and dropped the first A-bombs on Japan in August 1945. As relations between the USA and the USSR worsened after 1945, the USSR put more effort into its own research and, in July 1949, successfully developed its own atomic bomb, thus breaking the USA's nuclear monopoly. There then began a prolonged nuclear arms race as both the USA and the USSR produced newer and more destructive weapons, the USA trying to stay ahead and the USSR trying to catch up. From 1949 to the late 1980s, these two superpowers spent vast sums on these new weapons of mass destruction.

Why did tension between the USA and the USSR increase after August 1945?

The **Iron Curtain** was a term used to describe an imaginary wall of secrecy between the Soviet Union and western Europe. It was first used by the leading Nazi Joseph Goebbels in February 1945, but came into common usage after Churchill's speech in March 1946, in which he referred to an 'iron curtain' dividing eastern Europe from western Europe.

Eastern Europe and the Iron Curtain

As Stalin was determined that the Soviet Union would never again suffer invasion, Soviet strategic thinking became centred around controlling the countries of eastern Europe. Some officials, such as Molotov, also saw this as a way of achieving Soviet expansion and acquiring extra resources. Before the war, these states (with the exception of Czechoslovakia) had all been ruled by undemocratic, right-wing anti-communist regimes; of these, Hungary and Romania had become allies of Nazi Germany. Thus it was seen as vital to Soviet interests that these countries should be ruled by governments that would not be hostile to the USSR.

" WHO'S NEXT TO BE LIBERATED FROM FREEDOM, COMRADE ?"

A British cartoon of 1948, commenting on Stalin's takeover of eastern Europe.

This policy was put into operation as early as 1944, as Soviet troops pushed the German army out of eastern Europe. Once the Red Army was in control, anti-fascist coalition governments were set up, but the USSR insisted that local communist parties be given a significant role. As tensions between the 'Big Three' heightened in the years 1945–48, the Soviet Union increasingly insisted on the various indigenous communist parties being given a greater share of power. Over the next three years, these communist-dominated governments began to nationalise industry and land; later, they restricted opposition parties and frequently rigged elections. By 1948, Soviet control of these eastern European countries was largely complete, with the exception of Yugoslavia which, under Tito, remained independent. The actual process and speed of the Soviet takeover, however, varied from country to country.

Poland

Poland was one of Stalin's main concerns: it was the largest of the eastern European states and had twice been used as a corridor by German armies to

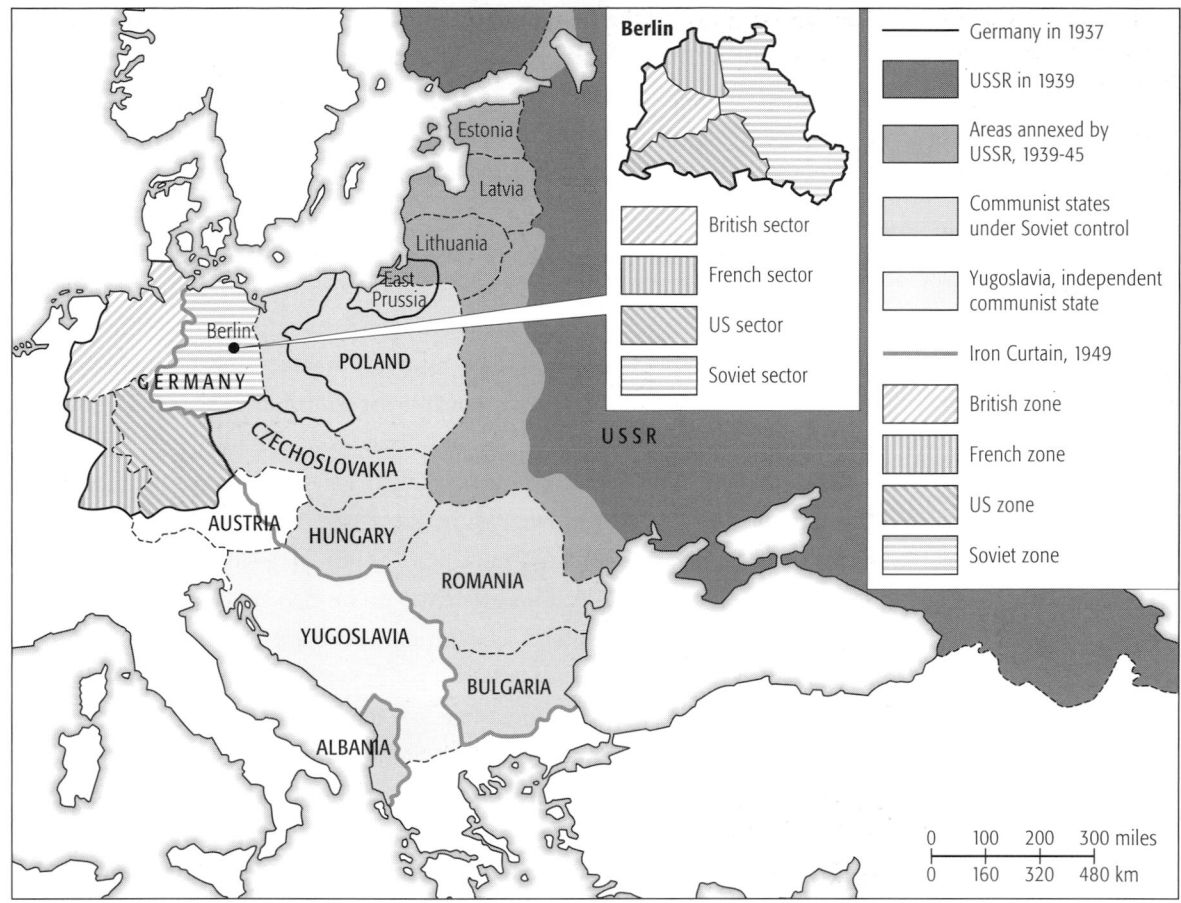

The Cold War division of Europe and Germany by 1948.

invade Russia. It had also been ruled by Pilsudski, a right-wing autocrat who had invaded the new communist state in 1920, with British and French backing. Much valuable Russian agricultural land was handed over to Poland in the Treaty of Riga, which ended this Russo-Polish War in 1921. It was largely this land that the USSR had claimed when Poland was divided up in the Nazi–Soviet Non-Aggression Pact of 1939.

When the Second World War began, many members of the Polish government fled to London to establish a government in exile. These conservative and strongly anti-communist London Poles were unlikely to form a post-war government that would be friendly to the Soviet Union. As the Red Army moved into Poland in July 1944, a rival, mainly communist, provisional government for Poland was set up in Lublin. Stalin was confident that these Lublin Poles, who had spent the war in exile in Moscow, would form a Polish government he could trust.

In August 1944, the Warsaw Uprising by the Polish resistance against the German occupying forces took place. This military operation against the

> Who, respectively, were the London and the Lublin Poles?

German army was seen by the USSR as an attempt by the London Poles to secure control of western Poland before the Red Army did. Though nearby, the Soviet forces therefore did nothing to help the uprising and German troops were able to crush it. By January 1945, the Red Army had liberated all of Poland and the Soviet authorities declared the Lublin Poles to be the new provisional government of Poland.

However, when the Allies met for their second major wartime conference at Yalta in February 1945, the issue of Poland was a major source of disagreement. At the first conference in Tehran in 1943, it had been agreed, at Stalin's insistence, that the USSR would be allowed to take land from Poland; in return, Poland would be given land from Germany. At Yalta, however, Churchill tried to minimise these land changes and both he and Roosevelt tried to ensure that the new interim Polish government would be formed around the London Poles. Eventually, in return for agreements about the transfer of eastern Poland to the USSR, Stalin consented to some of the London Poles joining the Lublin government; he also conceded that free elections would be held in Poland as soon as possible. (The problem with this concession was that most leading Polish politicians were strongly anti-Russian and unlikely to head a government friendly to the USSR.)

By April 1945, it was obvious that Stalin was unhappy with the agreement he had reached over the composition of the Polish government. So although he did allow some of the London Poles to join the Polish government at the end of June, it remained an essentially communist-dominated government. On 5 July, the USA and Britain reluctantly recognised this new government.

When Roosevelt died and was replaced by Truman in April 1945, the West began to take a harsher line over eastern Europe. At the Potsdam Conference in July, agreement was finally reached over the **German–Polish border**. Truman insisted that Stalin carry out the promise he made at Yalta regarding free elections in Poland. Elections were finally held in January 1947, but they were rigged. As a result of the growing communist control, the leader of the London Poles left the country.

The **German–Polish border** was set along the Oder–Neisse rivers. Both the USA and Britain thought that too much German territory was being lost.

Romania and Bulgaria

While events in Poland unfolded, Soviet control was also being established in Romania and Bulgaria. By late 1944, the Red Army had defeated all Axis forces in these two countries and, as with Poland, coalition governments dominated by communists were set up. In February 1945, Stalin insisted on his choice becoming prime minister of the new Romanian government and, by mid 1945, the communists were clearly in control. In 1947, they abolished the monarchy in Romania.

In Bulgaria, the Communist Party was small but strong. Its leader, Dimitrov, had led the Comintern for a time during the 1930s and had been briefly imprisoned by the Nazis. The communist-dominated Fatherland Front won the rigged elections that were held in November 1945. In September 1946, the monarchy was abolished.

Hungary

Stalin was initially less worried about the kind of government that might rule in Hungary. Free elections were held in November 1945, in which the non-communist, peasant-based Smallholders Party was the largest single party. However, as the Cold War developed, Stalin's attitude changed and the August 1947 elections were rigged. In November 1947 the new communist government banned all parties that were not pro-communist.

Czechoslovakia

The final steps towards the Soviet domination of eastern Europe were taken in Czechoslovakia. The Czech Communist Party was quite popular and won over 38 per cent of the vote in free elections in 1946. A coalition government of communists and non-communists was formed – although the prime minister was a communist, the foreign minister and the president were both non-communists. However, in mid 1947 a serious industrial and agricultural crisis developed and, with Cold War tensions running high, the communists staged a coup before the May 1948 elections. In the rigged elections that followed, the communists won a huge victory which virtually completed Soviet control of eastern Europe.

Communists sought to justify such measures in eastern Europe by pointing to events in western Europe in countries such as Denmark, France, Italy and Belgium – in Belgium, communists were even imprisoned for a time. The Soviet Union was also denied a place on the Allied Control Commissions established in Italy and Japan to oversee the post-war settlement in the former Axis powers.

The problem of Germany

The Soviet Union's main concern in Europe, however, was not eastern Europe but Germany. They knew that the buffer zone provided by eastern European countries would provide little security from a revived and aggressive Germany. Soviet policy was not initially focused on dividing Germany – France was alone in wanting this.

In 1945, the main disagreement between the Allies was over reparations from Germany, with the Russians wanting massive compensation for all the destruction they had suffered between 1941 and 1945. Disputes over this question arose at both Yalta and Potsdam. At Yalta, the Allies agreed on the

Which of the Allies wanted Germany to be divided permanently after the Second World War?

temporary division of Germany into four zones of occupation, even though the USA believed this would be impractical. At Potsdam, agreement was reached over German demilitarisation, denazification and democratisation.

Though the USA, Britain and France objected to the level of reparations desired by the USSR, it was also agreed at Potsdam that each country could take reparations from its own zone of occupation. As the Soviet zone in east Germany was mainly agricultural, it was further agreed that some industrial equipment and raw materials would be handed over to the Soviet Union from the three western zones of Germany occupied by the USA, France and Britain. (How the German problem was affected by and became part of the Cold War is examined in Chapters 11 and 12.)

Soviet aims in 1945

Historians are divided over what the Soviet Union's aims and motives were in 1945. Traditionalists argue that possibly as early as 1943 Stalin had decided on a policy of territorial expansion, as part of a deliberate strategy to challenge global capitalism economically, politically and militarily. Some traditionalists see Soviet expansion as indicative of a Soviet attempt to obtain world domination. Others suggest that, although there was no pre-planned strategy, Stalin took advantage of any opportunities to expand Soviet territory and deliberately tried to create divisions between the Allies in order to maximise his chances of success.

More recently, historians have argued that Stalin's main fear was of a revived Germany and that Soviet policy in Europe in 1945 was aimed at preventing this, either by co-operating with the West or, failing that, by taking steps to protect its eastern borders by controlling the newly liberated states of eastern and central Europe.

Behind the Iron Curtain

While the Soviet Union was in the process of establishing its control over the countries of eastern Europe, the Red Army began to dismantle some of the industries in those countries and raw materials were commandeered, especially from Germany's former Axis partners, Hungary and Romania. Despite Stalin's strong desire to see communist governments in them, he stopped short of supporting any social revolution in these countries in the years 1944–46, despite the often strong wishes of local communist parties and their returning leaders.

Before the Cold War developed properly, the Soviet Union's main desire was to be flanked by friendly governments and for a steady flow of industrial and agricultural produce to help redress the weakness of the Soviet economy by speeding up reconstruction. Any revolutionary upheavals or transformations in the eastern European states, Stalin believed, might jeopardise these aims as well as alienate the USA and Britain who, at first, seemed prepared to acquiesce in eastern Europe being mainly a Soviet sphere of influence.

The people's democracies

As the Cold War developed, however, Stalin's intentions changed and he moved towards establishing regimes in eastern Europe that were organised along political and economic lines similar to those of the Soviet Union. In 1947, **Cominform** was set up and, by mid 1947, a series of treaties (containing both economic and military terms) was concluded with these countries. From 1947 to 1949, the eastern European states were transformed into 'people's democracies'.

At the same time, the Stalinist model of state security, based on an extensive secret police system, was introduced under close Soviet supervision. In 1949, **Comecon** was established in order to co-ordinate the economic policies of the eastern European states and to establish closer links with the Soviet Union.

The only eastern European state to remain independent and so avoid becoming a Soviet 'satellite' was Yugoslavia, where Tito insisted on pushing for a socialist transformation before the Second World War had even finished.

Once Soviet control was established in eastern Europe, Stalin was determined to maintain it. Before his death in 1953, purges of communist parties in the people's democracies mirrored developments in the USSR and created carbon-copy Stalinist states. Yet, in many ways, this process of consolidation brought little lasting benefit to the Soviet Union. Most eastern European economies stayed relatively weak and soon needed Soviet assistance, while the buffer zone was made virtually obsolete as the USA quickly built up a nuclear weapons arsenal based on bombers and, later, on missiles.

The **Communist Information Bureau (Cominform)** was set up in 1947. In some ways it was a successor to Comintern (which Stalin had abolished in 1943). Its main tasks were to keep tight control of the communist parties ruling eastern Europe and to co-ordinate the international work of western communist parties.

The **Council for Mutual Economic Assistance (Comecon)** was set up in 1949 as the Soviet response to the Marshall Plan (see page 140). It was intended to co-ordinate the economic policies of all the eastern European states with those of the Soviet Union.

How did Cominform and Comecon help bring eastern Europe under closer Soviet control?

Historical sources

1 George Kennan, an important official in the US embassy in Moscow during the 1940s, writing after the war

Stalin's ambitions in the final stages of the war ran, of course, well beyond the objectives explicitly stated to the allies as the war came to an end, and beyond those that were implicit in the military advances of the Soviet armies at that time. What Stalin was really after was the expulsion of American influence from the Eurasian land mass generally, and its replacement by that of his own regime.

G. Kennan, *Russia and the West under Lenin and Stalin*, London, 1961, p. 386

2 A western historian's view on Stalin's aims regarding the problem of Germany after the Second World War

Stalin sought its [USA] long-term presence and aid in . . . Germany. It was Stalin who suggested the American occupation of a zone both in Germany and Austria, it was Roosevelt who hesitated . . . Stalin differentiated between British and American objectives in Europe. He perceived Churchill, quite accurately, as far more hostile to Soviet security arrangements than Roosevelt or, initially, Truman.

C. Kennedy-Pope, *Stalin's Cold War: Soviet strategies in Europe 1943 to 1945*, Manchester, 1995, pp. 193–94

Historical-source questions

1 What, according to Kennan in Source 1, was Stalin's objective concerning a US presence in Europe after the Second World War?
2 Why must the reliability of Source 1 be questioned?
3 To what extent does Source 2 contradict the views expressed in Source 1?

Summary questions

1 Identify and explain any *two* reasons for disagreements between the Allies in 1945.

2 Explain why Stalin decided to take control of the countries of eastern Europe after 1945.

The Cold War in Europe, 1945–91

11 The origins of the Cold War

◆ What was the Cold War?

◆ Why did the Cold War begin?

◆ How can the Cold War be explained?

Significant dates

1917	*November*	Bolshevik Revolution in Russia
1919	*March*	Communist International (Comintern) set up
1941	*June*	Nazi Germany invades the Soviet Union; Atlantic Charter
	December	Declaration of the United Nations
1943	*November*	Tehran Conference
1944		Bretton Woods Agreement
1945	*February*	Yalta Conference
	April	Roosevelt dies and is replaced by Vice-President Truman
	May	Red Army occupies Berlin; lend–lease aid to USSR ended by USA
	July	Potsdam Conference
	August	USA drops A-bombs on Hiroshima and Nagasaki
	December	Council of Foreign Ministers meets in Moscow; Ethridge Report

Born in 1882, Franklin Delano **Roosevelt** became a Democrat state senator in 1910, then governor of New York and, in 1933, president of the USA at the height of the Depression. He introduced the New Deal to cope with these problems and went on to win the presidential elections in 1936, 1940 and 1944. He was opposed to fascism and was prepared to make some concessions to allay Stalin's security fears after the Second World War. He died after the Yalta Conference in April 1945 and was succeeded by his vice-president, Harry S. Truman.

Overview

Distrust between the capitalist West and communist Soviet Union had been a feature of international politics since the Bolshevik Revolution of 1917. When Germany invaded the Soviet Union in 1941, the West and the Soviet Union put aside their differences and co-operated in a Grand Alliance against the common threat of Nazi Germany. But signs of strain soon began to emerge.

At the Tehran Conference in 1943, Stalin was concerned about the delay in opening a second front and there was disagreement over the futures of Germany and Poland. At the Yalta and Potsdam Conferences in 1945, these differences deepened – especially after Truman became president of the USA, following **Roosevelt**'s death. Tensions over Germany and the growing Soviet domination of eastern Europe were heightened after the USA dropped atom bombs on Japan.

What was the Cold War?

Antagonism and co-operation, 1917–43

The term **Cold War** is used to describe the antagonism between the United States and the West on the one side and the Soviet Union and eastern Europe on the other. This conflict existed during all, or most, of the period 1945–91. Its most obvious signs were the division of western and eastern Europe by the Iron Curtain, the emergence of two hostile political and military alliances (NATO and the Warsaw Pact), and an arms race which at times seemed to threaten nuclear annihilation.

Though direct hot war between the two **superpowers** was avoided, there were many international crises during the Cold War and several vicious hot wars involving the allies or 'client states' of the rival superpowers.

The 'great contest'

The long-term causes of the Cold War can be traced back to 1917 and the Bolshevik Revolution in Russia, which resulted in the emergence of the world's first state based on Marxist ideology. The revolutionary Russian republic directly challenged the capitalist world system by its attempts to stimulate and aid world revolution and to create a collectivist socialist economy. In 1919, Lenin and Trotsky showed that their calls for revolution in Europe were serious when they formed the Communist International (Comintern). Capitalist countries were suspicious and even fearful of this new state.

From 1917 to 1921, the new communist state was embroiled in a civil war which, as we have seen, involved armies from the USA and Britain – the Bolsheviks saw this as a deliberate capitalist attempt to destroy their revolutionary socialist experiment. Though the Bolsheviks emerged victorious, the USA (among others) refused to recognise the communist government. This was partly because by 1918 Wilson had already begun the USA's attempt to replace the old European state system with a new international order, under US hegemony, to make the world 'safe for democracy'. By 'democracy' Wilson meant an international liberal capitalism, based on individualism. The first concrete evidence of this had been his Fourteen Points, issued in January 1918.

The relative general economic backwardness of tsarist Russia, the First World War, the revolutions of 1917, the civil war and foreign intervention, and the Polish invasion of 1920–21 (backed by Britain and France) all combined to weaken communist Russia, which remained isolated after the failure of revolution elsewhere in Europe. The military attacks by other nations were

The **Cold War** was the term originally used in the fourteenth century about the conflict between Christian and Islamic states. It means hostile relations which, however, do not build up into a 'hot' war (involving actual military conflict). The term was popularised by US journalist Walter Lippmann and US politician and businessman Bernard Baruch in the years 1946–47.

The term **superpower** was first used in 1944 and refers to a country considered so powerful, because of its economic and military resources, that it can largely dictate and control international events to serve its own interests.

The **'great contest'** was a term used by the historian Isaac Deutscher to refer to the global conflict between the two rival social systems of capitalism and socialism. According to Deutscher, this contest began as soon as the Bolsheviks had established their power after the November 1917 Revolution.

What is meant by the 'great contest'?

The **Riga Axioms** refer to the views and policies of the US diplomatic experts, based in Riga (the capital of Latvia), who worked for the Division of Russian Affairs (DRA) during the 1920s. This had been set up by the US State Department which, despite refusing to recognise the new Soviet republic, wanted to discover Soviet foreign policy objectives. Latvia, formerly part of tsarist Russia but then an independent republic, provided a haven for Russian exiles opposed to the Soviet government. Their views greatly influenced those who worked in the Riga centre of the DRA to see Soviet aims as threatening world revolution. In particular, they warned the USA to take action against this threat. These views helped shape US policy towards the Soviet Union into the 1930s and 1940s.

George Kennan was born in 1904. He was a US diplomat who worked at the Riga centre of the US

replaced by economic embargoes in the early 1920s – all aimed, in the words of Winston Churchill, to 'strangle infant Bolshevism in its cradle'. In addition, some of Stalin's economic policies – especially in agriculture – had a negative effect on the relative strength of the Soviet Union.

The **'great contest'** between the USA and the USSR was one-sided as, in contrast, the USA had emerged economically and militarily strengthened from the First World War. Consequently, for most of the period 1921–41, Soviet communism was no serious rival to world capitalism and was overshadowed by the Great Depression, the rise of fascism and the threat of another world war. The Great Purge, however, strengthened hardline attitudes in the USA against the USSR, while the Soviet Union itself became increasingly suspicious of all capitalist states.

Significantly, the USA set up the Division of Russian Affairs, which was later responsible for the important **Riga Axioms**. The division was headed by Charles Bohlen and **George Kennan** and was much influenced by exiled Russians opposed to the Bolsheviks – they tended to stress the world revolution aims of the new Soviet state. The Riga Axioms assumed real influence after 1945, when the legacy of the Bolshevik Revolution of 1917 began to have an increased impact on international relations, although some historians have recently begun to reassess their overall significance.

The Second World War

Initially, in the period 1939–41, the views of US 'hardliners' such as Kennan and the Riga Axiomists seemed confirmed by Soviet actions like the conclusion of

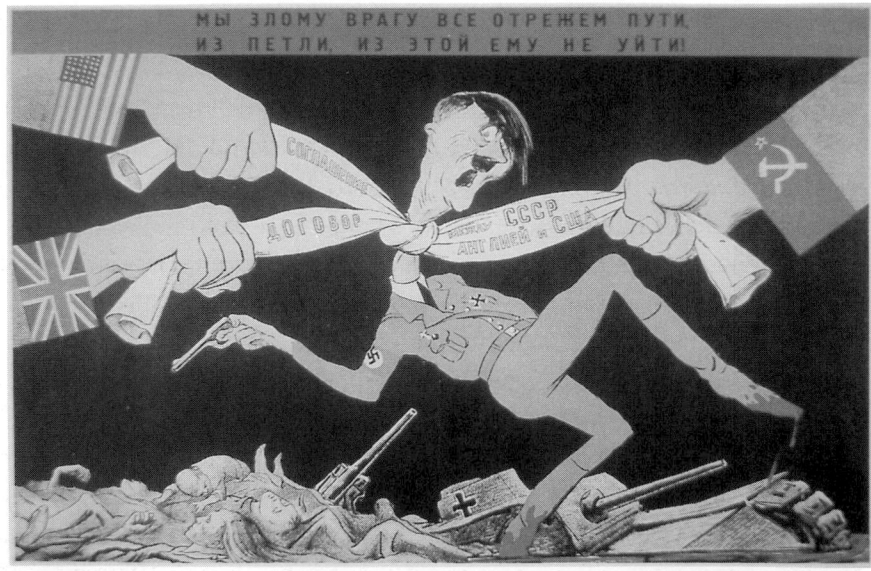

A Soviet cartoon from 1942, celebrating the unity and victories of the wartime Allies. This unity, however, began to break down even before the end of the Second World War.

the Nazi–Soviet Non-Aggression Pact, the partition of Poland, war against Finland and the Soviet takeover of the Baltic states (see page 102). Their views were supported by others such as Robert Taft and, especially, Joseph Kennedy, the US ambassador in London, who had supported the British foreign policy of appeasing Nazi Germany rather than forming an alliance with the Soviet Union.

However, their views were opposed by Joseph Davies, US ambassador in Moscow during 1937–38. He believed that the USSR was interested in co-operation in order to help stabilise Europe against Nazi aggression. He was also of the opinion that the Soviet Union was developing a form of state capitalism rather than socialism. Roosevelt saw Nazi Germany as more expansionist than the USSR and thought that at the end of the war a weakened Soviet Union could be persuaded to drop the idea of world communism in return for security guarantees and help in economic reconstruction (which in turn would also help the US economy). Roosevelt initially felt this was preferable to the continued existence of opposed or rival alliances, an arms race and the threat of future wars (although there is evidence that his attitude to the USSR's demands later began to harden).

Hence, when the USSR was attacked by Germany in June 1941 and then the USA by Japan in December 1941, the USA and Britain soon joined with the Soviet Union in a Grand Alliance, seeing Hitler as a more serious and immediate threat than Stalin.

The Tehran Conference

Though the outbreak of the Second World War seemed to temporarily end the USA/West–Soviet rivalry, problems soon began to emerge within the Grand Alliance. In particular, the delay in opening up a second front in Europe led Stalin to suspect that this delay was a deliberate decision on the part of the Alliance partners to ensure that the USSR was seriously weakened. The Russians were also concerned over Roosevelt's statements on US foreign policy which, he said, was based on 'democracy and economic freedom'. The Soviet Union remained suspicious of Roosevelt's **'open-door' policy**, based on 'free' world trade and 'equal' access to raw materials as they believed it was designed to benefit economically advanced countries, especially the USA.

However, as the war was still continuing, the Big Three managed to maintain their alliance. When they met at Tehran in November 1943, they agreed in principle that the Soviet Union (invaded three times via Poland since 1900) could have its 1918 border with Poland restored, while Poland's western border would move further west. They also agreed that no central European alliance would be allowed against the Soviet Union. These two points seemed to remove some of Stalin's main security concerns, though Churchill and Roosevelt were not in total agreement on these issues.

Division of Russian Affairs in the 1920s. His advice on policy options, which were based on his belief that the Soviet Union was intent on world domination, became known as the Riga Axioms. Later, in 1946, his 'Long Telegram' became the basis of the USA's Cold War policy of 'containment' of the Soviet 'threat'.

What was the Grand Alliance?

The **'open-door' policy** was the USA's way of demanding 'equal opportunity' in all foreign markets, via the establishment of free trade (thus abolishing all tariffs and preferential systems). However, because the USA was by far the most advanced economic power, such a policy of equal opportunity was more likely to lead to increased US global domination than to any 'mutual benefits' – especially for the relatively backward and weakened Soviet Union. This desire to extend US economic influence is sometimes referred to as 'dollar diplomacy'.

Why was Poland an important issue at the Tehran Conference in 1943?

Why did the Cold War begin?

Breakdown of the Grand Alliance, 1944–45

A photograph showing the Big Three (Churchill, Roosevelt and Stalin) at the Yalta Conference in February 1945.

Tensions, which finally led to the breakdown of the Grand Alliance and the start of the Cold War, began to emerge more sharply at the 1945 conferences held at Yalta in February and at Potsdam in July. There were four main areas of disagreement: Germany, Poland, economic reconstruction and nuclear weapons.

Germany

Although the war against Germany was still continuing when the Allies met at Yalta in February 1945, it was clearly nearly over as far as Europe was concerned. The problems which had emerged at Tehran – especially Poland and the fate of the eastern European countries – now had to be resolved. The conference agreed, quite amicably, to temporarily divide Germany into four zones of occupation, with an initial agreement (in principle) on reparations for the damage done by Nazi Germany, especially to the USSR.

The problem of Poland proved more difficult to solve; eventually, it was agreed that the USSR's demands regarding Poland's eastern borders would be met and that Poland would receive territorial compensation from Germany, up to the Oder–Neisse rivers. The Allies also accepted the Lublin provisional government for Poland, with the addition of some of the London Poles. However, when Roosevelt died in April 1945, the more optimistic spirit in which these agreements were reached soon faded, as Vice-President Truman took a more hardline approach to the Soviet Union.

In May, Truman abruptly ended the lend–lease aid to the USSR – this was a serious, as well as worrying, blow to the war-devastated Soviet Union. Then, at the Potsdam Conference in July 1945, Truman stated the USA would only agree to the Soviet Union extracting reparations from the eastern zone of Germany – which was mainly agricultural and therefore poorer – as well as receiving 25 per cent of the machinery from the three western zones. This was on condition that the USSR sent back to the western zones 60 per cent of the value of what it had received from them in the form of goods and raw materials (especially coal).

Poland and eastern Europe

The issue of Poland was complex; Stalin saw it as a life-and-death question for the Soviet state. In October 1944 Churchill and Stalin met in Moscow. They concluded the informal **'percentages' agreement** concerning influence in south-eastern and eastern Europe. Although Roosevelt was not present, he was briefed afterwards and made no objections; however, Poland was not mentioned at this meeting.

At Yalta, however, Roosevelt backed away from the prospect of a Soviet sphere of influence in eastern Europe. Stalin felt this was essential for Soviet security and was worried by the new US call for an 'open-door' policy and their suggestion that there should be no formal spheres of influence. Roosevelt, who had kept the earlier agreements with Stalin about eastern Europe secret from the US public, now suggested that the proposed United Nations Organisation should make decisions about these issues after the war was over.

These shifts persuaded Stalin to begin taking practical measures to ensure Soviet security interests in eastern Europe. When the Soviet Union failed to carry out the Yalta agreement on free elections in Poland, US suspicions about Soviet motives were aroused even further. Once Truman became president, friction increased and the USA became more determined to contain Soviet power whenever possible. The first sign of this was the abrupt ending of the lend–lease aid in May 1945 (although Truman's decision also had much to do with Congressional pressure to reduce expenditure, and applied to Britain as well).

Economic reconstruction

In view of the dreadful destruction suffered by the USSR, Stalin's priority after the war was economic reconstruction. Consequently he agreed, provisionally, to join the World Bank and the International Monetary Fund at the Bretton Woods Conference in 1944. The promise of a loan from the USA overcame his reservations about their growing influence. But when the USSR asked for a $6 billion loan in January 1945, the USA imposed conditions, such as opening eastern European markets to US capital. The USSR would not accept this **dollar diplomacy**.

At the Moscow Conference in October 1944, Churchill and Stalin concluded a **'percentages' agreement** about 'spheres of influence'. The percentage ratios for Britain and the USSR respectively in the eastern European states were as follows: Romania – 10:90; Greece – 90:10; Bulgaria – 25:75; Hungary – 25:75; Yugoslavia – 50:50. As the Cold War began, it soon became clear Stalin intended to impose Soviet political control (and Soviet-style economic and social systems) on those countries in the Soviet sphere.

Dollar diplomacy originally referred to heavy US investment in Latin American countries in the 1920s and 1930s. The USA's economic dominance was seen as giving it the power to determine diplomatic and internal politics in those countries in which it invested.

For this reason, Stalin placed more emphasis on reparations from Germany – at Yalta it was agreed that $10 billion would be a starting point for negotiation. Tension increased in May, when the lend–lease aid was ended without notice. A further Soviet request for a loan, in August 1945, was 'lost' by the US State Department. Consequently, the USSR allowed the December 1945 deadline for membership of the World Bank and the IMF to pass without signing up. Instead it decided to increase reparations from its own sphere of influence and this necessitated greater Soviet control of eastern Europe.

The US atomic bomb

The apparent, though partial, agreements on Germany, reparations and Poland were undermined in August 1945 when the USA exploded the world's first atomic bombs on Hiroshima and Nagasaki. More significant for relations between the USA and the USSR was the USA's refusal to share the technology with its Soviet ally.

At the Yalta Conference, Roosevelt had extracted a promise from Stalin to enter the war against Japan, once Germany was defeated. However, Truman and his secretary of state, James Byrnes, saw the A-bomb (tested successfully on 16 July 1945) as a way of ending the war against Japan without Soviet participation, as well as keeping US casualties to a minimum. This would pre-empt any Soviet demands for influence in Asia, which was seen as vital to US interests. The Potsdam Conference was delayed until 16 July, partly to give Truman a new powerful negotiating tool. This policy was opposed by the US secretary of war, Henry **Stimson**, who argued that the Soviet Union should be offered an atomic partnership if the USSR was prepared to make some concessions on eastern Europe.

In 1945, the USSR was only a regional power, unlike the USA, which was by then already a truly global power; significantly, the **USA's long-term aims** increasingly conflicted with the USSR's regional objectives. Stalin interpreted the refusal to share nuclear technology as a demonstration of US power to a seriously weakened USSR. This interpretation is supported by the revisionist historian G. Alperovitz, who argues that, because only the USA had nuclear weapons from 1945 to 1949, possession of the nuclear bomb was seen by Truman and his advisers as a 'negotiating tool' to force the USSR to accept its plans for post-war Europe and the world.

Stalin was very concerned about this nuclear monopoly and quickly authorised a speed-up in the development of a Soviet bomb. However, though the USSR was without its own atomic bomb until 1949, this did not overly affect Soviet policy in eastern Europe. Despite fears about the A-bomb, Stalin carried on with his plans to take over, possibly because he decided to listen to those of his advisers who said that the USA would not use nuclear weapons in Europe.

Stimson was one of several US diplomats who believed that, if Soviet fears were addressed, Stalin would not be bothered about establishing Soviet control in Europe. This had been Roosevelt's belief.

What was Stimson's view concerning the USA sharing its nuclear weapons technology with the USSR?

The **USA's long-term aims** were to ensure the spread of liberal capitalism world wide, to prevent anti-capitalist revolutions and to protect US interests around the globe.

Nonetheless, from mid 1944, as Soviet forces took back Soviet territory previously occupied by German forces, Stalin became increasingly aware of how damaged and weakened the Soviet Union was (see page 115). By the end of the war, the Red Army was about 11 million strong, while US forces totalled almost 12 million. Because of the need for rapid economic reconstruction, money had to be shifted from defence to industry. Accordingly, the Red Army was rapidly demobilised to under 3 million so that even in conventional terms the USSR did not pose a military threat that needed to be met with US nuclear weapons.

The discussion of other contentious issues at Potsdam was postponed, after it was agreed that regular meetings of the Council of Foreign Ministers would deal with these. When, in September and October 1945, Molotov would not agree to including a number of non-communists in the governments of Hungary, Romania and Bulgaria, Byrnes seemed prepared to make concessions on this, in order to secure a wider agreement. However, this was blocked by J. F. **Dulles**, a leading Republican, who supported the Riga Axioms. When the council met again in Moscow in December 1945, the Soviet Union agreed to include two non-communists in the Romanian and Bulgarian governments, in return for US recognition of these states. However, Byrnes was beginning to have doubts about making any concessions to the USSR as, before the December meeting, he had received the Ethridge Report, which he had commissioned and which was very critical of the USSR's 'imperialist' policies in Romania and Bulgaria.

> What were the main areas of disagreement at the 1945 conferences of Yalta and Potsdam?

How can the Cold War be explained?

The historical debate

There are various theories put forward by historians to explain the roots of the Cold War. Soon after the end of the Second World War, supporters of the orthodox view argued that the Cold War was a result of Soviet ideology which focused on the destabilisation of capitalist states. This placed responsibility for the Cold War on the USSR, with the West forced to adopt policies which 'contained' the 'communist threat'.

By the late 1950s, however, a new – revisionist – interpretation was emerging, which argued that the USSR was too weak to pose a real threat in terms of global expansion and that responsibility for the Cold War rested with the USA not the USSR. According to this argument, Stalin focused on internal policy and did little to promote international revolution. Instead, the Soviet Union was pushed into increasing its control over eastern Europe to counter US actions, which aimed to establish American domination through the 'open-door' policy. Having pushed to undermine the sterling area and the

Born in 1888, John Foster **Dulles** became an important Republican politician in the USA. He held various diplomatic and advisory posts before and during the Second World War. He was strongly opposed to any concessions to the Soviet Union at the end of the war and was a supporter of the Riga Axioms. He later became secretary of state (1953–59) and was a major influence on US foreign policy during the Cold War – he became known as one of the 'Cold War Warriors'.

imperial preference system (which gave advantages to British manufacturers selling to British colonies) during the war to reduce British influence, the USA now attempted to do the same in eastern Europe. The Soviet Union was, therefore, forced to establish greater control in the region in order to protect itself from the aims of US global dominance – a 'Pax America'.

A third opinion is offered by post-revisionists, who try to avoid placing blame on just one of the superpowers. One post-revisionist argument is that the Cold War was the result of confusions, especially in the aftermath of Roosevelt's replacement by Truman, when Truman's hardline policies deepened the suspicions of a Soviet government more accustomed to Roosevelt's conciliatory overtures. Other post-revisionist strands look at the role of nuclear proliferation, which impelled both sides to distrust each other. Class-conflict theorists, on the other hand, see the Cold War as the inevitable result of the global conflict between capitalism and communism. More recent research has begun to focus on how Stalin chose to ignore Litvinov's more moderate advice and take a harder line advocated by other counsellors.

What are the three main historical explanations for the start of the Cold War?

How do class-conflict theories explain the origins of the Cold War?

Historical sources

1 Winston Churchill, writing about the agreement made between himself and Stalin on 9 October 1944 in Moscow

We alighted at Moscow on the afternoon on October 9 . . . At ten o'clock that night we held our first important meeting in the Kremlin . . .

The moment was apt for business, so I said, 'Let us settle about our affairs in the Balkans. Your armies are in Rumania and Bulgaria. We have interests, missions, and agents there. Don't let us get at cross-purposes in small ways. So far as Britain and Russia are concerned, how would it do for you to have ninety per cent predominance in Rumania, for us to have ninety per cent of the say in Greece, and go fifty-fifty about Yugoslavia?' While this was being translated I wrote out on a half-sheet of paper: [various percentages relating to Romania, Greece, Yugoslavia, Hungary and Bulgaria] . . .

I pushed this across to Stalin, who by then had heard the translation. There was a slight pause. Then he took his blue pencil and made a large tick upon it, and passed it back to us. It was all settled in no more time than it takes to set down.

W. Churchill, *Triumph and tragedy*, Boston, 1954, pp. 226–28

2 Walter Lippmann, an American journalist, writing in the *Nashville Tennessean* on 15 March 1946

No atomic bombardment could destroy the Red Army; it could destroy only the industrial means of supplying it. The Russian defence to atomic attack is, therefore, self-evident; it is to overrun continental Europe with infantry, and defy us to drop atomic bombs on Poland, Czechoslovakia, Austria . . . The more we threaten to demolish Russian cities, the more obvious it is that the Russian defence would be to ensconce themselves in European cities which we could not demolish without massacring hundreds of thousands of our own friends.

E. G. Rayner, *The Cold War*, London, 1992, p. 12

Historical-source questions

1 According to Source 1, what was the British attitude in 1944 to increased Soviet influence in eastern Europe?
2 In what ways did Churchill later alter his views as expressed in Source 1?
3 What attitude does Walter Lippmann have in Source 2 to the US nuclear monopoly?
4 To what extent did other US politicians and diplomats share Lippmann's views?

Summary question

1 Identify and explain why the members of the wartime Grand Alliance began to have serious differences in 1945.
2 Compare the main points of at least *three* different historical explanations for the origins of the Cold War.

12

Early stages, 1946–49

Focus questions

◆ Was 1946 a turning point?

◆ How important were the Truman Doctrine and the Marshall Plan?

◆ What were the main points of tension in Europe from 1947 to 1949?

Significant dates

1946   *February*   Kennan's 'long telegram'; Baruch Plan fails
         March   Churchill's 'Iron Curtain' speech
         June   USA–Soviet negotiations on Export–Import Bank end
         July–October   Paris peace conference
         October   Communists win elections in Bulgaria
         November   Rigged elections in Romania result in communist victory

1947   *January*   Communists rig elections in Poland; Britain and USA merge German zones to form Bizonia
         March   Truman announces containment policy (Truman Doctrine)
         June   Marshall Plan announced
         August   Communists win elections in Hungary
         September   Cominform set up; Zhdanov delivers his 'Two Camps' speech

1948   *February*   Brussels Treaty Organisation
         February–March   Communist coup in Czechoslovakia after non-communists resign from government
         June   France joins its German zone to Bizonia, to form Trizonia; new currency introduced in West Germany; Yugoslavia expelled from Cominform; start of Berlin Crisis
         September   Parliamentary committee set up to draft the basic law for a separate West German state

1949   *January*   Comecon established
         April   NATO set up
         May   Berlin Blockade ends; West Germany (FDR) formally established
         August   Soviet A-bomb tested
         September   FDR government appointed
         October   Chinese communists take power; East German state (GDR) set up

Overview

Ongoing disagreements during 1946 continued the hostility between the East and the West, symbolised by Churchill's 'Iron Curtain' speech in March 1946. Events such as the economic crisis in Europe, electoral successes for the communists in Italy and France, and the Greek civil war led the USA to announce the Truman Doctrine and the policy of 'containment' in 1947. This was followed by US economic help for Europe (Marshall Aid). Before long, the term Cold War was being widely used. Growing Soviet power in eastern Europe, the Brussels Treaty Organisation formed by west European states and the merger of the West's zones in Germany saw relations between the USA and the USSR almost completely break down in 1948. The Soviet response was the Berlin Blockade, which the West countered with the Berlin Airlift. In 1949, NATO was set up, initially at the request of western European states, but it soon became dominated by the USA. Though the Berlin Blockade ended in May, Cold War tensions increased when the USSR exploded its first atomic bomb. By the end of 1949, Germany was divided into two separate states.

Was 1946 a turning point?

The growing divide, 1946–47

By the end of 1945, tensions between the Allies were already apparent. The problems that arose between 1946 and 1949 – Germany, atomic weapons, the economic crisis in western Europe and increasing Soviet control of eastern Europe – and the decisions made about them resulted in more serious divisions.

In 1946, western governments came to see increasing Soviet control in eastern Europe as the first step towards the spread of communism westwards. Some politicians believed in the possibility of communist takeovers in Greece, Italy and even France, where communist support was relatively strong. As early as February 1946, Byrnes began to urge the Iranian prime minister to resist any Soviet advances in that important oil-rich region.

February 1946 saw two significant developments. First, the failure of the **Baruch Plan** ended any hopes of an agreement on the control of nuclear weapons. Second, Kennan sent his famous 'Long Telegram' in which he argued that the USSR was a dangerous and expansionist state that would never co-operate with the USA. This meant that, no matter what the USA did, Soviet policy towards the West would not be altered in the short or medium term. This view rapidly became the basis of US policy and was the origin of the policy of 'containment' (the term was first used by Kennan) which emerged the following year, essentially reviving the Riga Axioms.

The **Baruch Plan** was a US plan, presented by Bernard Baruch to the UN on 15 June 1946, which was supposed to remove Soviet fears about the USA's nuclear monopoly by eventually placing such weapons under international control. An International Atomic Energy Authority would be set up to control all raw materials and atomic plants. However, the USA then insisted on its right to continue making nuclear weapons and to retain them for some time. Gromyko, the Soviet ambassador to the UN, called for a complete ban on nuclear weapons. The Baruch Plan, though adopted by the UN's Atomic Energy Commission on 30 December 1946, was vetoed by the USSR in the Security Council.

What did Kennan's 'Long Telegram' say about Soviet foreign policy?

Iron Curtain. The term was used to describe the boundary between capitalist western Europe and communist eastern Europe. As the Cold War deepened, the frontiers – especially in Germany – became physical and visible.

What was the significance of Winston Churchill's Iron Curtain speech?

In March 1946, Winston Churchill made his famous **Iron Curtain** speech in Fulton, Missouri. In this speech he supported the view that the Soviet Union was an expansionist state, arguing for an end to compromise and calling for a stronger Anglo-American alliance. This was an important shift away from the spirit of Yalta and Roosevelt's policy of co-operation with the USSR and coincided with Kennan's 'Long Telegram'.

In essence, Kennan was in favour of a 'fully fledged and realistic showdown with the Soviet Union' over developments in eastern Europe. As early as February 1945, he had argued that if the West was not prepared to 'go the whole hog' to block any expansion of Soviet influence in Europe, then the only alternative was to split Germany permanently in two and to draw a definitive frontier between East and West. He believed the world should be divided into rival spheres of influence and that the USA should conduct a propaganda war against the USSR and communism.

In 1945–46, Byrnes used international loans and credits to stabilise economies outside the Soviet sphere (such as France). The loans, amounting to $5,700 million, were used to reconstruct war-damaged industries. At the USA–Soviet negotiations about loans and credits to the USSR, Byrnes made it clear that, in return, the USA would expect to have a say in the economic reconstruction of eastern Europe and the removal of all trade barriers. This resulted in negotiations being broken off. The Export–Import Bank then transferred most of the money initially intended for the Soviet Union to France as the economic problems there were seen to be boosting the popularity of the French Communist Party. In addition, US economic support of the United Nations Relief and Rehabilitation Administration (UNRRA) was ended (much of which had gone to Poland, Czechoslovakia and Hungary) and applications from these countries for credits from the World Bank were turned down.

Economic crisis in western Europe

'Doves' is the term used to describe those who prefer to find peaceful ways to resolve differences; those who follow more hardline or aggressive policies are sometimes called 'hawks'.

What happened during 1946 to those US officials who believed the Soviet Union was willing to compromise over eastern Europe?

Most USA officials soon came to support Kennan's views – some **'doves'**, who believed the USSR was willing to compromise, were forced to resign. However, although a media campaign (helped by Churchill's speech) was launched about the 'new threat' from the Soviet Union, neither the Republican-dominated Congress nor the general public were yet convinced of the need to give large loans to economically weak allies or to increase the military budget to counter the Soviet 'threat'. The Republicans won the Congressional elections of November 1946 and actually voted to cut Truman's 1947 budget, including military expenditure.

However, the economic and political situation in western Europe in 1946–47 eventually persuaded Congress to support the more active and costly foreign policy desired by Truman's administration. By then, the economic plight of most European states after the devastation of the Second World War was serious (Britain's problems, for example, led to a shift from it being a world power to a junior partner to the USA). The loans made by the USA in 1945–46 had not produced the desired improvement and industrial production was still 20 per cent below that of 1939. Europe was then hit by a poor harvest in 1946 and a severe winter in 1946–47. Its population was both cold and hungry; the communist parties in France and Italy were also experiencing increased support.

George **Marshall**, who replaced Byrnes as secretary of state, estimated that western Europe would need $17 million of aid in order to recover, but the Republican Congress was still not convinvced. The turning point was the British announcement in February 1947 that, because of its economic problems, it would no longer be able to give economic or military aid either to Turkey or to the Greek royalists who were fighting a civil war against the Greek communists (in fact, the USA was already helping Britain with the costs).

Born in 1880, George C. **Marshall** became chief of staff during the Second World War and pushed for an Allied advance through France as the best way to defeat Germany. As well as being the architect of the Marshall Plan to aid the economic recovery of western Europe, he also headed the Marshall Mission to China, in an attempt to maintain the nationalist–communist alliance.

How important were the Truman Doctrine and the Marshall Plan?

Containment and the Truman Doctrine

By linking the issue of USA loans to the struggle against communism, **Dean Acheson** was able to gain support for Truman's policy of 'containment'. He argued that if Greece fell to the communists, then the Balkans and, ultimately, Africa and western Europe (especially France and Italy) would be undermined. This 'rotten apple' argument (based on the idea that one communist state would begin to 'spoil' its immediate neighbours) was similar to the **domino theory** which came to dominate US foreign policy in the following decades.

The change in policy from isolationism to containment was announced by Truman in his speech to Congress on 12 March 1947. In order to gain the support of the Republican Congress, he had to exaggerate the USA's differences with the Soviet Union and argue that the ideological struggle between democracy and communism was a crucial one. The USSR, he implied, was aggressively expansionist and therefore needed to be contained (although he did not directly mention the Soviet Union itself). This new policy – which came to be known as the Truman Doctrine – argued that all countries had to choose between the 'freedom of the West or the subjugation of communism'. Truman then announced US readiness to assist any country resisting 'armed minorities' or 'outside pressure'. Congress finally approved aid for Greece ($300 million) and Turkey ($100 million): in 1949, the Greek communists suffered a bloody defeat, while Turkey moved firmly into the western bloc.

Born in 1893, **Dean Acheson** was a convinced anti-communist. He helped develop the Truman Doctrine, the Marshall Plan and NATO, and from 1949 to 1953 was US secretary of state. He also encouraged support for nationalist China and US/UN involvement in the Korean War.

The **domino theory** is the argument that if one country is allowed to 'fall' to communism, then neighbouring states will be next to go, as with a line of dominoes. Similar to the 'rotten apple' argument – that one 'rotten' (i.e. communist) state will turn all the other ones 'bad' if it is not removed.

Historians have put forward various reasons why the policy of containment was adopted so quickly by the USA in the 1940s. In general, there was a feeling in the USA that appeasing Hitler in the 1930s had resulted in the Second World War and that there should be no repeat of this in relation to Stalin's regime.

Several other explanations have also been put forward. One is that, as the USA emerged from the Second World War as a truly global power with world-wide interests, political developments in other countries that were not totally pro-capitalism might endanger the power of the USA and should therefore be resisted (in the 1940s nationalist movements in European colonies were threatening vital sources of raw materials and markets). Another is that both USA industries and the military (the military–industrial complex) had bene-fited from the war economy and they believed that continued growth would be assured if a new threat appeared to take the place of the Axis powers. In addition, it was believed that such military expenditure might help stave off a new depression in war-torn Europe by creating jobs in factories and the military.

What did the Truman Doctrine have to say about the USA's role in 'containing communism'?

The Marshall Plan

As well as giving aid to Greece and Turkey, Congress decided to help revive the economies of the western European states through US credits and the revival of the key German economy.

In order to gain Congressional support, it was made clear that only coun-tries with capitalist economies would qualify for aid and it was pointed out that an expanded European economy would also be good for US exports. At the same time, it would allow the revival of the German economy within a European framework, thus preventing a new German dominance, which France in particular feared.

On 23 May 1947, Kennan gave his support to the idea and it was put for-ward as the Marshall Plan on 5 June 1947. Technically, it was open to the Soviet Union and the eastern European states, but the plan's political and eco-nomic criteria meant Stalin was unlikely to accept it. In fact both the USA and the USSR saw it as an attempt to weaken Soviet control of eastern Europe.

Congress only finally agreed to the plan in March 1948, (after the commun-ist coup in Czechoslovakia in February) and an interim payment of $4 billion was made. In August, the western European states calculated that they needed $28 billion, though the USA finally reduced this to $17 billion.

At first, the Soviet Union's response to the Marshall Plan was mixed. Although the USSR was not in favour of US economic and political domin-ation of Europe, it needed US capital and goods. The USSR took part in early discussions about aid, but the continued refusal by the USA, Britain and

France to consider German reparations led to the breakdown of talks. Because this disagreement threatened to delay the implementation of the Marshall Plan at a time when the economic situation in Britain and France was serious, it was decided to exclude the Soviet Union from further discussions and to exaggerate the differences between the two sides. By July 1947, the Soviet Union decided participation in the proposed scheme would involve too many risks and soon rejected further negotiations. Early positive responses from Czechoslovakia, Poland and Hungary were ended on 10 and 11 July, by a combination of Soviet pressure and Czech doubts. Bulgaria, Yugoslavia, Romania, Albania and Finland also rejected involvement between 9 and 11 July.

The Truman Doctrine and the Marshall Plan, on top of the other decisions of 1946–47, contributed to the collapse of the earlier Soviet policy of co-operation with the US and so – along with Soviet actions in eastern Europe – played a significant part in the split of Europe into two opposing camps.

> What connection was there between the Truman Doctrine and the Marshall Plan?

What were the main points of tension in Europe from 1947 to 1949?

From division to Cold War, 1947–49

Eastern Europe

As early as February 1946, the USSR began making attempts to increase its influence in eastern Europe. This was partly due to Stalin's desperation to rebuild the Soviet Union's war-devastated economy. During the summer of 1947, following the Truman Doctrine and the Marshall Plan, these efforts were stepped up, resulting in increasingly communist-dominated governments in Poland, Hungary, Romania and Albania. The USSR came to see Europe as being divided into two antagonistic camps and believed greater control of eastern Europe was essential for its security. This view was reinforced when many non-communist political leaders in these countries, believing the USA would intervene on their side, refused to co-operate with local communist parties.

Poland

In Poland, for example, Mikolajczyk, the new deputy prime minister and leader of the important Peasants' Party, was not keen to co-operate with the Polish communists and, as a result, elections due in February 1946 were postponed until January 1947. Communist manipulation ensured their victory, with Mikolajczyk's party winning only a handful of seats. The communists then took steps to strengthen their control over state bodies.

Bulgaria

Here, the Communist Party, via the Fatherland Front (a coalition of left and centre parties dominated by the Bulgarian Communist Party), ignored earlier Soviet agreements about allowing representatives of the opposition to have a role in government. After the October 1946 elections, the communists were mainly in control and, during 1947, they began resricting the activities of the main opposition party.

Hungary

Here, the right-wing Smallholders' Party (KGP) which won the October 1945 elections, formed a government with Ferenc Nagy as prime minister. He faced an alliance made up of the Communist, Social Democrat and National Peasant parties and so, on 5 March 1946, he was forced to set up a coalition government. But demonstrations against the government's economic policies forced the resignation of KGP deputies. The security forces (controlled by a communist minister) then closed down the opposition parties and initiated a purge; this culminated in the arrest of KGP deputies on counter-revolutionary charges. By the summer of 1947, Nagy had been forced to resign. New elections, held on 31 August 1947, resulted in a communist victory.

Romania

The communist government in Romania, headed by Dr Petra Groza, was recognised by the West after representatives of the National Peasants and the Liberals were included. However, the government was increasingly by-passed by the Soviet authorities and, after a stormy campaign (and vote-rigging) in November 1946, the communists and their allies won almost all the seats. During 1947, all three main opposition parties were closed down and later, on 30 December 1947, the king abdicated. The new People's Republic of Romania was then declared.

Czechoslovakia

The situation developed rather differently here as, before 1939, Czechoslovakia – unlike the other eastern European states – had been a parliamentary democracy. In addition, support for the Czech Communist Party and the Soviet Union was quite strong. In free and fair elections held on 26 May 1946, the communists won 38 per cent of the vote and a coalition government was formed.

Harassment of non-communists did not begin until the summer of 1947, when a serious economic crisis developed. The Czech government applied to the USA for financial assistance but, as Czechoslovakia had already rejected the Marshall Plan and Cold War tensions were developing, this application was rejected. The Czech Communist Party then put pressure on the coalition

Set up by Stalin in 1947, **Cominform** (the Communist Information Bureau) was intended to co-ordinate the different communist governments of eastern Europe and the communist parties in western Europe. Its HQ was originally in Belgrade in Yugoslavia, but shifted to Bucharest in Romania in 1948 when Tito was expelled for not following Stalin's line. It was abolished by Khrushchev in 1956.

The doctrine of the **two opposing camps** was the Soviet reply to the Truman Doctrine and was first government by calling for a more radical programme of economic reform, including nationalisations. When the communist minister of the interior began to appoint 'trusted comrades' to important police posts and to prepare show trials, most non-communist ministers resigned on 20 February 1948. The communists organised huge demonstrations against the government and then called a general strike on 24 February. All remaining non-communists ministers then resigned.

Gottwald, the leader of the Czech Communist Party, became prime minister after persuading Beneš, a non-communist, to support him and they formed a new government, replacing those who had resigned with supporters of the Communist Party. In new elections, the communists and their allies won over 66 per cent of the seats and Beneš was replaced.

Turning point in the USSR's foreign policy

On 22 September 1947, Soviet control of the eastern European countries was taken a step further when the communist parties of these states met in Poland. They agreed to set up the **Communist Information Bureau** (**Cominform**) and, under Zhdanov's influence, they condemned the Marshall Plan on the grounds that it was preparing to extend US power in order to launch a new world war. In his opening speech, Zhdanov spoke of the world being divided into **two opposing camps**. Cominform was intended to keep the communist parties in Europe under Moscow's control. This was a significant step and marked the end of the USSR's flexible and hesitant foreign policy in relation to US actions – even after rejecting the Marshall Plan, the Soviet Union had at first been undecided on what steps to take next.

The Truman Doctrine, the Marshall Plan and German reconstruction (see page 144) thus proved to be important turning points in the USSR's foreign policy. These policies also strengthened the position of those Soviet advisers who had been advocating a more aggressive and expansionist policy.

Yugoslavia

One exception to these developments in eastern Europe was Yugoslavia where **Tito** had already established a communist government, despite Stalin's 'percentages' agreement with Churchill (see page 131). Problems between the USSR and Yugoslavia arose when, in late 1947, Tito signed treaties with Bulgaria, Romania and Hungary agreeing to economic co-operation. Then in January 1948 Tito announced the formation of a customs union with Bulgaria, prior to the setting-up of a Balkan Federation. After an initial hesitation Stalin decided to oppose this and, though Bulgaria backed down, Tito refused to. As Tito was also refusing to prioritise the expansion of heavy industry, Stalin withdrew all Soviet economic and military advisers from Yugoslavia in

announced by Zhdanov at the first conference of Cominform at the end of September 1947. According to Zhdanov, the post-war world was divided into two camps: the Soviet-led anti-imperialist and democratic camp and the US-led imperialist and anti-democratic camp. He argued that the USA, via the Truman Doctrine and the Marshall Plan, was trying to dominate Europe and was also preparing for a new war to achieve world domination and that only the Soviet bloc was preventing this and trying to preserve world peace.

How did the establishment by the USSR of Cominform in 1947 contribute to a worsening of Cold War tensions?

Tito, whose real name was Josip Broz, was born in 1892. He became a leading member of the Yugoslav Communist Party after the First World War and during the Second World War he organised partisan resistance against the Axis forces. In 1945, he ignored Stalin's instructions to form a coalition government with non-communist parties and instead established a communist government. His continued differences with Stalin eventually led to Yugoslavia's expulsion from the communist bloc in 1948. From then on, Tito followed a policy of non-alignment.

March 1948 in order to topple Tito. However, Tito resisted, the Yugoslav Communist Party backed him and he then arrested Stalin's Yugoslav supporters. In June 1948, Yugoslavia was expelled from Cominform for 'bourgeois nationalism' and, under pressure from the Soviet Union, the other eastern European countries broke off diplomatic and trade links. This was followed by a purge of 'Titoists' in the eastern European communist parties.

Why did a split emerge in eastern Europe between Yugoslavia and the USSR?

At the same time, western communist parties were instructed to campaign against the Marshall Plan and protest strikes were arranged in France and Italy during the winter of 1947–48. Such actions tended to isolate these parties and led to their expulsion from the post-war coalition governments. It was clear that the Cold War was affecting internal as well as international politics.

With Cominform established, the Soviet Union pushed hard for 'people's democracies' to be established in eastern Europe, with planned economies run on the lines of the Soviet model. By the summer of 1948, non-communists had already been removed from coalition governments and political influence in all east European states via rigged elections, intimidation, arrests, show trials and political purges. Local communist party leaders were now increasingly replaced with those selected by Stalin, thus strengthening Soviet control over these satellite states. Such actions only helped to increase western support for Truman's policy of containment.

The continuing problem of Germany

Germany became one of the major factors for the worsening relations between the USA and the USSR. After 1945, it was clear Germany would be fundamental to the European (and even global) balance of power and thus it was of tremendous importance to Soviet security concerns. As the tensions grew into the Cold War, both sides feared Germany becoming part of the opposing camp.

At Potsdam, it had been agreed that, despite being temporarily divided into four Allied zones of occupation, Germany should be treated as one economic unit to be administered by the Allied Control Council. Berlin, deep inside the Soviet zone of Germany, was also to be divided into four zones and it was also agreed that the **Five Ds** should be applied to Germany. However, the still-unresolved question of reparations continued to cause problems between the Soviet Union and the other Allies. Tensions also arose over political developments in the Soviet zone when the Social Democrats (SPD) and the Communists (KPD) merged to form the Socialist Unity Party (SED) – the majority of ordinary SPD members in the eastern zone seem to have supported this. Of particular concern to the West was that about 30 per cent of SPD members in the western zones also favoured this merger and wanted the SED to become an all-German party. The western Allies refused to give permission for this.

The **Five Ds** were demilitarisation, de-nazification, democratisation, de-industrialisation and decentralisation.

A Soviet cartoon from 1949, showing the USSR's fears over the West's plans for Germany.

The main issue, however, was economic. The Soviet Union had liked the idea of the 'pastoralisation' of Germany, put forward by H. J. Morgenthau Jr, the US secretary of the treasury. This policy would have meant the destruction of German industrial power, creating a primarily agricultural economy. But the USA and Britain soon decided a revival of German industry was essential, partly because it was seen as essential for the recovery of the west European economies in general, and partly because they were unable or unwilling to prop up the German economy indefinitely.

In April 1946, General **Clay**, the US military governor, told the US State Department that he believed the Soviet Union was co-operating over the Potsdam Agreement and that it was not planning any aggression. However, Byrnes, the US secretary of state, decided to test this at the Paris meeting of the Council of Foreign Ministers which began later that month. He proposed that all four Allies should sign a pact to demilitarise Germany for 25 years. Although Molotov, the Soviet foreign minister, did not reject this, the meeting broke up because of the USA's continuing refusal to consider the question of reparations.

Then on 3 May 1946, because of lack of agreement on an all-German trade policy, Clay was told to stop all reparations deliveries to the Soviet Union. On 27 July 1946, Britain and the USA agreed to merge their zones to form one economic unit to be known as Bizonia; this took place in January 1947. On 6 September 1946, Byrnes persuaded the USA and Britain to call for a major reconstruction of German industry.

Born in 1897, Lucius **Clay** was commander of US forces in Europe and military governor of the US zone of Germany 1947–49. He is best known for his organisation of the Berlin Airlift.

Then in February 1947, Britain announced that, as well as being unable to afford continued support for the Greek royalists, it could no longer afford to pay the occupation costs or to prop up the German economy. They made it clear that Britain might have to pull out of Bizonia if German heavy industry was not revived. At the March–April meeting of the Council of Foreign Ministers, the question of reparations was raised again. Though Clay still favoured some concessions on this, Marshall was opposed, while Dulles claimed a revived west German economy would help the economic problems of France by creating a strong export market for French industry.

After the Truman Doctrine and the Marshall Plan, announced in June 1947, the USSR began to see these steps as attempting to build up the economy of a western Germany which had 75 per cent of the German population and the important industrial regions. Such a west German state might prove to be a military threat in the future, as it had in the past – especially if it were allied to what the Soviet Union perceived to be an increasingly hostile USA. Soviet fears about western plans for Germany led to a more hardline response. At the meeting of the Council of Foreign Ministers in London during November and December 1947 Britain and the USA agreed on one last attempt to revive the economy of a unified Germany.

However, as they had no intention of agreeing to Soviet demands for reparations (and knowing the USSR would not agree without reparations in the long term), they expected the talks to fail. They agreed that should this happen – which it did – they would develop Bizonia and introduce currency reform, as preliminary steps to the establishment of a separate west German state. In February 1948, the USA organised further discussions and, on 7 June 1948, the London Recommendations were accepted. These recommendations included France joining its zone to Bizonia to form Trizonia and proposals for an assembly representing the west German *Länder* to begin drafting a constitution for the new state. On 18 June, without consulting the Soviet Union, the West introduced the Deutschmark to replace the Reichsmark in west Germany; on 23 June, this was extended to west Berlin.

Länder was the name for the separate states which made up the Federal Republic of Germany.

Why did a crisis break out over Germany in 1948?

The Berlin Blockade

The Soviet Union, opposed to the idea of a separate west German state, tried to prevent this by putting pressure on west Berlin by cutting off all road, rail and freight traffic to west Berlin on 24 June 1948. The Berlin Blockade was the first open Cold War conflict between the two sides. However, though the USA transferred 60 B29 bombers (capable of dropping nuclear bombs) to Britain, no bombs were supplied and this crisis did not develop into a 'hot' war.

The Berlin Airlift

Instead, the Allies responded with the massive Berlin Airlift, in which tons of food, fuel and other basic items were flown from Trizonia into west Berlin to supply its 2 million citizens. The airlift was organised by General Clay and lasted for almost a year, until May 1949, when the obvious failure of the blockade finally led Stalin to call it off.

The Berlin Blockade, designed to make the West drop its idea of a separate west German state, actually speeded up the very thing it was intended to stop. The West portrayed it as an attempt by the Soviet Union to drive the Allies out of West Berlin in preparation for taking over the western zones of Germany. The prime ministers of the west German *Länder* who had, at first, been reluctant to accept the creation of a separate west German state, now agreed as a way of ensuring US protection against this Soviet 'takeover'.

In May 1949, the new Federal Republic of Germany was set up and its first government began operating in September 1949. On 7 October, the USSR finally accepted the division of Germany and announced the transformation of its eastern zone into a new state, called the German Democratic Republic. This division of Germany soon came to represent the division of Europe into two mutually suspicious and hostile camps. Soviet fears that the West wanted a revived Germany, closely allied to the USA, were later confirmed in 1955, when West Germany was allowed to join NATO.

> What was the immediate impact of the Berlin Crisis on the Cold War after 1949?

Military developments

When Roosevelt was US president, he had not believed that the Soviet Union was a serious threat to US security. Mindful of Russian history and fears – and of the fact that on several occasions the USSR had come close to defeat during the Second World War – he was prepared to make some concessions. In particular, he believed the Soviet Union desired three things: a sphere of influence in eastern Europe (and, if possible, those Middle Eastern and Asian states that also had borders with the USSR), reparations from former Axis powers (especially Germany) and US financial support in reconstructing the USSR. This did not mean he intended to give Stalin everything he wanted and he expected that any concessions on these issues would be on American terms.

However, Roosevelt's death and Truman's accession had allowed Byrnes to push for a tougher policy; he wanted to ensure that concessions would only be forthcoming if the Soviet Union accepted that the USA should be the strongest power, based on its nuclear monopoly. When US credits were not forthcoming, Stalin placed reliance on reparations. When these were persistently refused by the USA and Britain, the Soviet Union turned to the pursuit of security via tight control over eastern Europe and the development of its own atomic weapons.

Only a few contemporaries – such as General Clay and the historian Isaac Deutscher – publicly questioned the reality of the perceived military threat from the Soviet Union. They saw the USSR as militarily and economically weak. Most others accepted Kennan's ideas that the Soviet Union was a serious threat and needed to be contained. Many western European countries, as well as looking to the USA for economic assistance, also came to depend on its military strength. Britain, for example, wanted US help to support its interests in Europe and the Middle East, while France needed help to maintain its colonial position in south-east Asia. For its part, the USA was unwilling to take on this international military role (for its own reasons) and Truman's advisers came to believe that they could win the emerging Cold War by stimulating massive economic growth in the West which would then 'win' the eastern European states away from the Soviet Union.

Soviet actions in eastern Europe – especially the communist takeover in Czechoslovakia in February 1948 – led the western European countries to form the Brussels Treaty Organisation. By then, some US advisers, including Kennan, had come to believe that the tough stance taken by the West in 1947 had made the USSR ready to negotiate away its sphere of influence.

However, others (such as Clay, in March 1948) feared that the overall military weakness of the Soviet Union might lead it to launch a 'defensive' war in the near future, before the imbalance between the USSR and the USA became even greater. The CIA also issued warnings about the possibility of a pre-emptive strike by the USSR with the result that on 17 March 1948 Truman asked Congress to approve military training for all American men and selective military service for some.

By late 1948, however, Marshall and Kennan had both concluded that the limited response of the Soviet Union over the Berlin Crisis had shown the Soviet threat to be a political and not a military one. Consequently, they believed it could be contained by mainly non-military means, as Soviet power was at its peak and would soon decline, especially if the economic (as well as military) strength of the West was increased. After the Berlin Crisis was over, **Bevin**, the British foreign secretary, worked hard to include the USA in a European alliance. At the same time, the Berlin Crisis had shown that the USA was prepared to make a stand against the USSR and that Stalin was not prepared to risk a 'hot' conflict. Thus the USA was more than willing to agree to the setting up of a global military alliance. On 4 April 1949, the BTO became the North Atlantic Treaty Organisation (NATO), with the USA and Canada as new members. The treaty was signed in Washington and the USA was clearly its strongest member – in fact, from the beginning, NATO was based on the USA's nuclear monopoly.

The Soviet response to the increasing tensions which followed the Berlin

Ernest **Bevin** was born in 1881. He was a trade unionist and Labour politician. As general secretary of the TGWU, he helped plan the general strike of 1926. From 1940 to 1945, he was minister of labour and national service; from 1945 to 1951, he was foreign secretary and pursued a strong anti-Soviet, pro-US line.

Crisis was not mainly military but economic. In January 1949, it announced the formation of the Council for Mutual Economic Assistance (**Comecon**), which bound the east European states even more closely to the Soviet Union. The creation of NATO raised huge security concerns in the Soviet leadership as the USSR was, at most, only a regional power, whereas the USA was already clearly established as a global superpower. The victory of the Chinese communists, which led to the creation of the People's Republic of China in October 1949, did little to even up the relationship of the opposing forces in the Cold War as China was economically and militarily weak and needed Soviet assistance. This meant that China was not a comparable ally in the same way that Britain and France were for the USA. This left the USSR a much weaker superpower than the USA.

Soviet fears were increased when similar US-dominated treaties were created in the Pacific and the Middle East during the 1950s. These treaties, which gave an even wider spread of foreign bases for the USA, only served to underline the global isolation of the Soviet Union.

The nuclear arms race

A significant development in the Cold War, which gave a new dimension to international relations between East and West, occurred in August 1949 when the Soviet Union was able to explode its first atomic bomb. The US nuclear monopoly was thus ended and a nuclear arms race then began, as the USA was determined to keep well ahead of Soviet military capabilities, while the USSR (which had also been attempting to develop atomic weapons for some time) was equally determined to match US nuclear capabilities. By 1952, the USA had developed a much more powerful nuclear weapon – the H-bomb – which ushered in the thermonuclear age; by 1953, the USSR had matched it.

Comecon (the Council for Mutual Economic Assistance) was set up in 1949 to co-ordinate the industrial development and trade of the Soviet Union and its eastern European satellites and to prevent trade with the West. Initially, the Soviet Union insisted on preferential terms, especially in relation to the supply of raw materials which Stalin wanted for the reconstruction of Soviet industry. Later, under Khrushchev, the terms became more equal and, in 1964, a Bank for Socialist Countries was set up.

Historical sources

1 US Secretary of State, George Marshall, announcing his plan in an address at Harvard University

It is logical that the United States should do whatever it is able to do to assist in the return of normal economic health to the world, without which there can be no political stability and no assured peace.

Our policy is directed not against any country or doctrine, but against hunger, poverty, desperation and chaos. Its purpose should be the revival of a working economy in the world so as to permit the emergence of political and social conditions in which free institutions can exist.

E. G. Rayner, *The Cold War*, London, 1992, p. 16

2 Andrei Vyshinsky, the Soviet deputy foreign minister, speaking at the UN on 18 September 1947

The so-called Truman Doctrine and the Marshall Plan are particularly glaring examples of the manner in which the principles of the United Nations are violated, of the way in which the Organisation is ignored . . .

It is becoming more and more evident to everyone that the implementation of the Marshall Plan will mean placing European countries under the economic and political control of the United States and direct interference by the latter in the internal affairs of those countries . . .

An important feature of this Plan is the attempt to confront the countries of eastern Europe with a bloc of western European states including western Germany.

M. McCauley, *The origins of the Cold War, 1941–1949*, London, 1995, pp. 140–41

Historical-source questions

1 Which 'country or doctrine' does George Marshall implicitly refer to in Source 1?
2 Why did Marshall feel it was necessary to return 'normal economic health to the world'?
3 How do Sources 1 and 2 show differing views of US policies in 1947?

Summary questions

1 Identify and explain at least *two* reasons why the Soviet Union felt threatened by the Truman Doctrine and the Marshall Plan.

2 How dangerous to international peace was the Berlin Crisis of 1948–49?

3 Compare the importance of at least *three* effects of the Berlin Crisis on the development of the Cold War.

13 Fluctuating relations: Europe, 1949–68

Focus questions

◆ To what extent did relations between the two camps fluctuate in the period 1949–68?

◆ How did Khrushchev's 'peaceful coexistence' differ from previous Soviet foreign policy?

Significant dates

1950   *March* Stockholm Appeal

1952   *March* The 'Stalin Notes' on Germany; show trials in Czechoslovakia
November USA explodes H-bomb

1953   *January* Eisenhower becomes US president
March Stalin dies
June Workers' revolt in GDR
July USSR explodes an H-bomb

1955   *February* Khrushchev emerges as main Soviet leader
May West Germany joins NATO; Warsaw Pact formed; Treaty on Austrian neutrality
July Geneva Summit

1956   *February* Twentieth Congress of CPSU; Cominform dissolved
June Unrest in Poland results in reforms
October Hungarian Revolt
November Soviet troops invade Hungary

1957   *October* USSR launches Sputnik

1958   *November* Khrushchev's Ultimatum and the start of a new crisis over Berlin

1959   *September* Camp David meeting

1960   *May* Paris Summit; U-2 spy-plane incident

1961   *March* Soviet manned space flight
June Vienna Summit
August The Berlin Wall built

1964   *October* Khrushchev replaced by Brezhnev and Kosygin

1968   *April* Dubček begins Prague Spring in Czechoslovakia
July Warsaw Letter
August Bratislava Declaration; Warsaw Pact forces invade Czechoslovakia
November Brezhnev Doctrine

Overview

From 1949, with the communist victory in China and the start of the Korean War the following year, Cold War tensions shifted mainly to Asia because of the USA's concerns over the loss of China. In Europe, the Cold War was heightened by the USA exploding its first H-bomb, making the USSR feel more vulnerable in the light of the nuclear lead the USA was establishing.

However, Cold War tensions began to thaw after Stalin's death in March 1953, in spite of the USSR exploding its first H-bomb shortly afterwards. The new Soviet leadership soon announced a willingness to negotiate over Cold War problems, as did both **Eisenhower** and Churchill.

Relations between the two sides fluctuated, especially after West Germany joined NATO in May 1955. Even though the USSR responded by establishing the Warsaw Pact, the two sides concuded a treaty establishing Austria's neutrality. In July 1955, a summit meeting took place in Geneva at which general points of Cold War concern were discussed.

In 1956, the crises over Suez and Hungary renewed tensions and new disagreements arose over Berlin in 1958. These seemed resolved by the 1959 Camp David meeting. The relaxation of tensions was soon undermined by the **U-2** spy-plane incident, which broke up the 1960 Paris Summit. In November, Kennedy was elected president of the USA.

Renewed tensions over Berlin led to the construction of the Berlin Wall in 1961. Despite this (and the Cuban Missile Crisis of 1962), a Nuclear Test Ban Treaty was signed in August 1963. But, in 1968, came the Warsaw Pact invasion of Czechoslovakia and the announcement of the Brezhnev Doctrine.

To what extent did relations between the two camps fluctuate in the period 1949–68?

Stalin's foreign policy, 1949–53

In October 1949, with the creation of the Communist People's Republic of China led by Mao Zedong and then the start of the Korean War in 1950 (see Chapters 16 and 17), Cold War tensions shifted from Europe to Asia. In due course, the problems in Asia began to impact on the situation and subsequent developments in Europe. After the Berlin Crisis of 1948–49 and the formation of NATO in April 1949, Soviet nationalism increased in the USSR and generated a desire to cut off the Soviet bloc from all western influences.

In the early 1950s, the Soviet Union followed a dual-track foreign policy: while consolidating its control of the eastern European satellites, it also tried to limit the polarisation of Europe into two opposing Cold War camps. During this time, Stalin kept a firm control over foreign policy – especially as

Dwight **Eisenhower** was born in 1890. He commanded both the invasion of North Africa in 1942 and the Allied invasion of Europe in 1944. He was then appointed US army chief of staff and, in 1949, commander of NATO. He won the 1952 presidential elections. His views about the Soviet Union were similar to those of Truman. He helped end the Korean War, but authorised the U-2 flights over the USSR and also began the plans for an invasion of Cuba (later put into effect by Kennedy).

The **U-2** was a US reconnaissance (spy) aircraft which flew at an altitude which was beyond the range of Soviet fighters and ground-to-air missiles. At first, the USSR could do nothing about these US flights above their territory. However, improved air-to-air missiles finally allowed the Soviet Union to shoot one down and capture its pilot, Gary Powers. This incident ended the Paris Summit after only one day and prevented agreements on Berlin and a test ban treaty.

Molotov, who had been Soviet foreign minister and his closest adviser since 1939, lost his position in 1949.

The Stalinisation of eastern Europe

The effect of the dispute between the Soviet Union and Tito's Yugoslavia in 1948–49 was to strengthen Stalin's determination to control the eastern European bloc. As the quarrel intensified, many more government and Communist Party members were accused of betraying communism. This reached its climax in the early 1950s, with Titoists being accused by Stalin of working with the West in order to restore capitalism in Yugoslavia. There then began a witch-hunt for Titoists in the other eastern European communists parties, followed by a wave of purges and show trials, which affected even top party and state officials. In Czechoslovakia, for instance, **Rudolf Slansky** was the main victim. All this was part of Stalin's attempt to turn the bloc of eastern European states from a Soviet-dominated alliance into a tight monolithic bloc controlled from Moscow, with no deviation from Stalin's policies being allowed. Tito's links to the West thus served to give Stalin an excuse to extend Soviet control over eastern Europe. The purges did not last long after Stalin's death in March 1953, although Soviet control, resulting from this process of **Stalinisation**, remained.

Attempts to limit Cold War polarisation

After 1949, Stalin attempted to limit the emerging nuclear arms race by launching what became the first of several 'peace campaigns'. At the same time the Soviet Union began to put forward proposals for the neutralisation and demilitarisation of Germany and central Europe. These moves were greatly influenced by the huge amounts of money the Soviet Union felt it had to divert to its defence industry in order not to fall too far behind the USA which, though it too had demobilised (to 1.5 million) after 1945, had a clear nuclear superiority. In the period 1948–53, for example, the Red Army – which had been reduced to 2.9 million immediately after the Second World War – almost doubled in size.

According to the Soviet Union, these 'peace campaigns' were a continuation of pre-1939 Soviet attempts to maintain peace in Europe, evidenced by its joining the League of Nations in 1934, its support of collective security and its later attempts to form an anti-Nazi alliance with Britain and France (see pages 99–100). After 1945, Stalin and his advisers blamed the start of the Cold War on the actions of the West, but they did not believe it was inevitable that a 'hot' war would necessarily break out. Hence, Soviet encouragement of the mass peace movements (which campaigned in the West for disarmament and peace) seemed a logical way to attempt to limit the risk of western governments launching an attack on the Soviet Union. This approach, which began to take

Rudolf Slansky had been the general secretary of the Czech Communist Party, but in 1952 he and 13 other important communists appeared in a show trial during which all 'confessed' their crimes against socialism. All were found guilty, and Slansky, along with 10 others, was executed.

Stalinisation refers to the process in which eastern European communist parties – and states – were deprived of independent action and control. Instead, central control by the leadership (and ultimately from Moscow) replaced the democratic centralism that was supposed to exist. Later, both Khrushchev and Gorbachev tried to return to the original 'Leninist' norms or practice.

shape in 1949, reached its peak in the early 1950s with millions of activists campaigning across the world. A petition known as the Stockholm Appeal eventually received over 560 million signatures. Stalin hoped that such wide support would put pressure on western governments to reduce the international tensions created by the Cold War and to follow policies more to the liking of the USSR. Similar movements were also set up in eastern Europe, but were clearly communist-controlled.

Linked to this approach were Soviet attempts, after the establishment of NATO and the division of Germany, to turn Germany and Austria into a neutral central European zone. In 1950, in response to the West's announcement of the establishment of the European Defence Community (to include West Germany), the Soviet Union proposed new negotiations on the question of Germany. Stalin's proposals included reuniting and demilitarising Germany, after all occupation troops had been withdrawn. In March 1952, the 'Stalin Notes' were presented by the Soviet Union to the West: in the main, they offered the reunification of Germany in return for its neutrality. Though these proposals were repeatedly rejected by the West due to a mistrust of Stalin's motives, Stalin continued to make such offers until his death – even though the East German communists were unhappy at the prospect of losing their newly formed state.

Some historians have suggested that these proposals were merely propaganda ploys, in that the USSR knew they would be rejected by the West (given that the communist victory in China in 1949 and the start of the Korean War in 1950 both increased Cold War tensions). According to this school of thought, the USSR believed these proposals would please their supporters in Germany as well as some NATO countries (such as France, which had twice been invaded by Germany since 1900). Others have stressed these proposals were a continuation of post-1945 Soviet security policy and can thus be seen as both consistent and genuine.

In fact, one outcome of the start of the Korean War was to persuade Truman to act on the policy document **NSC 68**. This was drawn up by the State and Defence Departments after Truman had asked the National Security Council to reappraise the USA's Cold War policy. It called for a trebling of the USA's defence expenditure, so that the Soviet threat could be met anywhere in the world. Truman accordingly increased the defence budget from $13.5 billion to $50 billion. In 1952, plans were drawn up to increase NATO divisions from 14 to 50 and to establish US army, airforce and naval forces in Europe. As a result, US military power increased dramatically throughout western Europe. It was also decided to rearm West Germany, in case the Soviet Union should try to reunite Germany by force, and to expand NATO in Europe, by granting membership to Turkey and Greece.

What were the 'Stalin Notes'?

NSC 68 was the study of future US foreign policy initiated by Truman in January 1950. This considered four possible options, but recommended only one – that the USA should begin a massive armaments programme and oppose any 'communist aggression' in any part of the world. This was a classifed document until the 1970s.

What were the main proposals of the NSC 68 document?

These developments (and the security treaties signed with various Pacific states – see page 220) increased Stalin's fears and forced him to divert huge economic resources from industrial reconstruction and development into defence expenditure. Given the USSR's relative economic weakness, this produced much more negative results in the Soviet economy than US military spending did in the USA.

The 'thaw', 1953–55

When Stalin died in March 1953, the top communists decided to establish a collective leadership to avoid the domination of one individual. The new chairman (prime minister) of the Council of Ministers was Malenkov with Khrushchev as first secretary of the Communist Party. Also part of the new collective leadership were Molotov (foreign minister), Bulganin (minister of defence) and Beria (minister of internal affairs). In July 1953, however, Beria was accused of plotting to set himself up as dictator, arrested and shot.

This new leadership attempted to 'thaw' Cold War tensions. This thaw was one of the reasons why an armistice was signed in July 1953 to end the fighting in Korea. Soviet willingness to pressure North Korea to stop fighting and Eisenhower's desire for peace rather than victory represented a significant change in relations. As early as 1952 Malenkov called for 'peaceful coexistence' and in 1953 Beria spoke of Germany being reunited and becoming a neutral state. This thaw continued despite the escalation of the nuclear arms race, which took the form of the explosion of the first H-bomb in November 1952 by the USA, with the USSR following suit in July 1953. According to some historians, 1953 can be seen as the end of the first Cold War and the period 1953–68/9 as one of fluctuating relations between the two superpowers in which attempts to lessen confrontation and reach agreement were periodically frustrated by the emergence of new tensions and crises.

What is meant by the term 'thaw'?

Eisenhower and the New Look

This thaw developed despite the fact that the Republicans, led by Eisenhower, won the 1952 elections in the USA. Their New Look defence policy was, at least on the surface, a significant departure from that followed by Truman in the years 1945–53. The nature of Eisenhower's policy was symbolised by the appointment of J. F. Dulles as secretary of state; he continued to take a hardline stance on the Cold War, talking of the need for massive retaliation and **'brinkmanship'**. McCarthy (see pages 205–06) had supported the Eisenhower–Nixon ticket and had accused the Democrats of betraying the USA by allowing the 'loss' of China and the Soviet development of an H-bomb and so losing the USA's clear nuclear lead. Dulles attacked Truman's policy of containment as 'immoral' because it had abandoned all those living in the Soviet

By **'brinkmanship'**, Dulles meant that the USA should adopt a much more confrontational and aggressive stance towards the USSR and China, up to and including the use of nuclear weapons, based on the belief that the USA's nuclear superiority would force concessions from them. The 1952 election campaign, for example, had made promises to 'liberate' eastern Europe, based on a commitment to use nuclear weapons 'when necessary'.

bloc; he also called for the 'rolling back' of communism and the 'liberation' of eastern Europe.

This emphasis on the role nuclear weapons could play in the Cold War was linked to the Republicans' desire (as the party of big business) to reduce taxation while, at the same time, taking a more aggressive stance towards the Cold War – building up a stockpile of nuclear weapons was cheaper than maintaining large conventional forces.

Despite these statements, Eisenhower and Dulles continued in essence with Truman's containment policy – in the main, only the emphasis and style differed. Eisenhower was uneasy about the growth of the **military–industrial complex** within the USA and had serious doubts about using nuclear weapons; he believed nuclear war between the two Cold War antagonists would have 'results . . . too horrible to contemplate'.

In general, the new Soviet leadership believed the USA's New Look foreign policy was mainly rhetorical and remained keen to reduce tensions with the West. They were motivated by a strong desire to reduce USSR military expenditure in order to strengthen the economy and improve living standards. Despite this, the period 1952–62 encompassed several crises that seemed likely to take the two superpowers to the brink of war.

Germany

The new Soviet leadership was determined to continue with Stalin's attempts to achieve an easing of East–West relations, especially in relation to Germany. The possibility of giving up East Germany in return for a united but neutral Germany was preferable to the continued division of Germany and an escalating arms race and it became more attractive in June 1953 when the hardline policy followed by the East German rulers had sparked off a significant workers' revolt over low wage rates and living standards. The size of this Berlin Uprising required Soviet occupation forces to put down the demonstrations and strikes. Giving up East Germany seemed to make sense, as long as the Soviet's security fears were allayed by making central Europe neutral territory. East Germany cost the USSR money it could ill afford. As a result the Soviet Union was more concerned to keep Germany weak than to run part of it.

At the February 1954 meeting of the Council of Foreign Ministers, the Soviet Union again offered unification of Germany in return for its neutralisation. This offer was again rejected by the West because of the fear that a united Germany might ally itself with the Soviet bloc; in fact, one Soviet motive was to increase West German opposition to rearmament and NATO by offering reunification. The USSR tried to tempt West Germany with reunification provided NATO membership and rearmament were rejected. The Soviets then suggested that the USSR should join NATO with the idea of creating an

Military–industrial complex refers to the top US military leaders (the Pentagon) and the large US armaments companies. Some believe these have worked together to persuade US presidents that increased defence spending was vital when, in fact, this was not so.

How did Eisenhower's New Look policy differ from Truman's policy of containment?

organisation of collective security for the whole of Europe; this suggestion was inspired, in part, by Soviet fears that West Germany was about to be rearmed and allowed to join NATO. The West also turned this down.

How did Khrushchev's 'peaceful coexistence' differ from previous Soviet foreign policy?

The emergence of Khrushchev

The fall of Beria in July 1953 had not ended the power struggle that followed Stalin's death. In February 1955, after much manoeuvring, **Khrushchev** was able to bring about Malenkov's dismissal as Soviet premier – his place was taken by Bulganin, one of Khrushchev's closest allies. Like the rest of the Soviet leadership, Khrushchev had been profoundly affected by the Great Patriotic War. Fully aware of the human and economic devastation the Soviet Union had suffered and genuinely fearful of the risks posed by the escalating nuclear arms race, Khrushchev is particularly associated with his version of the traditional Soviet policy of 'peaceful coexistence' of East and West throughout the world.

However, his pursuit of this policy during the period 1955–64 was at times inconsistent. Unlike Stalin and the collective leadership that had replaced him in the years 1953–55 (both of which had followed a very cautious foreign policy), Khrushchev was more of a risk-taker. His more optimistic assessment of the Soviet Union's position was based, in part, on its possession of the H-bomb and recent developments in rocketry, which would soon result in the **Sputnik**. Khrushchev believed he was operating from a position of new, recently gained strength. Soviet rocket technology (which was more advanced than in the USA) helped balance the USSR's lack of allies, and thus airbases, around the world, so closing the gap between the two superpowers.

Nonetheless, Khrushchev tried to achieve real **detente** between East and West, so as to avoid the risk of a devastating nuclear world war. Khrushchev believed the situation in Europe was sufficiently stable for the Soviet Union to make concessions in peripheral areas and so he offered to pull Soviet troops out of Austria, provided the country's neutrality was guaranteed, and to return the Porkkala naval base to Finland (see page 102).

The Warsaw Pact, 1955

In May 1955, as feared by the USSR, West Germany became a member of NATO. Shortly afterwards the Soviet Union announced the formation of its own military alliance, the Warsaw Pact (so called because the treaty was signed in Warsaw). This pact was a mutual military assistance alliance between the Soviet Union and all its eastern European allies.

Born in 1894, Nikita **Khrushchev** fought in the Red Army during the civil war and later worked for the CPSU in Moscow. He was elected to the Central Committee in 1934 and was the chief political commissar with the Soviet army in the battle for Stalingrad. In 1949, he was appointed by Stalin to take charge of Soviet agriculture.

The **Sputnik** (meaning 'traveller') was the world's first orbiting satellite, launched by the USSR in October 1957. The Soviet Union went on to achieve a series of other space 'firsts', including the first man in space.

Detente is a French word which means a lessening of tensions. Normally applied to the years 1969–79, there were several such attempts between 1945 and 1991 to improve East–West relations.

What were the main features of Khrushchev's policy of 'peaceful coexistence'?

The formation of the Warsaw Pact marked the Soviet Union's final acceptance that the division of Germany was probably permanent. This did not mean that it had given up on the possibility of achieving European agreement on collective security – the Warsaw Pact even had a clause which stated that if a general European treaty on collective security was signed then the Warsaw Pact would be dissolved (Article 11).

Later that month, the western powers and the Soviet Union signed a treaty which ended the Allied occupation of Austria and established it as an independent but neutral state.

What was the Warsaw Pact?

The Geneva Summit

In July 1955, the first of a series of summit meetings between the leaders of the Big Four (the USA, USSR, Britain and France) took place at Geneva and seemed to mark the end of the Soviet isolation that had begun in 1945. This, the first meeting of the leaders since the Potsdam Conference in July 1945, was not important for any particular agreements, but for the spirit of friendship in which the meeting was conducted. The main items on the agenda were the issues of nuclear weapons and Germany. This 'spirit of Geneva' saw some general agreement on the need for less confrontation and more co-operation, and on a moratorium on nuclear testing.

However, Soviet proposals on disarmament and control of nuclear weapons (as well as renewed offers on the German question and European security) were again rejected. Khrushchev, in turn, rejected Eisenhower's 'Open Skies' proposal that each side allow the other to undertake aerial reconnaissance of military sites. But some progress was made – in September, the Soviet Union established diplomatic relations and trade links with West Germany. However, an offer by Adenauer, the West German chancellor, to 'buy' the GDR with credits and reparations for the USSR in return for allowing reunification was rejected.

The Twentieth Party Congress, 1956

The collective leadership that had taken over from Stalin in 1953 had immediately begun attempts to repair relations with Yugoslavia and to improve relations with its eastern European satellites. The Twentieth Party Congress of the CPSU, held in February 1956, was the first congress held since Stalin's death three years before. At the congress, Khrushchev announced his foreign policy, which had important implications for Soviet policy towards both Europe and the developing world, as he argued that in the new nuclear age peaceful coexistence was both possible and necessary.

Khrushchev also made another important, secret speech at this congress. Although it was intended only to make a domestic impact – to achieve 'de-

Stalinisation' or liberalisation – it soon caused serious problems in eastern Europe.

In this secret speech, Khrushchev attacked Stalin for his Great Terror of the 1930s and his cult of personality (see page 114). He also accepted that there could be 'national roads to socialism' that did not necessarily have to follow the Soviet model. This meant that the Soviet Union would accept eastern European states adopting policies different from those in the USSR, provided capitalism was not restored and Warsaw Pact membership was maintained.

In fact, as early as 1955, Khrushchev had made attempts to get Yugoslavia to return to the Soviet camp, blaming all the problems the two countries had experienced since 1948 on Stalin and Beria. However, Tito would only agree to restore diplomatic relations. In the same month as the congress, Khrushchev announced the dissolution of Cominform, from which Stalin had expelled Yugoslavia. This move was not only an approach to Yugoslavia, but also a step towards the loosening of Soviet control over eastern Europe as a whole.

This speech was soon unofficially circulated in the eastern European satellites where it encouraged reform communists who wanted to liberalise the authoritarian 'Stalinist' systems that had been imposed on their countries in the late 1940s and early 1950s. It also caused many communists and non-communists who desired a reduction of Soviet control of their countries to think that this would now be allowed. Two countries particularly affected were Poland and Hungary.

Why was Khrushchev's speech at the Twentieth Congress of the CPSU in 1956 so significant?

Poland

Protests by Polish workers angered at increased work norms turned into a serious riot in Poznan in June 1956, during which Polish security forces killed or wounded hundreds of demonstrating workers. The communist government of Poland (the Polish United Workers Party or PUWP) responded by moving towards a programme of reform and liberalisation, headed by **Gomulka**.

The Soviet leadership, in the context of the Cold War, feared the consequences of a Poland independent of Soviet control, so a meeting was arranged with Gomulka in Warsaw in late October 1956. At the same time, in order to put pressure on the Polish communists, Soviet troops in Poland held military manoeuvres.

Gomulka persuaded Khrushchev that he had no intention of leaving the Warsaw Pact or of dismantling the communist framework. By 21 October Khrushchev finally decided to trust Gomulka, calculating that no military intervention was needed to ensure Soviet security.

Gomulka had been the leader of the Polish communists, but was imprisoned during the eastern European purges of the late 1940s. At the time of the Poznan riot, he had only recently been released and rehabilitated, following Stalin's death.

Hungary

The situation in Hungary, however, was more serious. During 1956, following

Khrushchev's secret speech and the developments in Poland, protests became increasingly widespread. On 23 October, a massive illegal demonstration in Budapest, called in support of the Polish reform communists, soon spiralled out of control. The security police fired on the demonstrators and before long an armed revolt had broken out. This led to the government calling in Soviet troops for assistance. The fighting then spread to other major cities.

The initial Soviet response was to attempt a peaceful solution, along the same lines as their success in Poland. Consequently, Imre Nagy, a reform communist, was allowed to form a new government. His decision to allow the formation of opposition parties, however, as well as indications that he intended to take Hungary out of the Warsaw Pact, persuaded the majority of the Soviet Presidium into military intervention on 31 October. This was partly motivated by the fear that, if Hungary were allowed to leave the pact, other eastern European states might also try to follow suit, so breaking up the European buffer zone on which Soviet security depended.

Soviet insecurities were added to by the Suez Crisis, which resulted in the defeat of Egypt, one of the Soviet Union's main allies in the developing world, as well as ongoing problems with China and Yugoslavia. Consequently, after Nagy had announced Hungary's withdrawal from the Warsaw Pact on 1 November, the Soviet Union launched its military intervention on 4 November 1956. After some intense fighting, a new pro-Soviet government was installed, headed by Janos Kadar. In the purge that followed, many were expelled from party and state posts and Nagy was taken to the Soviet Union where, in 1958, he was executed.

That Khrushchev's main concerns were security-based is suggested by the fact that, once the situation had stabilised, Kadar actually implemented several of the reforms promised earlier by Nagy. In fact, Khrushchev was also prepared to accept a limited reduction in Soviet control. Another fact that supports this theory is that on 30 October, while the Hungarian crisis was still at its height, the USSR had issued a declaration promising a more equal relationship between the Soviet Union and the eastern European states. Once the crisis was over, Soviet armed forces were withdrawn from several Warsaw Pact states and bilateral and multi-lateral meetings were frequently held to help contribute to the shaping of Soviet foreign policy in Europe.

Sputnik and its impact, October 1957

On 4 October 1957, much to the surprise of the West, the Soviet Union launched the world's first satellite into space. In fact, Eisenhower had wanted the USSR to be the first to take this step, so that the USA would be seen as justified in developing its own **ICBM** system which was already well advanced. In reality, the USA's nuclear superiority continued to be overwhelming

ICBM stands for intercontinental ballistic missile, a rocket that could 'deliver' nuclear weapons across great distances. Sputnik technology gave the USSR its first lead in the nuclear arms race and allowed it to compensate for its lack of a worldwide system of airbases, such as the USA had.

throughout the decade – even by 1960, the USSR had only 4 ICBMs and 145 long-range bombers.

However, despite – or possibly because of – the Soviet Union's relative weakness, Khrushchev decided to pursue a more active foreign policy. He tried to get both West Germany and Britain to leave NATO by pointing out to them that membership increased the risk of them being involved in a nuclear war. He had been encouraged by the Geneva Conference and by the USA's reluctance to use nuclear weapons during the various crises of the mid 1950s (Hungary, Suez and the Taiwan Straits – for Taiwan, see page 230).

His turn to a more active, and risky, foreign policy was also an attempt to deflect internal criticisms of some of his economic policies. In June 1957, he had defeated an attempt by his opponents (dubbed the 'anti-party' group) to remove him and in early 1958 he strengthened his position by becoming prime minister while remaining secretary of the CPSU.

> How did the Soviet Union's launch of Sputnik in 1957 affect the nuclear arms race?

The Berlin Crisis, 1958–61

A second crisis over Berlin developed in November 1958 when, on 27 November, Khrushchev issued his first Berlin Ultimatum. This was an attempt to push the West into finally concluding a formal peace with Germany (as no treaty had yet been signed after the Second World War) and into agreeing that West Berlin should become an international, demilitarised area. He threatened that the Soviet Union would sign a separate peace with the GDR if such an agreement could not be reached; this would include handing over control of the access routes into West Berlin. Khrushchev had been encouraged by a statement made by Adenauer in March 1958 in which he had stated that an 'Austrian solution' might be acceptable.

These moves were intended to force the West to reopen negotiations on the future of Germany and especially to prevent NATO making West Germany a nuclear power. This was something the Soviet Union greatly feared and it was something that NATO had considered doing in 1949. At this stage, NATO already had nuclear-capable artillery and fighter bombers and the USA was rapidly building up its arsenal of tactical (short-range) nuclear weapons and ballistic missiles. However, as argued by J. L. Richardson, these Soviet actions were in part driven by the GDR leader, Walter Ulbricht, who threatened to take unilateral and possibly provocative action if Khrushchev did not try to do something about the existence of West Berlin which was, after all, deep within GDR territory.

Initially, Khrushchev had insisted on agreement being reached within six months, but the negotiations between the USSR and the West continued, on and off, until March 1959, when Khrushchev suspended the 27 May deadline. Negotiations continued in Geneva during the summer of 1959.

Camp David, September 1959

In an attempt to break the deadlock, Eisenhower invited Khrushchev to the USA for talks. These went well and Khrushchev withdrew his ultimatum, even though he was not given any indication that the West intended to make concessions. It was also agreed that further discussions would take place at the Paris Summit planned for May 1960.

The Paris Summit and the U-2 incident

By the time the leaders met in Paris, the situation had already altered. The USA had discovered, via its spy-planes, that the USSR was already well behind the USA as regards ICBMs, while West Germany was no longer prepared to make any concessions on West Berlin. Then, on 1 May 1960, came the announcement that a Soviet missile had successfully brought down a US U-2 spy-plane over the USSR. Eisenhower, embarrassed that his previous denials of spy-planes had been shown up and concerned at the effectiveness of Soviet missile technology, refused to apologise for the incident. At the same time, Khrushchev was facing criticism from China that he was following a 'soft' foreign policy in relation to the West. This combination of circumstances meant that the Paris Summit was doomed to failure.

What was the U-2 incident in 1960?

This photograph shows an exhibition in Moscow in 1960 about the shooting down of a US U-2 spy-plane and the capture of its pilot, Gary Powers. The incident angered the Soviet Union, embarrassed the USA and ended the Paris Summit.

The USSR proposed a confederation between the two Germanies, with both states leaving their respective military alliances (NATO and the Warsaw Pact) and demilitarisation of Berlin under United Nations control. The western powers countered by proposing a united Germany and all-German elections, along with some German disarmament. In reality, there was little hope of an immediate reunification of Germany, but what Khrushchev wanted was for the West to recognise the East German state as they had done with West Germany. The West refused to do so until free elections were held in the GDR; the stalemate continued for the next two years.

While these discussions were dragging on, an increasing number of East Germans migrated to the West. By 1959, these migrants numbered around 200,000 a year; many of them were technicians and other skilled workers. This clearly had a serious effect on the weak East German economy and Ulbricht began to press Khrushchev for action. In November 1960, he promised Ulbricht that any loss of trade with West Germany would be made up with Soviet purchases. On 18 January 1961, Ulbricht asked a Warsaw Pact conference for help to secure the position of the GDR and to force concessions from the West on Berlin to place the city under greater East German control and to prevent refugees crossing from one side to the other.

But at a conference held at the end of March, the Warsaw Pact countries did not support all of Ulbricht's requests. Khrushchev, encouraged by another Soviet technological first – the first manned space flight – and the failure of the US-backed Bay of Pigs Incident in Cuba (see pages 249–250), thought he might secure a better deal over Berlin with the new USA president, John F. **Kennedy**.

The Vienna Summit, June 1961

However, the first meeting between Kennedy and Khrushchev at the Vienna Summit in 1961 was not a success, as Kennedy still refused to make concessions on Berlin. At the end of June, Ulbricht requested another Warsaw Pact conference and Khrushchev gave provisional permission for Ulbricht to begin preparations for physically dividing Berlin.

Khrushchev then announced that he was reimposing the original six-month deadline. As tensions increased, the number of East German refugees increased dramatically and was soon almost double the rate for the 1950s. So, on 3–5 August, the Warsaw Pact urged the GDR to take action to secure the border with West Berlin. At first, it was a barbed-wire fence; then, as the West did not react, the GDR authorities rapidly completed the building of the **Berlin Wall** by 13 August. This became a very visible image of the Cold War division between East and West.

Born in 1917, John F. **Kennedy** belonged to the wealthy and politically powerful Kennedy family. He fought in the US navy during the Second World War and became a Democrat Congressman in 1947. In 1960, he became the youngest – and the first Catholic – president of the USA. He was a strong anti-communist but was also in favour of social and welfare reform in the USA. He was assassinated in November 1963.

The **Berlin Wall** was pulled down in November 1989.

Why was the Berlin Wall built in 1961?

This 1963 Soviet cartoon gives one reason for the building of the Berlin Wall in 1961. The sign reads: 'The border of the GDR is closed to all enemies.' The West German's dog's tail is depicted as a Nazi swastika.

Khrushchev's fall, October 1964

Born in 1906, Leonid **Brezhnev** became a secretary to the CPSU Central Committee in 1952 and joined the Presidium in 1957. He helped bring about Khrushchev's fall in 1964 and soon took over with Kosygin, at first having equal power. By the late 1960s, he was clearly the dominant ruler.

Many Soviet leaders were unhappy with Khrushchev's way of conducting foreign policy, but much more so with elements of his domestic policy, such as liberalisation and economic reforms. In October 1964, Khrushchev's opponents were able to secure a majority in the Central Committee for his removal. At first, power was shared between Leonid **Brezhnev**, the new first secretary of the CPSU, and Alexei Kosygin, the new premier.

Under Brezhnev and Kosygin, the de-Stalinisation and limited liberalisation associated with Khrushchev came to an end and economic policy became much more conservative. At the same time, the USSR began to move from being just a regional power to a position increasingly like that of a global superpower. This was achieved without the great crises in Cold War relations which characterised Khrushchev's conduct of foreign policy. The reason for this was because Brezhnev and Kosygin began to pursue a policy of detente.

Detente was essentially a continuation of the traditional Soviet policy of attempting to achieve peaceful coexistence with the capitalist West without the element of risk-taking that had been introduced by Khrushchev. By the mid 1960s, the Soviet and eastern European economies were attempting to make significant technological improvements and so desired more trade with the West. At the same time, Brezhnev and Kosygin hoped detente with the West would win acceptance of their eastern European bloc and help prevent any USA–China alliance directed at the Soviet Union.

Detente and the USA

The idea of detente appealed to the USA as it seemed a way of obtaining Soviet help in securing an acceptable settlement to the Vietnam War (see Chapter 19) and of curbing any expansionist aims the USSR might have. This policy was encouraged by Charles de Gaulle, the French president in the 1960s, who made several trade agreements with the Soviet Union and the eastern European states. These attempts led Brezhnev and Kosygin to revive the Soviet policy of attempting to achieve a pan-European collective security system, which it had been pursuing, on and off, since the 1950s.

Czechoslovakia and the Prague Spring, 1968

Despite the mutual good intentions, detente got off to a poor start in 1968 because of the crisis that arose over Czechoslovakia. In January 1968, the hardline Stalinist leader of Czechoslovakia, Antonin Novotny, was replaced by the reform communist Alexander Dubček. As the new first secretary of the Czech Communist Party, Dubček launched a series of political and economic reforms – known as the Action Programme – in April 1968. They were designed to achieve what he called 'socialism with a human face'. This Prague Spring, as it became called, alarmed hardliners such as Brezhnev who wanted to maintain strict party controls – both for the example it might set for domestic reforms elsewhere in the eastern bloc and because it followed closely on problems with Albania and Romania. The Soviet Union, worried about possible US reactions to the Czech crisis, were given to understand by Johnson, the US president, that it was seen as an intra-communist dispute.

Consequently, the Brezhnev leadership began to feel free to put pressure on Dubček to slow down his reforms and also to encourage the hardliners in the Czech party to oppose him. At the same time, the Soviets conducted a political campaign in the eastern European states to persuade them to side with Moscow. Despite these measures, the crisis continued and, on 14–15 July 1968, the leaders of five eastern European communist parties (the Soviet Union, the GDR, Hungary, Poland and Bulgaria) met in Warsaw to discuss the situation. On 15 July they sent the Warsaw Letter to the Czech Communist Party. This open letter stated that the internal developments in Czechoslovakia were of vital concern to the security of all the states signing the letter; in particular, they warned that Dubček's policies were allowing counter-revolutionary forces to threaten the existence of socialism in Czechoslovakia. Dubček's reply was to reassert his commitment to socialism and the Warsaw Pact, while defending his Action Programme which, he said, would continue.

At the end of July, Soviet leaders met with top Czech officials and, on 3 August, all the states that signed the Warsaw Letter met with Czech representatives, including Dubček, in Bratislava. They issued the Bratislava Declaration which confirmed their commitment to defending socialism in eastern Europe. In effect it seemed as if Dubček had been forced to limit his Prague Spring.

Brezhnev and other Soviet leaders, however, came to believe Dubček was either not able or not willing to deliver the promises he had been forced to make. Some had no intention of allowing the reforms, whilst others felt that there were many in Czech politics and society who wanted reforms to go further than Dubček would allow. In addition, the more hardline rulers in eastern Europe (Gomulka of Poland and, especially, Ulbricht in the GDR) were demanding that the USSR put a complete end to Dubček's reforms. At the same time, hardliners in the Czech party continued to urge the Soviet Union to intervene.

On 17 August, the Soviet Politburo decided that military intervention would be necessary, after all, to 'restore order' in Czechoslovakia. On 20–21 August, the five signatories to the Warsaw Letter sent a combined military force into Czechoslovakia. Instead of armed resistance, the Soviet-led force met passive resistance and peaceful protest. Dubček and some other leaders were arrested and taken to Moscow. After hard discussions, a joint statement was issued on 27 August, in which Dubček promised 'normalisation' of the situation – in other words, to end the Prague Spring and to return to pre-1968 methods of rule.

In November 1968 at a congress of the Polish Communist Party, Brezhnev issued what became known as the Brezhnev Doctrine in which he asserted that the independence of each of the eastern European states was limited by their duty to the Soviet Union, their own 'socialist' system and the security of the rest of the Warsaw Pact. As well as being an attempt to limit dissent within the communist movement, it was also intended to reiterate to the West that the Czech crisis was an internal matter within the Eastern bloc and not an example of Soviet expansionism.

Historical sources

1 Extract from J. F. Kennedy's broadcast of 25 July 1961 on the new crisis in Berlin

We cannot and will not permit the Communists to drive us out of Berlin, either gradually or by force. The fulfilment of our pledge to that city is essential to the morale and security of West Germany, to the unity of western Europe, to the faith of the entire free world.

The Atlantic Community . . . has been built in response to challenges: the challenge of European chaos in 1947; of the Berlin blockade in 1948; of Communist aggression in Korea in 1950 . . . The solemn vow each of us gave to West Berlin in time of peace will not be broken in time of danger.

E. G. Rayner, *The Cold War*, London, 1992, p. 42

2 Extract from a television broadcast on the Berlin question made by N. S. Khrushchev on 7 August 1961

In his recent speech [of 25 July] the President of the United States said that the USA faced a challenge of some kind from the Soviet Union, that there was a threat to the freedom of the people of West Berlin, that the Soviet Union was all but ready to use force . . .

What provisions of the Soviet draft of a peace treaty with Germany give the American President a pretext to contend that the Soviet Union 'threatens' to violate peace? Could it be those which envisage the renunciation of nuclear weapons by Germany, the legalising of the existing German frontiers, the granting of full sovereignty to both German states, and by their admission to the United Nations?

If anyone allowed himself to resort to threats it was the US President. He did not stop at presenting us with an ultimatum in reply to the proposal to conclude a peace treaty with Germany. As if to reinforce his threats, the President announced an increase in the strength of the US armed forces by 217,000 men.

E. G. Rayner, *The Cold War*, London, 1992, p. 43

Historical-source questions

1   What is meant by the terms 'Atlantic Community' and 'Berlin blockade' referred to in Source 1?
2   To what extent do Sources 1 and 2 present different views about the crisis over Berlin in 1961?
3   What was the outcome of this new Berlin crisis?

Summary questions

1   Identify and explain at least *two* reasons why the Soviet Union adopted the policy known as 'peaceful coexistence'.

2   Identify and explain at least *two* ways in which Soviet foreign policy altered after the fall of Khrushchev.

14

From detente to the Second Cold War, 1969–85

Focus questions

◆ Did detente mark the end of the First Cold War or was it merely a new phase?

◆ Why did a Second Cold War begin in 1979?

◆ How did the Second Cold War differ from the First Cold War?

Significant dates

1969	*January*	Nixon becomes president of the USA
	October	SPD/FPD win West German elections
1970	*March*	Nuclear Non-Proliferation Treaty comes into force; Moscow Treaty
1972	*February*	Nixon visits China
	May	SALT 1 signed
	December	Basic Treaty
1973	*June*	Brezhnev visits USA
	July	CSCE begins in Helsinki
	October	Yom Kippur War
1974		Portuguese Revolution
	July	Moscow Summit
1975		Independence for Portuguese colonies in Africa
	August	Final Act signed in Helsinki
1976		Soviet–Angolan Treaty
1977		Soviet–Mozambican Treaty
1978	*December*	USA recognises China
1979	*January*	Iranian Revolution; revolution in Grenada; revolution in Nicaragua
	June	Vienna Agreement
	December	Soviet troops intervene in Afghanistan
1980	*August*	Solidarity crisis in Poland
1981	*January*	Reagan becomes president of the USA; INF talks start
1982	*June*	START talks begin in Geneva
1983		Reagan's 'Evil Empire' speech
	March	Reagan announces SDI ('Star Wars') project

Overview

In the late 1960s, Cold War tensions were eased, as both sides seemed more willing to reach negotiated settlements. In 1970, agreements were reached about Germany, while 1971 saw a quadrilateral agreement on Berlin and China joining the UN. Relations between the USA, USSR and China further improved in 1972 when SALT 1 and an **ABM** treaty were signed. In 1973, US involvement in Vietnam ended and, despite war in the Middle East, the USA and USSR continued to hold weapons reduction talks and East–West trade increased. When Ford replaced **Nixon** in 1974, a SALT 2 outline was agreed. In 1975, the war in Vietnam ended and the USSR signed the Helsinki Declaration on Europe. Good relations continued under Carter at first. In 1979, the USA and China established diplomatic relations and Brezhnev and Carter signed SALT 2 in Vienna.

However, by the late 1970s, detente was beginning to unravel: it was seriously undermined in December 1979 when Soviet troops went into Afghanistan – this began what some historians have called the Second Cold War. Carter responded in early 1980 by blocking various exports to the USSR and by suspending ratification of SALT 2. Then in November, Reagan was elected president. In August 1981, he announced that the USA was stockpiling neutron bombs; later, he imposed economic sanctions on both Poland and the USSR, after martial law had been declared in Poland.

However, some bilateral talks still took place: in June 1982, there were START talks in Geneva. But in March 1983, Reagan made his 'Evil Empire' speech and announced the SDI ('Star Wars') programme. In November, NATO deployed Cruise and Pershing 2 missiles in Europe. The situation began to change in March 1985, when Gorbachev became leader of the USSR. In April, he announced a freeze on Soviet missile development.

> **ABM** systems (anti-ballistic missiles) are weapons used to shoot down enemy missiles.
>
> Born in 1913, Richard **Nixon** was a Republican politician and first entered the US Congress in 1947. He became a senator in 1950, and was a strong supporter of the anti-communist activities of the House of Representatives' Un-American Activities Committee during the early 1950s. In 1953, he became vice-president under Eisenhower. He was elected US president in 1968, and was re-elected in 1972. He was the first US president to visit Communist China and negotiated US withdrawal from the Vietnam War. He was forced to resign in 1974 because of the Watergate scandal.

Did detente mark the end of the First Cold War or was it merely a new phase?

Detente, 1969–79

By the late 1960s, several factors had emerged which made the US ready to follow a policy of detente with the USSR. The main reason was the growing impact of the Vietnam War (see Chapter 19) – both on the USA itself and on the USA's global position. In 1968, Nixon had won the presidential elections; though a hardline anti-communist for many years, he was prepared to limit the USA to a policy of containing communism if the overall consequences were beneficial to US interests. He believed that continuing the war in Vietnam was having an increasingly negative effect on the ability of the USA to maintain its economic and military superiority over the Soviet Union and realised that most Americans now wanted a withdrawal from Vietnam; he was also worried by signs that the US economy was beginning to decline.

He thus made detente – and an acceptable withdrawal from Vietnam – the main focus of his foreign policy. Much of the new diplomacy was carried out by **Henry Kissinger**. Throughout this period, he was Nixon's main foreign policy adviser. Kissinger also argued that US foreign policy should take account of the existence of other centres of power, such as China, Japan and western Europe. More importantly, both he and Nixon realised that Soviet assistance and co-operation would be needed to secure an acceptable settlement with North Vietnam.

At the same time, there were two main factors which were driving the Soviet Union to seek a better relationship with the USA. First, there were compelling economic reasons. By 1969, the Soviet economy was beginning to show signs of stagnating, even decline – in part due to bureaucratic inefficiency, but also because of the heavy burden of defence spending required to try to match US military developments. This situation was actually made worse in the 1970s as Soviet spending, both on defence and on aid to developing countries, was increased, with Brezhnev tending to ignore the signs of economic decline.

Second, there was a genuine fear that the risk of nuclear war had increased. This Soviet insecurity existed even though, by the late 1960s, the USSR had closed the **'nuclear gap'** with the USA – or at least had done so in some areas. For instance, the Soviet Union had 1,300 ICBMs to the USA's 1,054 – though this was no longer so important as ICBMs had become outmoded by **SLBMs**. Overall, the USA no longer had the overwhelming nuclear superiority it had had since 1945. The Soviet leadership believed the USA might be prepared to have serious talks on arms reductions. Previously, such talks had failed because the USA had only been prepared to agree to a freeze on armaments, which would maintain a situation of significant Soviet inferiority.

Finally, the Soviet Union was becoming increasingly concerned about the Sino-Soviet split which had grown wider since the early 1960s. In 1969, in fact, border disputes and armed clashes along the Ussuri River had almost resulted in war. The particular Soviet fear – beyond its increasing loss of control of the world communist movement – was the possibility of an anti-Soviet alliance between the USA and China which detente with the West would prevent. In fact, though Nixon and Kissinger had various reasons (including economic) for desiring a rapprochement with China, they did see it as allowing the USA to pull troops out of south-east Asia and to focus their attention and resources on the USSR, while China (still relatively weak in Asia) could be used to limit actions by the USSR and North Vietnam. When Nixon flew to

Born in Germany in 1923, **Henry Kissinger** was a professor at Harvard University, and acted as a government adviser. In 1969, he became Nixon's adviser for national security, and soon became his chief adviser on foreign policy. In 1973, Nixon appointed him secretary of state and Ford kept him on. In 1973, he shared the Nobel Peace Prize for his part in negotiating a ceasefire in Vietnam. He is particularly associated with the policy of detente, and his role as mediator in the Middle East. From 1969 to 1975, Kissinger chaired the National Security Council and, from 1973 to 1977, acted as secretary of state.

The **'nuclear gap'** was the relative superiority/inferiority in nuclear weapons between the two sides. The USA often claimed (incorrectly) that the Soviet Union was ahead – though the USSR did succeed in closing the gap in some areas.

SLBMs – submarine-launched ballistic missiles – were much more mobile and therefore harder to detect than land-based launching systems. The USSR could not keep as many nuclear submarines at sea as the USA because it lacked access to naval bases around the world.

China to meet Mao in February 1972, the Soviet leaders were afraid that any major disagreements with the USA might even result in a Sino-American military pact.

The Soviet Union saw detente as a means of consolidating its European position, while the USA thought detente was a useful tool in limiting Soviet power. Nonetheless, detente was a significant development and achieved its greatest successes in the early 1970s.

Nixon and Kissinger abandoned the policy of 'rolling back' communism, in favour of a policy of detente and **linkage**. The USA would accept the Soviet Union's closing of the nuclear gap, promise not to interfere in the Soviet sphere of influence, and offer western technology and investment. The price, or linkage, demanded from the USSR was to include help in extracting the USA from Vietnam, and acceptance that both superpowers had a mutual interest in maintaining stability in the developing world. Nixon believed that direct US involvement in the developing world could be replaced by giving weapons and training to US 'client' states, which could then deal with any regional problems by intervening on behalf of the USA. This idea – the **Nixon Doctrine** – had been developed as early as July 1969.

Between 1972 and 1974, four important summit meetings were held between the two Cold War superpowers. Initially, the Soviet Union remained suspicious of US motives in offering arms control just at the point when the USSR was approaching near-parity overall with the USA on nuclear weaponry. Some Soviet leaders saw this offer as an attempt to maintain and formalise the USA's superior system of global alliances.

SALT 1

In 1969, talks (Strategic Arms Limitation Talks or SALT) on limiting strategic nuclear weapons began hesitantly on the subject of arms control, not reduction. The fact that both sides had more than enough nuclear weapons to destroy each other resulted in a policy of deterrence being seen as sufficient. The intention was that new developments in weapons technology which might threaten this new stability would be curbed by these arms control talks. The USSR was particularly alarmed by the USA's big lead in ABM systems, and did not wish to compete in this area because of the massive costs involved.

These talks finished in May 1972, when Brezhnev and Nixon signed the SALT 1 agreement. Though no overall agreement on offensive weapons was reached, progress was made in some areas. In particular, there was to be a five-year freeze on all ICBMs, SLBMs, and long-range bombers, while each side agreed to having only two ABM sites (with no more than 100 missile launchers each). However, this last agreement was not as significant as it seemed, as neither side had any intention of developing an ABM system to that extent.

> Why was the Soviet Union concerned about the possibility of a diplomatic agreement between the USA and China?

Linkage refers to the US policy during the 1970s which tried to persuade the Soviet Union and China to co-operate in restraining revolutions in the developing world in return for concessions in nuclear and economic fields. However, while Soviet support was sometimes a factor, a wave of revolutions broke out, independent of Soviet control, so undermining this strategy.

> What did Nixon and Kissinger mean by linkage?

The **Nixon Doctrine** was a policy of delegation, declared in 1969, which was based on the idea that US 'client' states in the developing world would be given weapons to fight for US objectives in important regions, so avoiding the need for direct US military intervention – for instance, over 300,000 South Korean troops fought in Vietnam. The wave of revolutions in the late 1970s, however, led the USA to create a rapid deployment force, specifically for intervention in the developing world.

MIRVs (multiple
independently targeted re-
entry vehicles) are missiles
with multiple warheads,
each one capable of being
directed to a different
target.

What were the SALT 1
negotiations intended
to achieve?

SALT 1 also failed to include limitations on **MIRVs**; though the USA had developed these first, the Soviet Union soon developed and deployed their own system.

Despite this, SALT 1 was a significant move away from the earlier Cold War hostilities, and marked the beginning of a continuing process of arms control. The acceptance by the USA of the narrowing of the missile gap appeased the Soviet Union and so did much to reduce tensions between these two nuclear superpowers.

Detente in Europe

In Europe, the process of detente was aided by, and contributed to, developments in West Germany, which resulted in agreements to promote contact and trade between eastern and western Europe on the old problems of Berlin and the two Germanies. In October 1969, the Social Democrats (SPD), in alliance with the Free Democrats (FPD), won the West German elections – it was the first left-of centre victory since 1945. This SPD–FPD government, led by Willy Brandt, pursued a policy known as *Ostpolitik* (Eastern Policy) which was intended to reduce the barriers between the FDR and the GDR.

Brandt's abandonment of the Hallstein Doctrine, which stated that West Germany would not recognise any country which recognised the GDR, encouraged the USSR, which had, since the 1950s, wanted the West to accept the existence of the GDR and the Soviet bloc in eastern Europe.

In August 1970, the Soviet Union and West Germany signed the Moscow Treaty, which formally ended the Second World War. It also confirmed the division of Germany and the loss of pre-war east German territory to Poland and the Soviet Union.

This success was followed by the Final Quadripartite Protocol in 1972, which saw the USSR accept West German links with West Berlin, thus ending another long-standing dispute. Later, in December 1972, West and East Germany signed the Basic Treaty, accepting the de facto existence of the two German states – though West Germany did not give full diplomatic recognition to the GDR.

What was *Ostpolitik*?

So, by 1972, SALT 1 and *Ostpolitik* had done much to reduce tensions in Europe as regards nuclear weapons and Germany. However, the Soviet Union also wanted the West to accept the status quo in eastern Europe. This was partly achieved by the Conference on Security and Co-operation in Europe (CSCE) held in Helsinki in July 1973. Though it did not result in a formal peace treaty, there was a declaration of intent, known as the Final Act, which was eventually signed in 1975. This guaranteed the status quo in Europe.

However, the issue of human rights proved contentious and ultimately contributed to the abandonment of detente by the West. This was because the agreement on the European status quo was linked to Soviet concessions on human rights in the Soviet bloc, with the CSCE to monitor progress on this issue. In addition, after Brandt resigned in May 1974, his successor – Schmidt – restored closer links with the USA, and in particular accepted the modernisation of NATO's nuclear capacity.

Why did a Second Cold War begin in 1979?

The decline of detente

One problem with detente was that, even though the Soviet Union wanted stability in Europe, it also wanted to extend its influence in the developing world which, at this stage, was very limited in comparison with that of the USA. In particular, the Soviet leadership was keen to acquire allies with naval bases. The USSR had access to only six operational bases – all in the Soviet Union. Although the Warsaw Pact outnumbered NATO as regards the total number of ships and submarines, NATO's access to sea bases around the world meant they could keep twice as many submarines at sea than could the Warsaw Pact. For the same reason, the USSR was able to operate only 6 aircraft carriers, compared to NATO's 20.

The USSR had made some progress in the Middle East when, after the Six Day War in 1967, the USSR had replaced all equipment lost by Nasser's Egypt and had sent thousands of military advisers. In return, Egypt had granted the USSR naval rights in some ports and some airbases. Thus, for the first time, the Soviet Union was able to counter US activities in the Mediterranean.

During the early 1970s, the Soviet Union had built on this, to become an important ally of several Arab states. This attempt by the Soviet Union to extend its influence into what had long been seen as a western sphere had a negative effect on East–West relations. In fact, as early as May 1972, the USA was already trying to weaken the Soviet Union's new position in the Middle East – immediately after signing SALT 1, it asked Iran to get Iraq to break its ties with the USSR.

However, Sadat (who replaced Nasser as ruler of Egypt in 1970) was angered by the USSR's refusal (because of its wish to continue detente) to help recapture territory lost to Israel in 1967; in retaliation, Sadat expelled all Soviet military personnel from Egypt. This had deprived the USSR of its most important naval and air bases in the developing world. Despite sending military supplies to Egypt and Syria after the Yom Kippur War had broken out in October 1973 and urging other Arab states to support Egypt and Syria, Soviet influence in the Middle East soon declined. More importantly, the USA was angered by the fact that the USSR had not passed on information about the possibility of an imminent Arab attack on Israel and that, once begun, the

How did events in the Middle East contribute to a decline in detente during the 1970s?

Soviet Union had tried to involve other Arab states. As a result, the USA deliberately excluded the Soviet Union from the subsequent Middle East peace negotiations.

Detente continued to crumble because the USA made it clear that it intended to maintain its global power base, while the USSR was equally determined not to accept its inferior position as regards allies in the developing world. In addition, a wave of revolutions began to break out in several developing-world areas – especially in the Middle East, Africa and Central America. The USSR tended to see these as presenting opportunities to improve its international position.

Problems also arose in relation to SALT 1 because several systems were not covered by the treaty – Trident, MX missiles, the B1 bomber and Cruise missiles. Though relatively short of money, Nixon decided these should be rapidly developed.

However, in the years 1973–74, Nixon's ability to pursue detente was restricted by decisions taken by Congress. The growing Watergate scandal, and the secrecy with which Nixon and Kissinger conducted much of their foreign policy, led Congress to assert its independence and control – for instance, in 1973, it blocked Nixon's plans to send US troops to Cambodia. More importantly, Congress insisted that any further agreements with the USSR should only be made if the Soviet Union made concessions on human rights in eastern Europe. Later, Mao's death in 1976 slowed down Sino-American negotiations which had been used to put pressure on the Soviet Union.

President Ford, who had taken over from Nixon in August 1974, found that Congress placed the same restrictions on his foreign policy. He responded to these developments by refusing to use the word 'detente'.

However, another important factor in shifting the USA away from detente was its own growing economic problems. The cost of Vietnam, allied to increased competition from the expanding Japanese and West German economies, had produced the USA's first balance of trade deficit since 1900. The situation was made worse by the big increase in oil prices which followed the Arab–Israeli War of 1973. The declining US economy obviously had serious implications for the future maintenance of US military power.

One consequence of this was Congress's reluctance to approve extra funds to enable Kissinger to counter Soviet diplomacy in Africa in the second half of the 1970s. Following the revolution in Portugal in 1974, the Portuguese colonies of Angola, Mozambique and Guinea-Bissau were granted independence, after many years of guerrilla warfare waged by independence groups. In Angola, the biggest group, the MPLA, was backed by Moscow, while the USA and China supported other groups. When the USA and China stepped up arms supplies to their groups, the USSR did the same, while Cuba actually sent combat troops to help the MPLA. When China withdrew, Congress rejected Kissinger's plea for extra funding and, in 1976, Angola signed a treaty with the USSR; in 1977, Mozambique followed suit. The USSR also established close relations with the new pro-Soviet government in Ethiopia. All these successes enabled the Soviet Union to overcome at last its great inferiority in regard to friendly naval bases outside its own territory.

Events in Europe also took a worrying turn for the USA in the period 1974–77. In 1974, the Portuguese revolution (which overthrew the right-wing dictatorship there) and the fall of the Greek military dictatorship resulted in both these countries having new left-wing governments containing many who wanted withdrawal from NATO. This coincided with the growing popularity of 'Eurocommunist' parties in France and in Italy. Thus, by 1976 even Kissinger was saying he would no longer talk of detente.

Carter and the Democrats

At first, **Carter** – who defeated Ford in the 1976 US presidential elections – followed a rather inconsistent foreign policy. He avoided the use of anti-Soviet rhetoric and announced that the USA would no longer give automatic support to repressive regimes simply because they were anti-communist. Carter relied on two advisers: Cyrus Vance, who was secretary of state, and Zbigniew Brzezinski (a Pole), who acted as national security adviser. This was a problem because, although they both saw the Soviet Union as being the crucial factor in international relations, they had conflicting opinions on how to conduct negotiations.

Vance thought a revival of detente was possible as soon as Brezhnev was replaced by younger communist leaders because he believed they wanted to end the Cold War confrontation. He also saw SALT 2 as a way of allowing the USA to solve its own economic problems by cutting the defence budget.

Brzezinski, however, had a very different attitude to the Soviet Union: he did not trust its leaders and believed only superior US strength would force the USSR to make acceptable agreements. For him, therefore, SALT 2 had relatively little importance. In fact, Brzezinski believed that a new arms race would ruin the Soviet economy – CIA experts reported that it was extremely weak – and so cause serious problems for the Soviet Union and its control of eastern Europe.

Soon, developments in the developing world (especially in Ethiopia) led Carter and Brzezinski to conclude that the USSR was attempting to improve its geopolitical position by taking advantage of the USA's economic problems and its post-Vietnam reluctance to risk involvement in another developing-world regional conflict. Carter alarmed the USSR by supporting the campaign for human rights in the Soviet bloc and by making very far-reaching calls

Born in 1924, James **Carter** served in the US navy until 1953, when he began to run his family's large peanut farms. He was a Democratic state senator and then the governor of Georgia, before becoming US president in 1977. He was convincingly defeated by the Republican candidate, Reagan, in the 1980 presidential elections.

How did the attitudes of Vance and Brzezinski to the USSR differ?

for arms control, which seemed designed to perpetuate the USSR's overall inferiority.

By 1978, Brezhnev was clearly ill and the Soviet Union was stagnating, both economically and politically. Meanwhile, events in the developing world resulted – without Soviet involvement – in several changes. In April 1978, in Afghanistan, communists took power; in January 1979, the shah of Iran (an important regional ally for the USA) was toppled by an Islamic fundamentalist revolt, led by the Ayatollah Khomeni; and in Central America and the Caribbean, left-wing and pro-Soviet governments took power in Nicaragua and Grenada.

However, as early as 1977, Carter had begun to modernise and extend US nuclear superiority. Though he had cancelled the B1 bomber, he then used the money to develop the new Stealth bomber and Cruise missiles. In fact, US defence expenditure actually increased under Carter. When the West German leader, Schmidt, told Carter he wanted European theatre (intermediate-range) Europe-based nuclear weapons included in SALT 2, Carter and Brzezinski refused. In March 1977, Vance informed the USSR about this: in late 1977, the USSR then began to deploy their newly developed SS-20s in eastern Europe. These missiles actually replaced the SS-4 and SS-5 missiles, which were inferior to the USA's Pershing 1 missile which had been deployed by the USA since 1960. More importantly, US satellites soon found all 39 of the SS-20 sites (the SS-20s were a retaliatory weapon).

These events in the developing world and Europe led the Republicans to begin to criticise Carter for not resisting what they saw as a new Soviet offensive. This growing pressure soon resulted in a revival of Cold War hostilities. Carter responded by taking a more hardline approach: he began to talk of the possibility of undermining communist rule or Soviet influence in China, Vietnam, Somalia, Iraq, Algeria and Cuba. In January 1979, the USA decided to deploy Pershing 2 and Cruise missiles in Europe (in fact, the initial decision to deploy had been taken in 1975, before the USSR had deployed the SS-20s). As well as increased US expenditure, it was significant that these new weapons were counter-force (first strike) weapons, unlike the Soviet SS-20s.

SALT 2

The SALT 2 negotiations opened in Vienna in June 1979. It was agreed to set a limit of 2,400 for missile launchers (both ICBMs and SLBMs) and heavy bombers for each side. A limit on the number of MIRV launchers was also agreed. However, some in the USA then began to claim that the USSR had actually achieved superiority over the USA as regards ICBMs. According to a number of papers produced by the independent Stockholm International Peace Research Institute (SIPRI), although the USSR did have a lead over the USA as regards delivery systems and megatonnage, the USA had – and always had had – a clear superiority as regards technology. The accuracy of US weapons was far superior: the SS-18 was only equivalent to the USA's old Minuteman, while the MX was twice as accurate as the SS-18. Also, 79 per cent of the USSR's ICBMs were on land, compared to 25 per cent for the USA, while 54 per cent of the USA's were on submarines, compared to 21 per cent for the USSR. (The rest of the USA's ICBMs were 'offsite' and not easily detectable by the USSR.)

Eventually the USA delayed ratification of SALT 2 when a Soviet combat brigade was discovered in Cuba. In fact, the USA had actually agreed to the presence of a small Soviet force at the end of the Cuban Missile Crisis (see pages 249–51) – but the New Right in the USA now pressed Carter to force the USSR to withdraw it. When Brezhnev refused, relations continued to deteriorate. The period of arms control, and thus of detente, was nearing its end.

Afghanistan, December 1979

Increased Soviet activity in Afghanistan's internal politics and the decision to send in Red Army divisions, as requested by the pro-Soviet Afghan government, put the final nails in the coffin of detente.

The Afghanistan government had been recognised by the West when it came to power after an internal coup and Afghanistan had unofficially been accepted by the West as a zone of special interest to the USSR, in view of their common border. Carter (acting on Brzezinski's advice) thus took the Soviet Union by surprise when he described it as 'the greatest threat to world peace since the Second World War'. The USSR claimed it had only intervened after

> Why did the Soviet Union claim to be surprised at the USA's reaction to its military intervention in Afghanistan?

A Soviet tank in Afghanistan. The decision to send in Soviet troops in December 1979 was one factor behind the start of the Second Cold War.

The **Afghan civil war** developed in 1979 when many traditionalist groups decided to resist the radical reforms of the new government.

Pakistan (with US support) and Iran had become involved in the **Afghan civil war**. In fact, Moscow feared having a fundamentalist Islamic state so close to its own Islamic republics, especially if it was allied to either the USA or China. Brezhnev also believed that failure to respond would lead other communist states to believe that the Soviet Union was no longer willing to resist US power. The USSR believed it was important to retain as many friendly states as possible, given its inferiority in relation to the USA – the Soviet Union had 11 significant allies outside Europe, while the USA had over 50.

US domestic politics

According to the historian F. Halliday, the Second Cold War can be explained, not so much by Soviet actions, but by developments in the USA and the developing world. In the USA, the south and west became increasingly important economically and demographically during the 1970s as most of the USA's aerospace and military industry was located there. This area had traditionally been the home of more extreme conservative politics, favouring high military spending and a virulent anti-communist foreign policy, as well as military intervention in the developing world. This area provided the base for the emergence of the New Right, itself a reaction to **US economic decline** and the wave of revolutions which swept the developing world in the 1970s.

US economic decline in 1980 meant there was no increase in GNP, inflation was running at 10 per cent and unemployment at 7.5 per cent.

By 1980, the New Right (a coalition of Republicans and neo-conservative Democrats) dominated Congress and were allied to the Pentagon and arms manufacturers. They claimed that since Vietnam US military strength had declined – though as early as 1968 the US military had begun to plan Cruise, MX and Trident missiles and the B1 bomber, while the decision to deploy Cruise and Pershing 2 had been taken as early as 1975. With about 7 million people directly employed in the armaments industry (and about 10 per cent of the population indirectly employed) a big increase in military spending was seen as a way of at least temporarily halting the economic downturn. However, Halliday's explanation remains a minority one, and most historians have seen the Soviet Union's military intervention in Afghanistan (which initially involved over 85,000 Red Army troops) and other events in the developing world as being more important than changes in US domestic politics.

How did the Second Cold War differ from the First Cold War?

Carter's reaction to the Soviet intervention in Afghanistan – and his return to traditional Cold War language and politics – turned out to be the first step in what some historians have called the Second Cold War. In January 1980, Carter (under increasing pressure from the Republican New Right) demonstrated US anger at the USSR's actions in Afghanistan by blocking various exports to the USSR, including much needed grain deliveries. He also confirmed the non-ratification of the SALT 2 treaty, and called for a boycott of the 1980 Olympics due to be held in Moscow. The USSR was further worried by the USA agreeing, for the first time ever, to supply China with military equipment.

In July 1980, Carter signed a presidential decree which considered the possibility of a limited war focused on specific military targets in the USSR, which were more vulnerable as 79 per cent of its ICBMs were land-based, and so easier to detect and hit, while the corresponding figure for the USA was only 25 per cent. A rapid deployment force was also set up for intervention in the developing world, while Carter went back on election promises to withdraw troops from South Korea.

Despite Carter's tough stance, **Reagan** was elected president in November 1980. Reagan's Republican administration, which took office in January 1981, committed itself to 're-establishing' US world power by increasing US nuclear superiority, which would then allow greater US intervention in the developing world. This was linked to expanding the US economy in general, and the military–industrial complex in particular. Despite the weakness of the US economy in 1981, Reagan increased military expenditure by 13 per cent in 1982, and by more than 8 per cent in each subsequent year. He justified this expenditure by claiming there was a 'window of vulnerability'. He claimed **Soviet military expenditure** on armaments had greatly increased during the 1970s, and was now greater than the USA's. Yet, according to SIPRI, the Soviet Union had never outspent the USA and had not made any sudden increase in the 1970s. At the same time, the CIA's budget was increased even more. The Reagan administration began to talk of 'surgical' nuclear strikes, while US communications were strengthened to resist any Soviet nuclear response. In Europe, he even considered the use of the neutron bomb and chemical weapons.

Detente was dismissed as a failure, and Moscow was blamed for breaking those agreements that had been reached, especially in relation to its perceived – and actual – increased penetration of developing world areas, such as Afghanistan. More importantly, Reagan immediately implemented an extremely vigorous anti-Soviet policy, in tune with his long-held anti-communist views. As a result, US–Soviet relations deteriorated to a low level.

Reagan's foreign policy sent out mixed messages. In 1982, he appointed George Shultz who, as secretary of state, was soon calling for new arms controls, yet in 1983 Reagan referred to the USSR as the 'evil empire'; then, within a year of this, he was offering 'constructive negotiations', but only when the USA had achieved a new superiority.

This approach worried Andropov, the new Soviet leader, who feared that the US policy would risk a real crisis between the two superpowers – especially

Born in 1911, Ronald **Reagan** was an actor and a convinced anti-communist who played a leading role during the McCarthy period. From 1967 to 1974, he was Republican governor of California and was closely associated with the New Right. He became US president in 1981 and is particularly associated with the start of the Second Cold War. Later he played an important role in the end of the Cold War.

Soviet military expenditure in the 1970s had increased by 2 per cent per annum, which was less than the annual increase in GNP. Because the USSR's GNP was about half that of the USA, it needed to spend double the proportion of its GNP just to match US developments. Overall, in 1980, NATO and other anti-USSR states spent a combined total of $305 billion on defence, compared to a Warsaw Pact expenditure of $201 billion.

when Reagan announced a five-year programme of $180 billion to modernise US strategic nuclear forces, especially in Europe. The first area to receive attention was the intermediate-range nuclear weapons in Europe. Since late 1977, the Soviet Union had been deploying SS-20 intermediate-range weapons in eastern Europe in an attempt to close the gap between themselves and the USA as regards these theatre nuclear forces (TNFs). The SS-20s replaced the older SS-4 and SS-5 TNFs which the USSR had deployed to match the earlier US deployment of Thor and Jupiter missiles. Partly in response to pressure from west European governments, the USA had adopted a 'twin-track' policy in 1979 – **Pershing 2** ballistic missiles would be deployed in West Germany, while ground-launched **Cruise** missiles would be placed in several European countries, including Britain. However, the USA had made the initial decision to deploy these new weapons before the Soviet Union had introduced the SS-20s. At the same time, the USSR was informed that no action on this would be taken if the SS-20s were removed. The USSR was alarmed by these new US weapons as they were much quicker and more accurate than existing weapons and thus much more difficult to combat: they were counter-force or first strike weapons rather than retaliatory weapons like the SS-20s, which were not even as accurate as the Pershing 1 missiles which the USA had deployed in 1960.

In 1982, at the Intermediate Nuclear Forces (INF) talks, Reagan put forward a new policy known as the 'zero option', whereby both parties agreed to put an end to future increases in armaments, but the Soviet Union rejected this. In fact, according to SIPRI, this zero option (freeze) would have retained a clear US/NATO superiority, as NATO had 1,000 medium-range nuclear bombers and 17,000 nuclear warheads while the Warsaw Pact had, respectively, 550 and 6,000. The USA also had a large lead in the more important SLBMs. In June 1982, following a vote by Congress, discussions to reduce strategic nuclear weapons – Strategic Arms Reduction Talks (START) – also began in Geneva. Then, in March 1983, Reagan announced the **Strategic Defence Initiative** (SDI or 'Star Wars') project. This would have made all offensive nuclear weapons redundant. The USSR feared this meant they would soon have no nuclear deterrent – they saw the improved balance of forces as being wiped out and believed the USA would no longer be interested in arms reduction talks.

In November 1983, NATO began to deploy the Pershing 2 and Cruise missiles. As a result, the USSR broke off all further talks; at the same time, the START negotiations were also called off. Overall, 1983 was the worst year in Cold War relations between the two sides since the Cuban Missile Crisis of 1962. In fact, the USA had deliberately broken off these and subsequent talks in the hope that the USSR would eventually pull out.

Pershing 2 and **Cruise** were 'new generation' nuclear weapons which were much quicker and harder to detect. This was especially true of the Cruise missiles, which could be launched from mobile missile carriers. The Soviet Union had nothing to match these.

The weapons being developed by the **Strategic Defence Initiative** or SDI (also known as the 'Star Wars' project) would make it impossible for the USSR to respond to a US strike because any Soviet missiles fired in retaliation would be destroyed by the SDI missiles before reaching the USA. US fears of being damaged through nuclear war were thus removed as there would no longer be a possibility of a Soviet counterattack.

What was the 'Star Wars' project?

Women peace protesters outside the US missile base at Greenham Common in Berkshire, England. They were trying to prevent the deployment of US Cruise missiles, which were seen to be dangerously escalating the Cold War arms race.

Poland

The Second Cold War, and the situation in Europe, became even more tense after December 1981, when the Polish government imposed martial law in an attempt to stop the growth of the independent Solidarity trade union movement. Although the USSR ruled out direct military intervention, Moscow did put pressure on the Polish leadership for a tough response. Moscow feared that if Poland was able to develop a more democratic system other east European states might try to follow suit; there was also the danger that the people of the Soviet Union might try to dismantle the mechanisms which guaranteed the power of the leadership of the CPSU in the USSR itself.

In addition, the USSR still saw Poland as an important part of the Warsaw Pact and hence of Soviet defences. The USSR still felt militarily vulnerable in Europe: although the Soviet Union had an army of 3.7 million (as opposed to the USA's 2 million), the bulk of the Red Army (44 divisions) was deployed on the Soviet Union's borders with China, with only 31 divisions in eastern Europe. Furthermore, some 60 per cent of Soviet divisions were said by the CIA to be less than 50 per cent of the required size, while 80 per cent were believed not to be combat-ready. In all, the combined NATO armed forces totalled 4.9 million, while the combined figure for the Warsaw Pact was 4.7 million.

The USA responded by imposing economic and trade sanctions on both Poland and the Soviet Union which they wanted west European states to apply as well. Yet this conflicted with the interests of several of these states, which still wanted detente – and trade – with the Soviet Union. In particular, western Europe was keen to maintain the natural gas pipeline which would carry gas from the USSR. Some west European states were also alarmed by the 'Star

A demonstration in Warsaw organised by Solidarity, a trade union independent of the communist government of Poland. Such developments were one sign of the eventual collapse of the eastern European regimes in 1989.

Born in 1931, Mikhail **Gorbachev** studied law at Moscow University and then worked as a communist official. In 1978, he became a member of the Central Committee of the CPSU and took charge of agriculture. By 1980, he was a member of the Politburo and supported Andropov, who became general secretary of the CPSU in 1983. Gorbachev himself became general secretary in 1985 and began a programme of reform to revive and modernise the Soviet economy and to liberalise the political system. He was awarded the Nobel Peace Prize in 1990 for the leading role he played in ending the Cold War.

Wars' project, while others were unhappy about the implications of Reagan's belief that all unrest in the world was the work of the USSR. This led the USA to increase its support of 'reliable' right-wing dictatorial or repressive regimes, such as El Salvador, and to support various terrorist groups, especially in Central America.

Soviet domestic politics

In the years 1982–85, the Soviet Union was going through a tense political transition. Andropov, who had succeeded Brezhnev in November 1982, died in February 1984; his replacement, Chernenko, died in March 1985. This coincided with increasingly serious economic problems, as the technological gap between the Soviet Union and the West widened (especially in micro-electronics and computers). Essentially, apart from the inefficiencies resulting from too much bureaucratic and central control, the attempt by the Soviet Union to keep up with US military might had distorted and weakened its economy. By the late 1980s, the Soviet economy was more like that of a less developed country than that of an advanced industrial country. The new Soviet leader, elected by the Central Committee of the CPSU on 11 March 1985, was Mikhail **Gorbachev**. He had already concluded that the USSR could no longer afford to follow each nuclear escalation made by the USA.

1 A joint Soviet–American communiqué, issued after the Moscow Summit meeting in July 1974

[Both sides are] deeply convinced of the imperative necessity of making the process of improving US–Soviet relations irreversible . . . The two sides continue steadfastly to apply their joint efforts . . . in such important fields as: removing the danger of war, including particularly war involving nuclear and other mass-destruction weapons; limiting and eventually ending the arms race, having in mind as the ultimate objective the achievement of general and complete disarmament under appropriate international control; contributing to the elimination of sources of international tension and military conflict; strengthening and extending the process of relaxation of tensions throughout the world; developing broad, mutually beneficial co-operation in commercial and economic scientific-technical and cultural fields.

E. G. Rayner, *The Cold War*, London, 1992, p. 73

2 Henry Kissinger, commenting on the policy of detente

Detente did not prevent resistance to Soviet expansion: on the contrary, it fostered the only psychologically possible framework for such resistance. [President] Nixon knew where to draw the line against Soviet adventure whether it occurred directly or through proxy . . . The United States and the Soviet Union are ideological rivals. Detente cannot change that. The nuclear age compels us to coexist. Rhetorical crusades cannot change that either.

H. Kissinger, *The White House years*, London, 1979, pp. 237–38

Historical-source questions

1 According to Source 1, what were the main objectives of detente, as agreed at the Moscow Summit in July 1974?
2 To what extent do Sources 1 and 2 agree about the objectives of detente?
3 How useful is Source 2 for assessing US aims concerning detente with the Soviet Union?

Summary questions

1 Identify and explain *two* factors which contributed to the emergence of detente.

2 Compare and assess the importance of at least *three* factors which contributed to the decline of detente in the late 1970s.

15

The end of the Cold War, 1985–91

Focus questions

◆ What role did Gorbachev play in ending the Second Cold War?

◆ Was the end of the Cold War also the end of the 'great contest'?

Significant dates

1985   *March* Gorbachev elected general secretary of the CPSU
        November Geneva Summit

1986   *October* Reykjavik Summit

1987   *December* Washington Summit

1988   *May* Moscow Summit

1989   Eastern European governments collapse or are overthrown
        December Malta Summit

1990   *November* CFE Treaty

1991   *July* Moscow Summit
        August Unsuccessful coup against Gorbachev
        December Collapse of the Soviet Union; CIS formed

Overview

In November 1985, the first summit between Gorbachev and Reagan took place in Geneva and the second took place at Reykjavik in October 1986. Progress was made on the issue of arms reductions, although this was partly undermined by US deployment of the new B52 bomber. In December 1987, the Washington Summit ended with the signing of the Intermediate Nuclear Forces (INF) Treaty.

In 1988 the Geneva Agreement ended the Afghan War. The Moscow Summit at which Gorbachev announced his unilateral decision to greatly reduce Soviet forces also took place in this year. By the end of 1989, after Gorbachev announced he would not stop reforms, most eastern European regimes had fallen. At this point, the USA agreed to end most restrictions on

US–Soviet trade. In 1990, Germany was reunited and the Conventional Forces in Europe (CFE) Treaty was signed. In March 1991, the Warsaw Pact was dissolved and later in the year START was signed. By the end of the year, Gorbachev – and the USSR – were gone and the Cold War had finally ended.

What was the significance of Gorbachev becoming general secretary of the Soviet Union in 1985?

What role did Gorbachev play in ending the Second Cold War?

The significance of Gorbachev

Gorbachev's election as general secretary of the CPSU in March 1985 turned out to be the beginning of the end of the Cold War – and, as it turned out, of the Soviet Union itself.

Though the latter result was not Gorbachev's intention, he certainly did set out to end the Cold War. His main concern was to end the stagnation of the Soviet economy, then to revitalise it, thus ensuring the security of the Soviet system. Gorbachev realised that the financial burden of maintaining the military power of the USSR was too great and that its effect on the Soviet economy would ultimately undermine Soviet security. He also calculated that the USA's huge budget deficit meant they too could not maintain their increased defence expenditure for much longer.

Gorbachev's 'new thinking'

Gorbachev's domestic policy was shaped by his policies of **perestroika**, **glasnost** and **demokratizatsiya** and he applied his policy of *novoe myshlenie* (or 'new thinking') to foreign affairs. He argued that continuing the arms race was pointless, as one side's advance was simply matched – or even bettered – by the other. He believed that political accommodation, not military power, would enable problems to be solved and real security to be achieved.

Gorbachev's new foreign policy was based on his belief – also applied domestically – that human rights, democracy, non-violence and freedom of conscience should become the basis of diplomacy. As part of this, he decided to state publicly what had, in fact, long been the reality of Soviet foreign policy: that the ideology of class war should not shape the Soviet Union's diplomacy.

In some ways, the 'new thinking' policy contained elements of traditional Soviet foreign policy in that it aimed for peaceful coexistence and detente with the West. But Gorbachev's new policy was also markedly different: for example, he dropped the dual-track policy of peaceful coexistence to ensure Soviet security combined with the desire for the peaceful long-term victory of socialism across the world. Gorbachev's stated aim now was simply Soviet security – Khrushchev's idea of a peaceful but competitive coexistence was clearly

Perestroika was the policy of restructuring launched by Gorbachev. Though it soon came to be used to describe his general intention to modernise the USSR, it was initially aimed at the Soviet economy. His main aim was to make the economic system more modern and to improve productivity.

Glasnost was the policy of openness adopted by Gorbachev, who wanted past mistakes and current problems in the USSR to be voiced in public, including criticism of the leadership of the Communist Party and its policies in the media.

Demokratizatsiya refers to Gorbachev's attempts to make the Soviet political system more democratic. Elections were reformed to give greater choice to the voters, and political organisations and clubs (at first, left-of-centre but soon liberals as well) were allowed to operate outside the control of the Communist Party. Gorbachev also tried to make the government and the soviet system more independent of party control.

What were the main aspects of Gorbachev's 'new thinking' as regards Soviet foreign policy?

abandoned. Gorbachev's new approach was signalled by his appointment of Edvard Shevardnadze (who was a liberal reform communist from Georgia) as foreign minister.

At his first Central Committee meeting in April 1985, Gorbachev announced his intention to reopen arms control talks with the USA and spoke of the need to withdraw Soviet troops from Afghanistan. He also gave an early indication of his belief that the arms race need not continue, as all that was needed for Russia's security was the military capacity to threaten an effective counter-attack. This was a return to Khrushchev's approach and, more importantly, it was a clear rejection of the policy of parity followed by Brezhnev.

At the Twenty-seventh Party Congress in February 1986, Gorbachev talked about global interdependence and spoke publicly for the first time of the need to abandon the policy of competitive peaceful coexistence. At the Nineteenth Party Conference in June 1988, he began a public debate about the mistakes of previous Soviet foreign policy (such as the invasion of Czechoslovakia in 1968) and opened up some archives for historical research.

Why were some communists opposed to Gorbachev's domestic and foreign policies?

Although his ideas and approach made him extremely popular abroad, they caused growing criticism from more conservative quarters within the Soviet Union. These elements were determined to maintain the monopoly of power held by the political elite in the USSR and believed that increased democracy in the Soviet Union would undermine Soviet control of eastern Europe. In the main, these hardliners wished to continue with the Stalinist system of rule.

Reagan's response

Reagan's approach to the USSR began to moderate at the same time and contributed to an improved relationship between the two superpowers. The whole nature and direction of the nuclear debate began to alter and negotiations became increasingly meaningful. The overall result was a growing and genuine political accommodation between the two statesmen in the second half of the 1980s and they agreed to resume the arms control negotiations which had ended after the Soviet Union had walked out in November 1983.

Gorbachev was quick to take steps to push the pace: in April 1985, he froze further deployments of the SS-20s; in August he declared a temporary halt to Soviet underground nuclear testing; in September, he proposed that the USSR and the USA reduce all strategic nuclear weapons stocks by 50 per cent; and in October, he announced plans for a reduction in the number of Soviet missiles in eastern Europe.

The four summits, 1985–88

Over the next three years, Reagan and Gorbachev held four US–Soviet summits on arms control.

Geneva, 1985

The first meeting took place in Geneva in November 1985. Although no significant agreements were reached, it was the first such summit that had been held for six years. Besides establishing a good personal relationship between Reagan and Gorbachev, it was significant for Gorbachev's statement that 'nuclear war cannot be won and must not be fought'. Any practical agreement on the reduction of Soviet ICBMs was prevented by the Russians' continuing fear of Reagan's 'Star Wars' plans. Reagan also rejected Gorbachev's suggestion that they issue a joint statement promising that neither side would be the first to launch a nuclear attack – this was because the USA wanted to keep the option of responding to a conventional attack with nuclear weapons. However, they did agree to promise to prevent any war between themselves and not to seek military superiority.

After the summit, Gorbachev continued to push the pace and, in January 1986, he took the USA by surprise by proposing the total elimination of all nuclear weapons by the end of the century. Other offers – to eliminate all ICBMs in 10 years and to withdraw all tactical nuclear weapons from Europe – followed, with the USA making counteroffers. In April 1986, he suggested new talks on the reduction of Warsaw Pact and NATO conventional forces. In May, Gorbachev officially launched his 'new thinking' policy, despite Reagan's continued refusal to drop the development of the Strategic Defence Initiative (SDI).

However, relations between the two superpowers deteriorated in the first half of 1986. Increased tension because of US aggression in Libya and Afghanistan was made worse when, in May, Reagan announced that the USA would not stick to the still unratified SALT 2 agreement because of the continued Soviet presence in Afghanistan. A dispute over spying in August 1986 (western secret service agents in the USSR identified several KGB agents operating in the USA and Britain) resulted in the USA expelling 25 Soviet UN employees and warning the USSR not to retaliate. After the Soviet Union backed down – they did not expel any CIA agents operating in the USSR – Reagan agreed to a second summit.

Reykjavik, 1986

The atmosphere of the second Reagan–Gorbachev summit was, predictably, not so good natured. Once again, the USA's SDI was the main item of contention. Ever since the SDI had been announced by Reagan in March 1983, the Soviet Union had seen it as violating the **ABM Treaty of 1972** and thus escalating the nuclear arms race (see page 170).

Gorbachev tried to move the talks from consideration of reductions and limitations to complete nuclear disarmament; in response, Reagan called for

In the **ABM Treaty of 1972** the USA and the USSR agreed not to deploy new ABM systems, which were extremely costly.

the complete elimination of all ballistic nuclear missiles within 10 years. Agreement was reached in principle that strategic nuclear weapons should be cut by 50 per cent and that medium-range nuclear missiles in Europe should be withdrawn.

However, the continuing arguments about the SDI finally caused the summit to break up: Reagan refused to abandon it and Gorbachev said further reductions on the part of the USSR could not happen without this taking place. It seemed a deadlock had been reached. After the summit, the USSR expelled 5 US diplomats and the USA retaliated by expelling 55 Soviet diplomats.

The deadlock was broken by Gorbachev in February 1987, when he offered to accept the NATO policy of the zero–zero option on the deployment of SS-20s, Pershing and Cruise missiles in Europe. This meant, in essence, that both sides would withdraw their missiles from Europe – a complete reversal of what, for 10 years, had been Soviet policy on this issue. This was a big concession by the Soviet Union, as their SS-20s had been deployed to try to even up the balance of forces, which was again upset by the more sophisticated US Pershing 2 and Cruise missiles. Gorbachev's critics in the USSR saw this as a dangerous surrender. In November, Gorbachev acknowledged that human rights needed to be improved in the Soviet bloc and that the Iron Curtain should be lifted; he also spoke of the need to avoid superpower confrontation in the developing world.

Washington, 1987

As a result of Gorbachev's concession, a third summit meeting took place in Washington in December 1987. This meeting resulted in the signing of the INF Treaty, which agreed that all land-based intermediate and shorter range nuclear missiles would be withdrawn from Europe. This was the first arms agreement to be signed since 1979; it was also a unique agreement in that never before had arms reduction talks led to the elimination of an entire category of nuclear weapons. In practical terms this accounted for about 5 per cent of the total number of nuclear warheads in existence. The INF Treaty was also historically important because, for the first time in arms control agreements, both sides accepted verification procedures, which included access to data and the witnessing of weapons destruction. The arms race was not just slowed down by the INF Treaty, but was actually reversed. At this stage there were signs that the Cold War would end through a mutually agreed settlement.

Moscow, 1988

Before the next summit meeting, Gorbachev had taken another step towards easing tensions between East and West by announcing, in February 1988, that the Soviet Union would withdraw its forces from Afghanistan, without insisting on any guarantees on the type of government which might then come to power in that country. This had long been insisted on by the USA and had been resisted by previous Soviet leaders (including Gorbachev at first). By April 1988, an international conference in Geneva on this issue had resulted in an agreement to end all foreign involvement in the Afghan civil war. Gorbachev even hinted that Soviet troops might soon be withdrawn from eastern Europe. By February 1989, after almost 10 years of fighting, the last units of the Red Army had left Afghanistan.

Despite this, the Moscow Summit held in May 1988 achieved little as, once again, arguments about the SDI project blocked any agreement on the reduction of strategic nuclear weapons. By then, Gorbachev had effectively destroyed Reagan's attempt to depict the Soviet Union as an 'evil empire' and Reagan had stated publicly that his view of the USSR had changed. In fact, Gorbachev was soon scoring higher opinion poll ratings in the USA than were US politicians and what became known as 'Gorbimania' hit western Europe, as people responded to his attempts to end the arms race and his talk of a 'common European home'.

This perception of Gorbachev as the main peacemaker was enhanced by statements he made in December 1988 in which he said that Soviet forces would be reduced by 500,000 over the following two years and that Soviet troops would be gradually withdrawn from the GDR, Czechoslovakia and Hungary. Gorbachev said that no reciprocal moves from the USA would be required. Significantly, perhaps, Gorbachev made these announcements without first discussing them with the Soviet defence minister.

Why was Gorbachev's announcement in 1988 that Soviet troops would withdraw from Afghanistan seen as an important step in reducing Cold War tensions?

What were the four summits which took place between the Soviet Union and the USA in the years 1985–88?

From Reagan to Bush

The November 1988 USA presidential elections were won by George Bush. After he took over in January 1989, the pace of improvement in US–Soviet relations slackened off for a time, as Bush believed Reagan had made too many concessions. When he met Gorbachev in July 1989, he was reassured by Gorbachev's statement that the USSR had no desire to challenge the USA's global dominance. Soon, Baker, the new secretary of state, developed a good relationship with Shevardnadze. By now, the Soviet Union was desperate for US financial assistance and Shevardnadze was instructed to indicate that the USSR was ready to sign the START treaty, without needing any reciprocal US concessions.

The Gorbachev Doctrine

Historians have seen the Soviet withdrawal from Afghanistan as part of a clear policy on the part of the USSR of disengaging from the developing world in order to avoid confrontation with the USA, based on a desire for security through co-operation and improved relations. One historian has called it the 'Gorbachev Doctrine'.

However, Gorbachev's actions here and in relation to nuclear disarmament and eastern Europe have also been described as the 'diplomacy of despair'. This argument maintains that the Soviet Union was forced to make more defence cuts than the USA, even though it was in an inferior military position, because of its economic difficulties.

How can Gorbachev's foreign policy be seen as a 'diplomacy of despair'?

Was the end of the Cold War also the end of the 'great contest'?

The collapse of eastern Europe, 1988–89

Part of Gorbachev's 'new thinking' was based on the idea that the Soviet Union and eastern and western Europe shared a 'common European home'. He stressed the common history and culture of Europe and argued that the security of Europe as a whole could only be resolved by pan-European initiatives and bodies.

Of particular importance was Gorbachev's public abandonment, in March 1985, of the Brezhnev Doctrine of 1968. He made it clear that Soviet troops would not be sent into any eastern European state, either to defend an existing regime or to crush reform communists or mass popular movements. He reiterated this at a Warsaw Pact meeting held in April 1985.

When Gorbachev came to power in 1985, most regimes in the Soviet bloc seemed reasonably secure and stable and many of Gorbachev's critics blamed the collapse of these states, in only four years, on Gorbachev's policies.

What was the significance of Gorbachev's abandonment of the Brezhnev Doctrine in 1985?

As part of his approach, Gorbachev encouraged his policies of *perestroika*, *glasnost* and *demokratizatsiya* in the eastern European satellites. While many citizens in these countries were keen to enjoy the new freedoms being allowed in the USSR, several eastern European governments had grave doubts about these policies. Those of the GDR, Bulgaria, Romania and Czechoslovakia tried hard at first to limit news of Gorbachev's reforms in the Soviet Union. The ruling communists in Poland and Hungary, however, welcomed the new opportunities for reform.

Poland and Hungary

In Poland, Solidarity (banned in 1981 when martial law was declared) was legalised in January 1989; in April, it agreed with the government on a package of political and economic reforms. These included elections to be held in June which resulted in a clear victory for Solidarity. In August 1989, the new Polish parliament elected the first non-communist prime minister to rule in eastern Europe in over 40 years.

In Hungary, reform communists had for some time been carrying out their own Gorbachev-style policies. These moves increased in the late 1980s and, in 1989, it was agreed that multi-party elections would be held. (The invasion of Hungary in 1956 had partly been a reaction to such reform.) Gorbachev accepted these developments in both countries.

East Germany

It took developments in the GDR to accelerate the pace of change in the rest of eastern Europe. Hungary's decision to open its border with Austria in August 1989 sparked off a crisis in East Germany. By September 1989, thousands of East Germans were crossing to West Germany through Hungary and Austria, provoking an economic crisis similar to the one that had led to the building of the Berlin Wall.

Honecker, the East German leader, unlike Ulbricht in 1961, could not rely on Soviet support, a fact made clear by Gorbachev's visit in October when he urged Honecker to carry out political and economic reforms. Demonstrations in support of democracy spread across the GDR and, on 18 October, Honecker resigned as leader of the Communist Party, to be replaced by Egon Krenz.

The demonstrations grew even bigger, culminating in a massive demonstration – numbering 500,000 – in East Berlin on 4 November. At this stage, Gorbachev indicated that the GDR must form closer ties with West Germany, pointing out that the USSR could no longer afford to subsidise its economy. On 7 November, the GDR government resigned and, on 8 November, Krenz decided to open the Berlin Wall. This breaching of the Berlin Wall was the

The dismantling of the Berlin Wall, November 1989. This act came to symbolise the collapse of communism and the end of the Cold War.

most dramatic example that the Cold War and Soviet control of eastern Europe were nearing their end. Thousands of Berliners rushed to cross the border of what was no longer a divided city.

Czechoslovakia and Bulgaria

These events in East Germany stimulated mass protests in Czechoslovakia and Bulgaria. In Czechoslovakia, in particular, the atmosphere was reminiscent of the Prague Spring of 1968. The communist government resigned and a multi-party system was established – ironically, the chairman of the new federal parliament was Alexander Dubček. As a result of this 'velvet revolution', Vaclav Havel, a dissident, became president. In Bulgaria, too, mass demonstrations led to the government's resignation and the emergence of a multi-party democracy.

Romania

The one exception to these peaceful revolutions was Romania, where Ceaucescu, the country's leader, tried to use the army to crush demonstrations. After the riots spread to Bucharest, the government fell. Ceaucescu was subsequently executed.

The USA signalled that they would have no objections if Gorbachev sent in Soviet troops to help the Romanian army against Ceaucescu. However, Gorbachev's only intervention in eastern Europe was to continue to encourage liberal reforms. (Earlier, on 27 October, the Warsaw Pact had declared there would be no military intervention to support unpopular governments.)

Although Gorbachev hoped that the new governments would be reform communists or socialists which would establish democratic socialism in eastern Europe, all he could be sure of was that the old-style communist governments had gone. The Soviet Union allowed the dissolution of its security zone that had been the foundation and main aim of its foreign policy since 1945 and which had played a large part in the start of the Cold War. This collapse of the Soviet bloc was a clear indication of how serious the decline of the USSR was, both internally and externally, by the end of the 1980s. All these eastern European states had been heavily in debt to the Soviet Union, thus adding to its own economic problems.

How did developments in East Germany contribute to the final collapse of the eastern European bloc?

The Final Act, 1990–91

Further arms reductions

The collapse of the eastern European regimes – and hence of the Soviet buffer zone – played a big part in ending the Cold War. In December 1989, at the Malta Summit, Gorbachev and Bush officially declared the end of the Cold

War. This symbolic statement came about when Gorbachev announced that the USSR no longer saw the USA as an enemy. The USA offered the USSR economic help, and informal agreements were reached on the future of eastern Europe, Germany and the Baltic republics. (On the last issue, Gorbachev was prepared to consider a loosening of their ties to the USSR but not, at first, their independence.) They also agreed to work towards reducing the size of conventional forces in Europe. After the Malta Summit, Shevardnadze stated that the Cold War had been 'buried at the bottom of the Mediterranean'.

What was the main significance of the Malta Summit in 1989?

The question of Germany remained a serious security concern for the Soviet Union. At first, Gorbachev hoped to avoid German reunification, believing that – with the uncertain political and diplomatic policies likely to emerge in eastern Europe – a divided Germany would be less of a security threat. The Soviets were also concerned that NATO would extend its membership eastwards, right up to the Soviet Union's borders. By February 1990, however, Gorbachev had accepted that it was up to the Germans to decide whether they wanted reunification. He hoped that if reunification took place the new Germany would remain neutral. However, Kohl, the West German chancellor, made it clear that a united Germany would join NATO. In May, the GDR signed a reunification treaty and the West German deutschmark became the common currency in July.

Gorbachev was also beginning to negotiate on the withdrawal of Soviet troops from the eastern European states. To ease this process, the USA offered much needed financial assistance but, essentially, Gorbachev had to agree to everything that Bush had wanted – in particular accepting the reunification of Germany – in order to get the financial assistance. Once again, Gorbachev acted without prior discussion with the Soviet foreign minister or the military.

In the end, Gorbachev – under strong pressure from the West and having obtained some **concessions** – accepted reunification of Germany (and its membership of NATO) in September 1990 and it finally took place on 3 October 1990. German unification soon came to symbolise the end of the divisions that had existed in Europe since 1947.

The **concessions** were that the former West German army would be reduced and no NATO forces would be deployed in the former GDR.

In November 1990, the CFE Treaty, which led to a reduction in troop deployments, was signed. At the same time, further talks were begun on the reduction of nuclear weapons. This resulted in the START treaty, which was signed at the Moscow Summit in July 1991, ten years after it was first drawn up. Considerable cuts in the size of US and Soviet strategic nuclear stockpiles were agreed and talks for a START 2 treaty were begun.

The collapse of the Soviet Union

Initially, when some Soviet republics – especially the Baltic republics – began to push for independence, the USA stated that it was not in favour of the break-up of the Soviet Union. It seemed to prefer Gorbachev's plans for a looser confederation to those of Yeltsin, who intended to break up the USSR into 15 separate nation states, each with its own government. The USA preferred to deal with one central power and feared the possible consequences of the instability which might result from any break-up; the USA was also keen to support Gorbachev because it wanted Soviet support in the Gulf War against Iraq (Iraq was allied to the Soviet Union and several thousand Soviet troops were stationed there).

Consequently, when violent clashes between protesters and the security forces occurred in Lithuania and Latvia in January 1991, the USA did not respond by breaking off relations with the Soviet Union. After continued tension in the Baltic republics in February, Bush decided not to travel to a summit which was to have been held in Moscow, though he did visit the USSR later that year. By May 1991 Gorbachev was beginning to think that US economic aid promised to him would not be given after all.

Though the implementation of CFE Treaty was speeded up, resulting in the USA announcing $1.5 billion in credits for the USSR to purchase grain, tensions began to resurface. This stemmed from US insistence that further significant economic aid would not be forthcoming unless the Soviet Union moved to a market, or capitalist, economy. Matters were made worse when the KGB claimed to have evidence that the USA was attempting to bring about the disintegration of the USSR.

As we have seen, developments under Gorbachev – especially the loss of eastern Europe and the acceptance of Soviet nuclear inferiority – had alarmed his critics in the Soviet leadership. Their fears were increased in July 1991 when the Warsaw Pact was dissolved, leaving NATO still in existence and now unchallenged. A group of political and military leaders who were opposed to plans to give more power to the Soviet republics (which had been given mass support in a referendum in March 1991) decided to overthrow Gorbachev. The plotters feared that this move to weaken central control would result in the disintegration of the USSR.

In August 1991, these plotters launched their attempted coup while Gorbachev was on holiday. At first, Bush seemed prepared to accept the coup. Then he changed his mind and made contact with Yeltsin who, as the newly elected president of the Russian republic (the biggest and most important of the 15 republics that made up the USSR), was potentially Gorbachev's successor. Yeltsin put himself at the head of popular protests against the coup. This, together with the fact that the bulk of the army and security forces refused to support the coup, resulted in its failure.

Although Gorbachev remained Soviet president, his position was increasingly undermined by Yeltsin, who used his control of Russia to hasten the

The former Soviet Union and its republics.

collapse of the Soviet Union. The USA accepted that the strong nationalist feelings that had emerged meant that the break-up of the Soviet Union was inevitable as it was becoming clear that Gorbachev was losing control.

In December 1991, Russia – along with the important republics of Belorussia and the Ukraine – declared the formation of the Commonwealth of Independent States (CIS). Significantly, they informed Bush of their decision before they informed Gorbachev. On 25 December 1991, Gorbachev announced his resignation as president of the Soviet Union in a television broadcast.

With this step, the Soviet Union – which had already broken up in practice – was declared formally to have ended. This left the USA with supreme global power after almost 75 years of struggle – the 'great contest' was over or, as expressed by Fukuyama (a US official), the 'end of history' had arrived, resulting in the final victory of 'liberal' capitalism. Others, such as R. Crockatt, have seen 1991 as the end of 50 years of war between the USA and the USSR – a war that had clearly been won by the USA, with its greater economic strength.

What is meant by the claim that the collapse of the Soviet Union in 1991 was the 'end of history'?

US power

Historians are still debating the causes of the collapse of the Soviet Union and thus the end of the Cold War. There were clearly many long-standing economic and political weaknesses within the Soviet Union itself which played a big part in its eventual downfall. These included bureaucratic control of the economy which resulted in much inefficiency and waste, and rates of productivity significantly lower than those achieved in the West. Its undemocratic political system alienated large sections of Soviet society and it would seem that Gorbachev's reforms came too late to save the system. However, it does appear that earlier US policies – especially maintaining and deepening the nuclear arms race – contributed to the distortion and ultimate collapse of the Soviet Union's economic and political structures.

Though the collapse of the Soviet Union has left the USA as the only remaining superpower, China remains controlled by a communist party and, as a nuclear power with a large population and a rapidly expanding economy, China has the potential to become a rival superpower in the near future.

Historical sources

1 Mikhail Gorbachev, explaining his 'new thinking' in relation to Soviet foreign policy

In late May 1986, we discussed the new role of Soviet diplomacy at a conference held at the ministry of foreign affairs . . . Today, I consider this meeting the starting point for the full-scale implementation of our 'new thinking'.

We realised it was vitally necessary to correct the distorted ideas we had about other nations. These misconceptions had made us oppose the rest of the world for many decades, which had negative effects on our economy . . .

Gorbachev, *Memoirs*, London, 1996, pp. 402–03

2 Extract from a news report of February 1991

At a meeting of the political and consultative committee of the Warsaw Treaty Organisation in Budapest on 25 February, foreign and defence ministers from Bulgaria, Czechoslovakia, Hungary, Poland, Romania and the Soviet Union unanimously approved and signed a protocol cancelling the validity of all military agreements, organs and structures of the Warsaw Treaty with effect from 31 March.

Moves to dissolve the military alliance, which were first apparent at a Warsaw Pact summit meeting in June 1990, were intensified after January 1991. They were followed by reports on 11 February that the Soviet President

Mikhail Gorbachev had written to leaders of member states recommending 'the liquidation of Warsaw Pact military structures by 1 April'.

E. G. Rayner, *The Cold War*, London, 1992, p. 88

Historical-source questions

1 What did Gorbachev mean in Source 1 when he referred to previous Soviet foreign policy having had 'negative effects on our economy'?

2 To what extent can these 'negative effects' explain the 'new thinking' of Gorbachev's foreign policy after 1985?

3 What was the 'Warsaw Treaty Organisation' referred to in Source 2?

Summary questions

1 Identify and explain *two* factors which led Gorbachev to adopt a new foreign policy after 1985.

2 Compare the importance of at least *three* factors which contributed to the collapse of the Soviet Union and the communist governments of eastern Europe.

The Cold War in Asia and the Americas, 1949–75

16

China and the Cold War

Focus questions

◆ What attitude did the USA take to communism in China before 1949?

◆ How did the communist victory in China in 1949 affect the Cold War?

Significant dates

1921	CCP founded
1923	GMD–CCP alliance
1925	Jiang Jieshi becomes leader of GMD
1931	Japanese invasion of Manchuria
1936	Sian Incident; formation of GMD–CCP United Front
1937	*July* Japanese invasion of China
1945	*December* Marshall Mission negotiates GMD–CCP truce
1947	'Red Scare' in USA
1949	*January* Communists capture Beijing
	August–September USSR explodes, then announces, first Soviet A-bomb test
October Communist victory
1950	*February* Klaus Fuchs spying revelations; Sino-Soviet Treaty; McCarthy begins his campaign in the USA
March Alger Hiss spy trial
April NSC 68

Overview

At first, the USA was not overly concerned about the civil war in China between the People's National Party (GMD) and the Chinese Communist Party (CCP) which broke out in 1927. Japanese aggression – first against Manchuria and then against mainland China – led the USA to give support to Jiang Jieshi's nationalist government after 1941.

In 1945, the USA and the Soviet Union encouraged the two sides to form a coalition government which culminated, in December 1945, in a truce brought about by the US Marshall Mission. When the truce broke down in early 1946, the USA at first continued to support Jiang Jieshi. When communist victory seemed imminent in 1948, however, the USA began to slow down its aid.

The USA tended to see communist China as Stalin's tool and refused to recognise Mao's government. The 'loss' of China compounded the growing Cold War in Europe and the loss of the USA's nuclear monopoly earlier in the year was seen as a defeat for Truman's policy of containment.

The Sino-Soviet Treaty in 1950 increased US concerns about the communist threat and contributed to the McCarthy 'witch-hunts' in the early 1950s. It also led Truman to order a review of USA foreign policy, resulting in the document known as NSC 68.

What attitude did the USA take to communism in China before 1949?

Early Soviet involvement

The Chinese Communist Party was formed in 1921; one of its founder members was **Mao Zedong**. In its early years, the CCP was advised by the Soviet government to co-operate with Sun Yatsen and his nationalist Guomindang party. When Sun died in 1925, he was succeeded by Jiang Jieshi who soon moved the party to the right.

In 1927, Jiang began what turned out to be a protracted civil war against the CCP. Despite receiving military advisers and equipment from Nazi Germany, Jiang was unable to crush the communists. This civil war was complicated by Japanese aggression against China. In the Sian Incident in 1936, some of Jiang's own officers forced him to form a United Front with the CCP against the Japanese invaders, but Jiang remained more concerned with weakening the communists.

US involvement

Before 1937, the USA had not placed much importance on events in China. Japan's invasion of China in 1937, however, caused them concern, given that there was growing competition between Japan and the USA in the Pacific region as both saw China and the Pacific as an important area for raw materials and trade.

When Japan attacked Pearl Harbor in December 1941, the USA decided to aid Jiang's government against the Japanese, even though they were supported by Nazi Germany – this shows the importance the USA placed on China and the Pacific. By this time, there were 2 million Japanese soldiers in China (over 50 per cent of Japan's armed forces). Jiang was much encouraged by the USA's entry into the war against Japan.

Despite **US military aid**, Jiang's forces were not very effective and were

Born in 1893, **Mao Zedong** was a librarian at Beijing University who became active in the May Fourth Movement, which protested against Japanese demands for Chinese territory after the First World War. He was a founder member of the Chinese Communist Party in 1921 and, by 1924, he was a member of its Central Committee. In October 1934, he led the Long March of the communist Red Army to the north of China in order to avoid destruction by the GMD. In 1935 he was elected chairman of the CCP, a post he retained until his death in 1976. Under him, China became a one-party state.

What was the outcome of the Sian Incident in 1936?

US military aid took the form of military equipment (which reached Jiang via the Burma Road); later, the USA built airfields in south-eastern China which allowed more supplies to be brought in, as well as allowing US bombers to destroy Japanese naval and merchant shipping.

soon pulled back to the south; the Chinese Red Army, however, stayed behind enemy lines where it was able to launch increasingly effective guerrilla warfare campaigns which put them at the head of resistance to the Japanese.

As the Japanese began to lose the war, they retreated from south China, northwards into Manchuria. This enabled the Chinese communists (who were operating behind enemy lines) to move into these areas – by 1945, they controlled 18 such 'liberation areas'. These were essentially rural areas where the majority of the Chinese population were peasants and, as in the **Jiangsi and Yanan soviets**, the CCP quickly initiated popular social reforms.

The Japanese occupation of China ended in August 1945 when the USA dropped atomic bombs on Hiroshima and Nagasaki, and the Soviet Union declared war on Japan and invaded Manchuria.

By then, it was clear that a full-scale civil war was about to break out again between the GMD and the CCP. (In fact, the United Front had not lasted long – from 1938 onwards, Jiang had put more and more effort into trying to crush the communists.) After August 1945, the GMD and the CCP rushed to be the first to move into the northern cities and areas that had been occupied by the Japanese and to seize the weapons of surrendering Japanese troops. The communists were much closer to the surrendering Japanese troops as Jiang's forces had retreated some 1,500 km to the south.

Jiang hoped that US backing would enable him to take control of all of China once again. For its part, the USA did not want to see the Chinese communists win this war and so create a new communist state in China. They already had serious differences with Stalin's Russia and were concerned that a communist China might frustrate their plans for the Pacific region – it would certainly end the Soviet Union's isolation. To prevent this, the USA organised a massive airlift of nearly 100,000 GMD troops to the key cities and ports along the coast and sent US troops to China.

Despite giving this aid, the USA (along with the USSR) did not want Jiang to renew the civil war – they wanted to prevent the communists from gaining power. They advised him to form a coalition government with the CCP. In December 1945, General George C. Marshall was sent to China to arrange a truce between the two sides and to broker an agreement on power sharing. Marshall realised the GMD could not win an outright victory and feared the renewal of civil war might encourage the Soviet Union to intervene in China on the side of the CCP. He pointed out to Jiang that, if he formed a coalition now while the GMD were stronger than the CCP, then he would have majority control. At the same time, Stalin – in order not to upset the West and so risk jeopardising agreements on eastern Europe – instructed Mao to agree to join such a coalition government. However, a section in the CCP pushed for an immediate military solution.

The **Jiangsi and Yanan soviets** were two areas where the communists had been in control since the 1930s.

Why did the USA airlift Jiang's troops to the major cities and ports in China after Japan had surrendered in August 1945?

What did the USA's Marshall Mission to China try to achieve?

At first the Marshall Mission was successful in that both sides signed a truce. However, this success was short-lived as the truce broke down in January 1946; by June 1946, the civil war was again in full swing.

It looked as though the GMD would win – they had an army of 3 million and were supported by US money, training and equipment, an airforce and, thanks to the US airlift, had control of all the major cities, ports and railways. In addition, most foreign governments – including Soviet Russia – recognised Jiang as the legitimate ruler of China. The communists, in contrast, had only about 1 million troops, no airforce, controlled no important cities and were not even backed by Stalin's USSR, which was still urging the CCP to form a coalition with Jiang and the GMD.

Significantly, though, communist control of rural areas meant they had close contact with the majority of the population and their determined resistance to the Japanese invaders had earned them considerable respect from the Chinese people. Jiang's government, on the other hand, was corrupt and inefficient, and his ruthless suppression of all opposition suggested that he was intent on establishing a military dictatorship.

Jiang's failure to carry out the military and social welfare reforms suggested by the Marshall Mission was one of the reasons why the truce broke down – the CCP accused Jiang and the USA of bad faith. Initially, the USA had said it would not continue to give aid to Jiang if he refused to initiate some social reforms. At first, even though no reforms were taking place, the USA continued to send Jiang massive military aid because of the Truman Doctrine and the policy of containment (which committed the USA to supporting any regime that was anti-communist).

Despite this support, China was not seen as being as important a priority as Japan in the USA's overall foreign policy in Asia. After 1945 the USA had chosen to prioritise support for Japan so that it might act as an anti-communist state in Asia. It was this policy which helped swing Mao round to supporting those communists who had, all along, pressed for military action. The Red Army, now under the control of Lin Biao, was renamed the People's Liberation Army (PLA).

Despite early setbacks, the PLA was in a much stronger position by the end of 1947. By now, morale in the GMD-held cities was crumbling as a result of the combined effects of GMD corruption, inflation and strikes – the strikes were often organised by local communists who had survived GMD purges and Japanese executions (purges and executions took place wherever Jiang or the Japanese captured communists). As the situation deteriorated, more and more GMD troops deserted to the PLA, taking their weapons with them. At this point, the USA (which had so far given Jiang over $200 million in military aid) concluded that the GMD were virtually defeated. By now Truman was

Why did the truce between the Guomindang and the CCP break down in early 1946?

prepared to leave Jiang to his fate as China was no longer seen as having any real strategic significance for the USA.

Early in 1948, despite the emerging Cold War in Europe, Marshall, now secretary of state, persuaded Truman to stop any further aid to Jiang. The PLA continued its successes in 1948 and, in January 1949, captured Beijing. In April, Jiang's capital, Nanjing, fell to the communists and Jiang fled to Taiwan (then known as Formosa) with China's entire gold reserves and 200,000 troops. On 1 October 1949, Mao proclaimed the birth of the new People's Republic of China.

How did the communist victory in China in 1949 affect the Cold War?

Impact on the USA

By October 1949, the Cold War tensions after the Berlin Crisis of 1948–49 (see pages 146–47), began to shift to Asia. When the USA decided in 1948 not to continue supporting Jiang, it still had a nuclear monopoly. As we have seen, this monopoly ended in August 1949 when the USSR unexpectedly exploded its first atomic device. The communist victory in China, following shortly after, led to accusations that Truman's government was 'soft' on communism in China and was therefore responsible for the 'loss of China'.

In the summer of 1949, Mao had declared that China would move from its neutral position to one closer to the USSR (it was known as his 'lean to one side' policy). Initially, because of past disagreements with Stalin, Mao had approached the USA for assistance, but Truman refused to recognise his new government. Mao had no choice but to turn to the USSR for economic aid. Despite Stalin's earlier disagreements with Mao over the CCP's decision to continue the civil war in China in 1946, he accepted Mao's request and in February the Soviet Union and China signed a 30-year Treaty of Friendship, Alliance and Mutual Assistance (or the Sino-Soviet Treaty).

However, this aid was rather limited (partly because of the Soviet Union's own immediate post-war economic problems). In all, only $300 million was offered over 5 years and most of this was in the form of credits, not cash; in addition, interest was to be charged. More valuable was Stalin's offer of technical advice and assistance – in total, over 10,000 engineers and planning experts were sent to help Mao restore the Chinese economy and to begin a slow socialist transformation. Later, in 1953, under the influence of these Soviet advisers, China launched its First Five-Year Plan. In exchange, Stalin insisted that joint Sino-Soviet companies be established to give the USSR more control and to guarantee a flow of funds back to the USSR. More significantly for the future, Stalin refused Mao's request for nuclear weapons.

What did China receive from the Soviet Union as a result of the 1950 treaty?

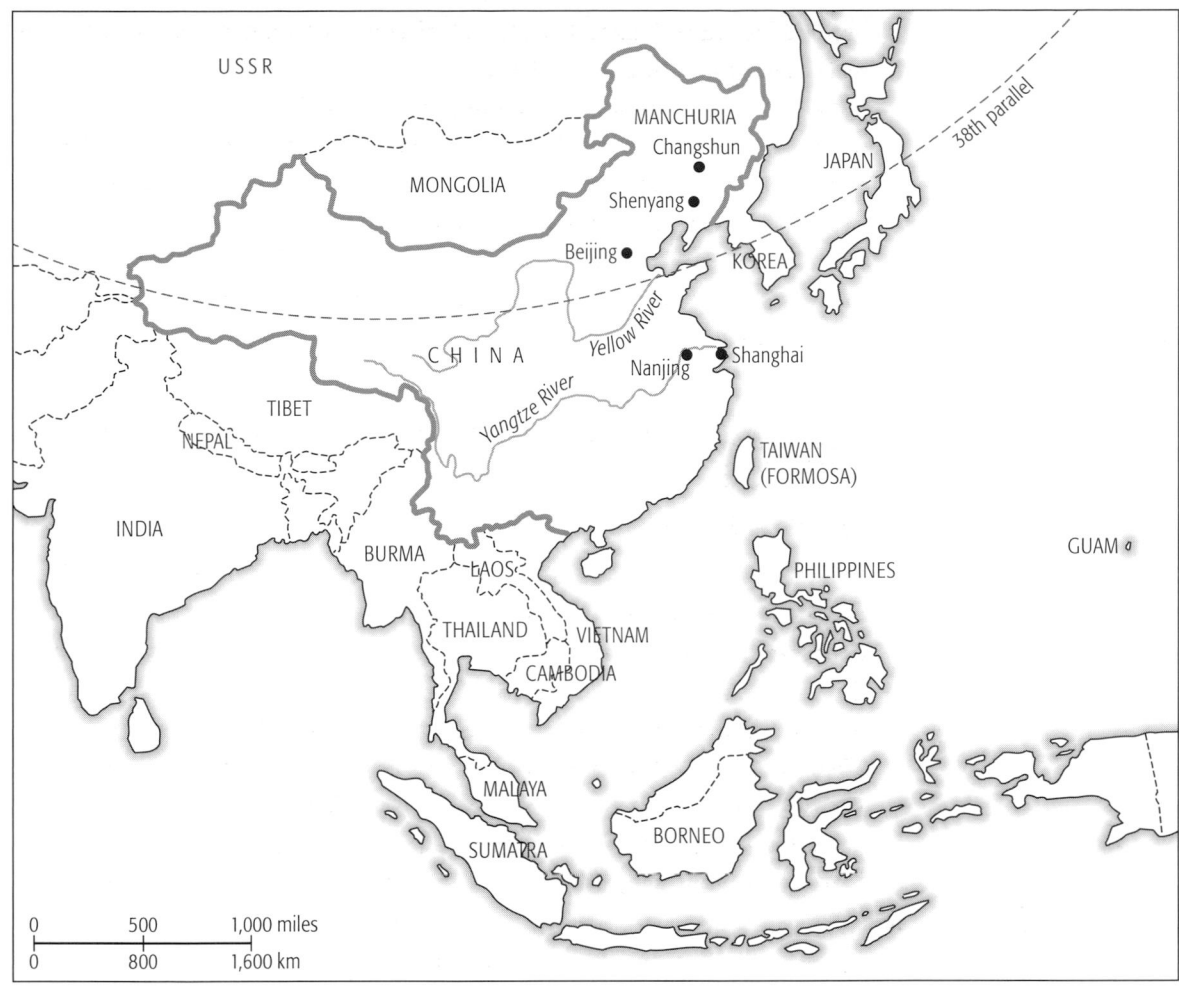

China and Asia in 1949.

The US government's initial response to this treaty was cautious. Dean Acheson, the secretary of state, thought that establishing good relations with Mao might be beneficial to US interests – despite his dislike of communism. Although the USA still refused to recognise the new People's Republic of China, recognising instead Jiang's regime in Taiwan as the legitimate Chinese government, it stopped short, at first, of guaranteeing Jiang US military help should Communist China decide to retake the island. Acheson even argued that recognising Mao's government might help break up its new friendship with the Soviet Union, but this was not possible in the anti-communist hysteria that was about to be stirred up during the early 1950s by the Republicans.

McCarthyism

These developments in China heightened Cold War tensions and helped trigger the launch of **McCarthy**'s anti-communist crusade within the USA. It was

Born in 1909, Joseph **McCarthy** became Republican senator for Wisconsin in 1945. In 1950, when it seemed he might not be re-elected in 1952, he began his campaign against suspected communists in the US administration. In particular, McCarthy (who was a Roman Catholic from an ordinary social background) turned his hatred on the liberal east coast 'establishment' which tended to hold the most important administrative posts. Dean Acheson personified all that McCarthy hated – he was a Protestant, came from an upper-class family and had gone from an elite private school to one of the best universities. In 1954, McCarthy began to lose credibility after he failed to supply any proof during a televised hearing. He then went on to accuse the army and even Eisenhower. He died in 1957.

How did events in China contribute to what became known as McCarthyism in the USA?

The **Un-American Activities Committee** was originally set up in 1938. In the early 1950s, it was used by Senator McCarthy in his campaign against communism in the USA. His early activities had pushed Truman into issuing Executive Order 9835 (a 'loyalty' test for civil servants) and had persuaded Congress (despite Truman's opposition) into passing the McCarran–Nixon Internal Security Act (to get all communist organisations to register with the government). Once in charge of the committee, McCarthy's 'Red Scare' took off, despite the Senate's Tydings Committee reporting in 1950 that his claims were a 'fraud and a hoax'.

aimed initially at the government's foreign policy advisers in the Far Eastern division of the State Department, but soon began to affect most sections of American society.

In November 1948, despite criticism of his China policy, Truman won the presidential elections. This was the fifth consecutive victory for the Democrats. One result was that party politics in the USA became increasingly bitter, with the Republicans accusing the Democrats of being 'soft' on communism, especially after the Soviet Union's development of atomic weapons and the 'loss' of China in 1949.

Once the Cold War truly began in 1947, a 'Red Scare' started to grip increasing numbers of Americans. One of the consequences of this in government circles was the introduction of loyalty tests for federal government employees (in which they had to swear an oath of loyalty to the government); a Loyalty Review Board was set up to hear appeals against dismissal. The Congress, elected in 1946, responded to Cold War tensions by making greater use of the House of Representatives **Un-American Activities Committee** (HUAC). In 1947, it had turned its attention on Hollywood actors, screen-writers and directors and ordered ten leading figures in the film industry to appear before the Committee.

Initially, the Hollywood Ten (some of whom had once been members of the small Communist Party of the USA or CPUSA) refused to discuss their politics and several important actors (such as Katherine Hepburn, Lauren Bacall and Humphrey Bogart) set up the Committee for the First Amendment to support their refusal to testify. However, media campaigns and statements by churches and other religious groups stirred up the public and soon the Screen Actors Guild (the film actors' union) began to operate a blacklist against suspected communists (from 1947 to 1952, its president was the actor Ronald Reagan).

This 'Red Scare' spread to schools and universities, some of which began to require that all teachers and lecturers swore an oath of loyalty, and reading lists were investigated by HUAC. In 1948, several lecturers and professors were dismissed for alleged links with the CPUSA. In 1949, this scare spread to American unions when the Congress of Industrial Organisations (CIO) expelled several communist-led trade unions.

After the Sino-Soviet Treaty was signed in February 1950, the Republican Party decided to step up its campaign against Truman in the run-up to the November 1950 presidential elections. Truman was partly to blame for his predicament because he had deliberately exaggerated the communist threat in 1947 in order to get congressional approval for aid to Greece and Turkey and, later, for the Marshall Plan (see pages 140–41).

In February 1950, the British announced that Klaus Fuchs (who had

Hollywood film stars protesting against the witch-hunt organised by McCarthy and the Un-American Activities Committee. Humphrey Bogart and Lauren Bacall can be seen in the centre.

worked on the USA's atomic bomb **Manhattan Project**) had been heading a spy ring which had passed nuclear secrets to the Russians. The month before, in January 1950, Alger Hiss, a government official, had been found guilty of passing classified US information to the Soviet Union during the late 1930s (the Republican congressman Richard Nixon had played a major role in exposing this). Both these spy scares were used by McCarthy to further his cause. He claimed that he had a list of 205 State Department officials who were members of the CPUSA. He also said that Acheson, the secretary of state, had this list but had taken no action against these officials. (Later, he reduced the number of accused officials to 57, a pattern he repeated many times – he would publicly brand people as communists, or communist sympathisers, with no hard evidence, and then change his story.)

NSC 68

The events of 1949 in Asia, combined with growing Republican criticism of his foreign policy, led Truman to call for a complete review of his administration's Cold War policies in January 1950. He believed that, if nothing else, the review would help undermine McCarthy's claims that his administration was 'soft' on communism.

The National Security Council, which carried out the review, produced its report (known as NSC 68 – see also page 154) in April 1950. The report stated

The **Manhattan Project** refers to the Allied military atomic research project set up by Britain and the USA soon after the outbreak of the Second World War, as British and US scientists had warned their respective governments that German scientists might be developing a nuclear bomb. Even before the USA entered the Second World War in 1941, the research project (code-named 'Manhattan') was set up in the USA. Millions of dollars were spent and the project was under the authority of US General L. Groves, with the main scientist being Professor J. R. Oppenheimer of the USA. The first atomic device was exploded in the New Mexico desert on 16 July 1945. After the Klaus Fuchs spying revelations, Oppenheimer became one of the victims of McCarthy's witch-hunts.

that US policy under Truman was broadly in line with the assessment of the Soviet threat made by Kennan in his 'Long Telegram' of 1946 (see page 138). It upheld the view that the Soviet Union was a military threat because of its commitment to worldwide revolution and because it was a 'totalitarian dictatorship'. The document also pointed out the continuity of Truman's policies since 1947: his commitment to 'contain' communism where it already existed, to erode its influence and power and, eventually, to bring about its ultimate downfall.

The report put forward the view that the best strategy to follow in Asia would be to build Japan into a regional power centre which could, in alliance with the USA, block any moves by the Soviet Union and China (which was seen as Stalin's junior partner, simply carrying out his instructions). Following this strategy, along with strengthening western Europe, was seen as the best way to create a global balance of power favourable to US interests.

What did NSC 68 say about US interests in Asia?

One significant change of direction, however, was signalled by the suggestion that US foreign policy objectives could only be met by a huge increase in US military strength. Until now, the USA had relied on using its dominant position in the global economy to wage, and win, the Cold War.

Now, according to this report, the USA needed to expand both its conventional and nuclear forces. It urged an immediate acceleration in the quest to develop the hydrogen bomb in order to restore the USA's nuclear monopoly lost in 1949. The authors of the report argued that possessing a new type of nuclear weapon would allow the USA to deny the USSR any balance of power and so ensure that the Soviet Union would lack the ability to make an effective Soviet response to US policies.

Another significant departure made by the NSC 68 was the suggestion that the policy of containment (which was based on the belief that, in the long term, the USSR was not a serious threat) should be replaced by one of confrontation. By confrontation they meant attempting an offensive 'roll back' of communism in Asia as well as in eastern Europe and, eventually, the Soviet Union itself.

Finally, NSC 68 was also important in that it recommended that the USA should have powerful military forces on a permanent basis, even though it was not technically engaged in a war. (During times of peace, the USA had previously always reduced its military strength.)

Though Truman broadly accepted this analysis and set of proposals, he calculated that the US electorate would be unlikely to accept the massive increase in taxes and cuts in welfare spending that would be necessary to implement these recommendations. For this reason, Truman put the report's recommendations on hold until the Korean War broke out.

Historical sources

1 Extract from the NSC 68 document, produced by the USA's National Security Council in April 1950

The Soviet Union is animated by a new fanatic faith antithetical to our own and seeks to impose its absolute authority over the rest of the world . . . The Kremlin is inescapably militant because it possesses a worldwide revolutionary movement and because it is a totalitarian dictatorship. It is quite clear from Soviet theory and practice that the Kremlin seeks to bring the free world under its domination by the methods of war.

O. Edwards, *The USA and the Cold War*, London, 1997, p. 64

2 Zhou Enlai, premier and foreign secretary of communist China, in a statement to the Chinese News Agency on 18 March 1950

The whole world knows that the US Government, in an attempt to annex China, has supported Jiang Jieshi in waging large-scale civil war, denying the Chinese people any opportunity to live in independence and peace. The US Government is supplying the Jiang Jieshi brigands with aircraft to bomb the mainland of China. It is employing similar methods in support of the puppets Bao Dai, Syngman Rhee and Quirino in undermining national independence movements in Vietnam, South Korea and the Philippines. Acheson says to the Chinese people: 'Why don't you ask for American aid?' But from their personal experience the Chinese people have realised what American so-called 'aid' means. It means death for millions; it means the loss of national freedom and rights.

E. G. Rayner, *The Cold War*, London, 1992, p. 24

Historical-source questions

1   What do you understand by the terms 'new fanatic faith' and 'the Kremlin' in Source 1?
2   What considerations should be made before accepting as fact the claims of Source 1?
3   Who was Jiang Jieshi, mentioned in Source 2?
4   What post was held by Acheson, referred to in Source 2?
5   Why must the reliability of Source 2 be questioned?

Summary questions

1   Identify and explain any *two* ways in which the victory of the Chinese communists in 1949 affected the development of the Cold War.
2   Identify and explain any *two* limitations in the way the USSR supported communist China in the period 1937–50.

17

The Korean War, 1950–53

Focus questions

◆ What caused the Korean War?

◆ What impact did the Korean War have on the Cold War?

Significant dates

1945	*August*	Korea divided along the 38th parallel; Allied Council set up by the Big Four to administer Japan
1948		Soviet troops leave North Korea
1949	*June*	US troops leave South Korea
1950	*January*	Acheson's Defence Perimeter speech
	June	Start of Korean War; US resolution accepted by UN Security Council; Inchon counteroffensive by MacArthur
	October	Truman decides on invasion of North Korea; Chinese troops intervene to help North Korea
1951	*April*	MacArthur sacked
	July	Peace talks begin
	August	US military alliance with the Philippines; Anzus Pact
	September	Treaty with Japan
1952	*May*	US occupation army leaves Japan
1953	*January*	Eisenhower becomes president
	March	Stalin dies
	July	Armistice signed

Overview

In 1945 Korea was temporarily divided into a communist North and capitalist South. In June 1950 the North attacked the South in an attempt to reunify the country. The USA, which was backing the South, was able to use the Soviet Union's boycott of the UN Security Council to persuade the UN to agree to send an army to help the South.

After early victories, the North was pushed back by US/UN forces, commanded by the US General **MacArthur**. Once the North had been pushed out of the South, the US/UN forces invaded the North. As they approached the border with China, a massive Chinese army went in to aid the North.

A clash over strategy, followed by insubordination, led Truman to sack MacArthur. Soon a stalemate in the Korean War was reached. This continued for almost two years, until an armistice was signed in July 1953. In the meantime, the USA had arranged a series of military alliances in the Pacific, designed to secure what it called the Defence Perimeter. Crucial to this was the reconstruction of Japan.

What caused the Korean War?

Korea lost its independence in 1910, when it was taken over by Japan. It remained a Japanese colony until August 1945. When Japan surrendered at the end of the Second World War, US and Soviet troops had moved, respectively, into the South and North of Korea, which was temporarily divided along the 38th parallel for the purpose of dealing with surrendering Japanese troops.

As the Cold War began to develop in Europe, the USA and USSR were unable to reach agreement on the reunification of Korea – they could not agree on what form the government should take, the type of economy it should have or on the alliances it should make. The American and Russian zones of occupation became, in practice, two separate states – this was formalised in 1948. The communist and industrial North was ruled by Kim Il Sung and the capitalist and mainly agricultural South was ruled by Syngman Rhee.

Both regimes were extremely authoritarian and both leaders (both of whom intended to remain as leader in any future reunification) were nationalists who resented the division of their country and who wanted to bring about reunification as soon as possible.

The Soviet Union – which wanted unification of Korea under Kim – withdrew its troops from Korea in the autumn of 1948 and the USA – which wanted the unification of Korea under Rhee – finally withdrew its troops from Korea in June 1949.

Neither side seemed too concerned about Korea's immediate future. Stalin had been worried, because of the USSR's common border with Korea, about the kind of regime which might rule after 1945: with Kim Il Sung in charge of the North, his security concerns seem to have been satisfied. In January 1950, the US secretary of state, Dean Acheson, did not include South Korea in his list of countries that the USA would automatically defend against any communist aggression in his Defence Perimeter speech (see below). Truman supported

Born in 1880, General Douglas **MacArthur** fought in the First World War and became the youngest commander in the US army in France. In 1930, he was promoted to chief of staff and, during the Second World War, was in charge of the military campaign against Japan in the Pacific. He took the formal surrender of Japan in 1945, and was in charge of the administration of Japan until 1951. In 1950, at the age of 70, he was appointed commander of the UN forces in Korea, but was dismissed in 1951 for opposing Truman's strategy and for acts of insubordination.

Why was Korea divided into North and South after the Second World War?

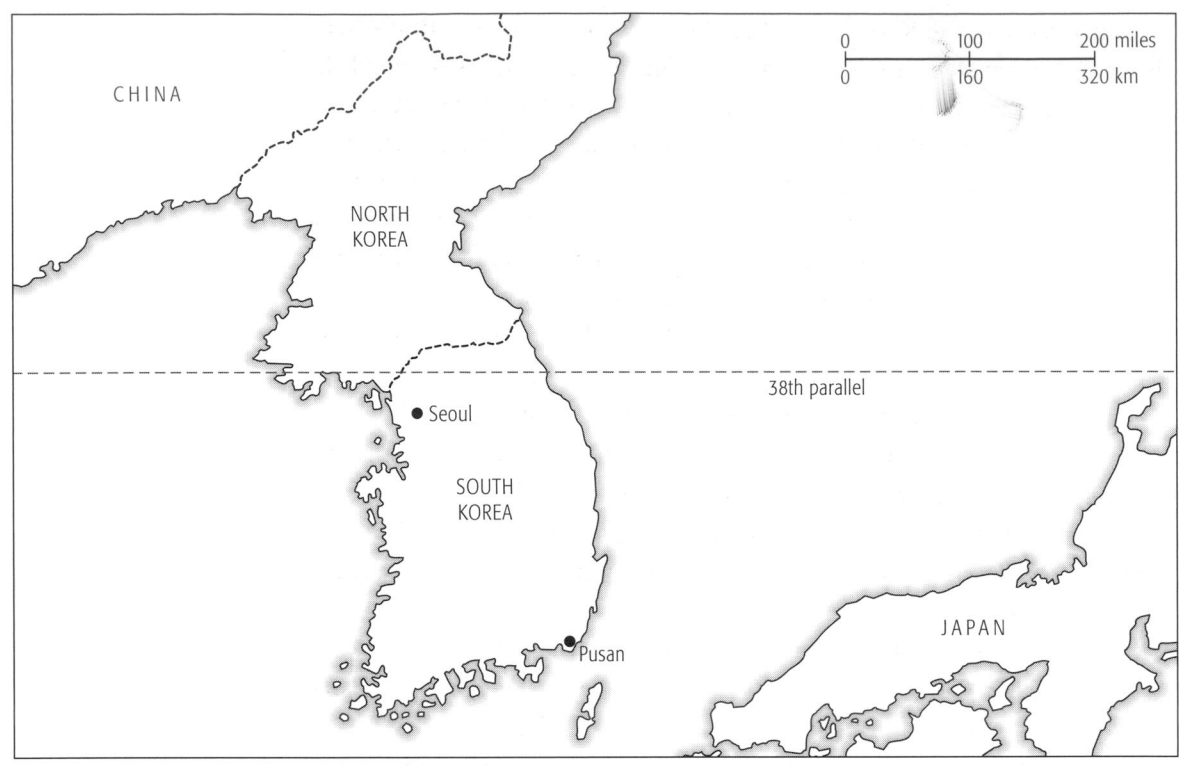

The division of Korea in 1950, before the start of the Korean War.

The **defensive perimeter** was the US military strategy developed in relation to Asia: war plans were drawn up to defend a crescent of off-shore Pacific islands against any possible communist threat from the Soviet Union or China. These islands were Japan, the Ryukyu islands, Guam and the Philippines. These formed an inverted U-shape, and all had US airbases and garrisons.

him in believing that mainland Asia was outside the USA's Pacific **defensive perimeter**. Economically, Korea was felt to have little real significance.

The Korean War began in June 1950, when a large North Korean army began its invasion of South Korea, in an attempt to reunite the country; there is some evidence to suggest that a similar invasion was being prepared by the ruler of South Korea. When the attack happened, it was not obvious that it would become an important turning point in the Cold War.

Soviet expansionism

Since the collapse of the Soviet Union and the end of the Cold War, access to previously restricted documents show that it was Kim Il Sung who was the driving force behind the North's decision to invade the South. Both Stalin and Mao were informed in advance by Kim of his intention to attack. In January 1950, following Acheson's Defence Perimeter speech, Stalin gave his cautious approval to Kim's plans. Later, Soviet military experts helped to draw up the final plan of attack and, in May and June, Stalin sent military advisers and equipment to the North. However, Stalin made it clear to Kim in April 1950 that if the USA became involved in the war the Soviet Union would not intervene directly to help him.

Stalin's decisions on Korea – like those he made on Berlin in 1948–49 were ultimately shown to have been based on serious miscalculations of the likely response from the USA. While Stalin was keenly aware that the Soviet Union could not fight another war, he believed that the successful reunification of Korea under Kim's communist government would strengthen Soviet security by ensuring a friendly state on the USSR's borders. It would also give the USSR access to Korean hydroelectric power and raw materials, at the same time denying Japan (the USA's most important Pacific ally) these things.

Though Mao also had some knowledge of Kim's plans, he too did not want to risk getting involved in a major war. Despite the fact that Kim had fought with him against the Japanese in Manchuria, Mao was uneasy about his close alliance to the USSR. At the time, Mao was more concerned about establishing communist rule in China after years of instability and destruction and in dealing with the threat posed by Jiang Jieshi's regime in Taiwan, which Mao wanted to invade. For these reasons, Mao refused to make any firm guarantees of military assistance.

Thus it was Kim – not Stalin or Mao – who pushed for the attack in June 1950. He was encouraged by Rhee's unpopularity and evidence of growing support for the communist party in the South. He believed most Koreans would see him as a national hero if he reunited the country. He resented the USA's post-war attempts to rebuild Japan, which had ruled Korea harshly, as a pro-western regional power and, mindful of US backing for Jiang Jieshi in China's civil war, feared the same assistance might be given to South Korea. However, Kim was a risk-taker and calculated that it was better to act than to wait for the USA to build up the South.

Several historians have argued that the 1950 invasion was in many ways a continuation of a much longer civil war between the north and the south of the country. Between 1945 and 1950, before the war began, there had been several border clashes between the two states, in which over 100,000 Koreans had died.

The US historian, B. Cumings, argues that the North Korean invasion was the result of Kim's strong nationalist and revolutionary ideals and had very little to do with Soviet wishes. This view is supported by the fact that Kim had made several proposals to Stalin since early 1949, all of which had been rejected.

Eventually, Kim was able to persuade Stalin that an invasion would result in a quick victory, as Rhee's unpopularity would lead to a popular uprising in support of the North and unification. Kim was also encouraged in pushing ahead with his invasion plans by Acheson's Defence Perimeter speech.

US strategy

Importance of Japan

The main focus of US policy in Asia was Japan, which was seen as vital in 'containing' the threat of Soviet expansion across the world. After August 1945, the Big Four set up a joint Allied Council to administer Japan, but the real power lay with the USA which was the only ally with an army in Japan. Soviet requests for the temporary division of Japan into four zones of occupation, as in Germany, were immediately turned down.

From 1945 to 1947, the Allies concentrated on the demilitarisation and democratisation of Japan, and some of its huge *zaibatsus* were broken up. However, by 1947, with the start of the Cold War, US strategy towards Japan altered. Control of Japan was seen as crucial for the balance of power in the whole Asian region, especially in view of its vast industrialist potential. Thus it was seen as essential to tie Japan into a close alliance with the USA and to rebuild its economic strength. Japan rapidly became the focus of US policy in Asia.

Japan's industry and agriculture were badly damaged in the closing stages of the war, leading to the growing popularity of the Communist Party of Japan (at this stage the Japanese government was a caretaker one appointed by the USA). The USA's reaction was to rebuild Japan's economy and remove earlier restrictions on industrial production. In 1948, government employees in Japan lost the right to strike, while US occupation authorities began to arrest trade unionists suspected of being communists or communist sympathisers. In 1949, following a wave of industrial strikes over wages and the harassment of activists, the communists won over 3 million votes in the elections. In response, the US Congress voted to give $500 million in aid for the purchase of food and raw materials for Japanese industry. As part of its policy to 'buy' Japanese support, the prosecution of Japanese war criminals was also quietly dropped and the USA made it clear that it would soon withdraw its occupation forces and that the terms of the peace treaty would not be harsh.

The defensive perimeter

In line with Truman's policy of containment, the USA decided that communism should be contained on the periphery of Asia – China, South Korea and even, for a time, Vietnam were not seen as vitally important to US security. This policy – which became known as the defensive perimeter strategy – included drawing up war plans to defend a belt of offshore Pacific islands in Asia (including Japan, Guam and the Philippines) against any further Soviet expansion. It was decided that in order to make effective military resistance possible, the USA should maintain or build airbases and garrisons on these islands. The USA was also concerned about possible developments in Malaya

What were the main parts of the USA's defensive perimeter strategy?

and Indonesia. Generally, the USA favoured independent states with pro-US, anti-communist governments and, initially, had not supported the return of the former European imperial powers, such as France (**Indochina**) and the Netherlands (Indonesia).

As the Cold War developed, between 1945 and 1950, it was also decided that anti-communist forces in China, South Korea and Vietnam should be given substantial financial assistance. At this time, US policy was firmly against deploying US troops in any conflict on the Asian mainland.

By 1950 it had become clear that the US strategy in Asia to contain communism had not been very successful. Although Japan was already showing signs of a strong economic revival and was closely allied to the USA, China had been 'lost'. At the same time, communist forces were clearly growing in popularity and strength in Indochina (see Chapter 18), and it was clear that Kim's regime was determined to use force to bring about Korean reunification under his leadership.

This lack of success was partly because most of the USA's resources were devoted to Europe, which was seen as being of greater strategic importance than Asia. However, the communist movements in Asia were much more popular than those in Europe; this popularity had a lot to do with the communists' links to those demanding national independence from colonial powers such as France. This, even more than the relative lack of US aid, was the major reason why communism in Asia proved so much more difficult to contain.

The US response

Truman's immediate reaction to the North Korean invasion on 25 June 1950 was to rush military supplies to South Korea. Just two days later, on 27 June, the USA – taking advantage of the USSR's boycott of the UN Security Council (in protest at the USA's refusal to allow communist China a seat) – pushed a resolution through the UN Security Council calling for military action to be taken by UN members against North Korea. On 30 June, Truman ordered US troops based in Japan into South Korea.

Although this was, in theory, a UN military venture – 15 other UN members, including Britain, sent troops – it was essentially a US enterprise. The vast majority of troops involved were non-Korean (260,000 out of just under 300,000 UN troops were American) and both the UN and South Korean forces were placed under the command of US General MacArthur, who was directly accountable to Truman, not to the UN.

The reasons for these US actions were varied: one major reason for US involvement was the belief that Kim was not acting independently, but merely as Stalin's puppet in his attempt at world domination. Truman acted on what became known as the domino theory – if South Korea fell to the communists

Indochina refers to the federation of states in south-east Asia which until 1954 were part of the French empire. The main countries were Vietnam (Annam, Tonkin and Cochin China) and Cambodia, which were made part of the Union of Indochina in 1887; Laos was added in 1893. After the Second World War, France offered more self-government – though Cambodia and Laos accepted this, it was rejected by those who wanted Vietnam to be a totally independent country. In 1954, France was forced to withdraw completely from Indochina, and the three states became independent. However, this area then became part of the Cold War, and a 'hot' war continued until 1975.

Why was the USSR boycotting the UN and why was this important for the conduct of the Korean War?

then the rest of Asia would follow, with the Near East and even Europe next under threat. A firm response was also seen as providing evidence of the USA's determination to resist communism anywhere in the world. It also provided an opportunity for the US government to gain public acceptance for the NSC 68 proposals which had been drawn up just two months before.

The war

Initially the war went extremely well for North Korea, and the US/UN forces were pushed relentlessly backwards throughout the summer of 1950. By August, the North Koreans had captured Seoul, the South Korean capital, and, by September, had conquered all of the country apart from an area around the south-eastern port of Pusan.

In this desperate situation, MacArthur launched a seaborne counter-invasion at Inchon, well behind North Korea lines; soon, he was pushing northwards to the 38th parallel. At the same time, UN forces began to fight their way out of Pusan and begin pushing the North Koreans back.

The original US war aim was merely to expel the North Koreans from the South, across the 38th parallel. However, in October 1950, Truman decided to instruct MacArthur to invade North Korea – the USA had clearly moved beyond a policy of containment to one of 'roll-back', as outlined in NSC 68. To the USA an easy victory seemed possible, as intelligence reports suggested that neither the Soviet Union nor China would intervene to help the North Koreans; they were also motivated by the attractive proposition of a united, pro-American Korea on the USSR's border. In addition, Truman was keen to prove, after the 'loss' of China, that he was not 'soft' on communism, even though some NSC 68 supporters feared the recommendations (to greatly increase military expenditure) had not yet been implemented sufficiently to risk military confrontation with the USSR.

MacArthur quickly captured Pyongyang, the North Korean capital, and continued to push north. By November 1950, he was approaching the Yalu River, which marked the border between North Korea and China. As we have seen, Mao wanted to keep out of the Korean War but, as US troops approached the Chinese border, he came under increasing pressure from Stalin and from sections of the CCP leadership to take action to defend Chinese independence and national security. With no official diplomatic contact with the USA, Mao had no way of knowing whether or not the USA planned to invade through North Korea. His decision to send troops to aid Kim was done in the hope this could be prevented by fighting in Korea. The tension in China was heightened by fears that Jiang, with US military help, might choose this moment to launch an invasion of mainland China from Taiwan.

Why did China become involved in the Korean War?

Some of the many civilians affected by the fighting in the Korean War. In all, over 500,000 civilians in the North and South were killed.

At first, a small force of Chinese volunteers crossed into North Korea on 25 October to help stop MacArthur's advance. When MacArthur renewed his advance, over 250,000 Chinese troops crossed the Yalu River.

During December, the US/UN forces suffered heavy losses and, after a successful counteroffensive, Chinese and North Korean forces recaptured Pyongyang and, in January 1951, pushed south and retook Seoul. For a time, Truman and his administration considered MacArthur's call for using nuclear weapons against China. In the end, after strong opposition from Attlee, the British prime minister, and concern that such action might end in a nuclear war with the Soviet Union, this option was rejected.

The fear of nuclear war with the Soviet Union was based on the incorrect assumption that Stalin had ordered the Chinese in and that Stalin would honour the Sino-Soviet Treaty of 1950 if China was attacked. Instead, Truman and Acheson decided to revert to the original US policy of simply expelling North Korea from the South. The USA was now committed to fighting a limited war which they believed the Soviet Union would not oppose.

In fact, as soon as the war had started, Stalin had withdrawn all Soviet military advisers from North Korea and had recalled Soviet ships on their way to

North Korea with military supplies – this was a clear sign that he had no wish to be dragged into a war with the USA. At the end of 1950, despite US advances up to the Chinese border, Stalin broke promises he had made to Mao on providing air cover and military equipment for the advancing Chinese troops. Even when he did decide to give some help to China and North Korea, Stalin made sure that the help was limited and that no Soviet personnel would be directly involved in the fighting, though Soviet advisers remained in Korea and others helped to supervise airbases.

What was Stalin's role in the origins and early stages of the Korean War?

Although Truman had now settled on fighting a limited war, this was not a strategy shared by MacArthur. After he publicly criticised Truman's policies, he was dismissed as military commander in April 1951. Despite Republican support for MacArthur's views and public criticism, Truman stuck to the new policy that Korea was not the place to risk an all-out war against communism. By then, superior US/UN air power and greater military resources enabled the West to launch two successful counterattacks in February and March 1951. The result was another successful US/UN push just across the 38th parallel.

At this point, however, the two sides reached a military stalemate – although talks about a truce began in Panmunjon as early as July 1951, they dragged on until 1953. This was for the most part because the USA tried to insist that North Korean and Chinese prisoners of war should not necessarily be repatriated to their home countries but should stay in South Korea (or even be sent to the USA). Stalin also put pressure on Kim and Mao to gain as many concessions as possible from the USA concerning North Korean security. By 1952, with many of the NSC 68 recommendations already implemented – especially in relation to the H-bomb – some in the US military believed the USSR could now be defeated. For this reason they took a tough stance at the peace talks. Stalin, though, was not prepared to be bullied – he calculated that the USA could not win a conventional war against China and North Korea and had information that the USA would not use nuclear weapons.

The stalemate was ended in 1953. In January, Eisenhower became president and warned China, via the Indian ambassador, that the USA would now consider using the A-bomb if no progress was made at the talks taking place at Panmunjon. This was part of what was called the 'New Look' US foreign policy and was closely associated with Eisenhower and his secretary of state, J. F. Dulles. In public, Dulles spoke openly about 'brinkmanship', based on US willingness to use nuclear weapons (see page 155). As we have seen, in practice this proved to be more rhetoric than reality and there was not much difference between the policy of brinkmanship and Truman's earlier policy of containment.

What was China's involvement in the Korean War?

After Stalin's death in March, China and the USA compromised on the prisoners-of-war issue and an armistice was signed in July 1953. The main part of the agreement was that a line, roughly along the 38th parallel, would be the border between North and South Korea. Thus, after three years of war and almost 10 million people either dead or injured, very little had changed. However, continuing Cold War hostilities and the ongoing enmity between North and South Korea have meant that no permanent peace settlement has yet been signed, although the two countries are now beginning to co-operate with one another.

What impact did the Korean War have on the Cold War?

The USA and NSC 68

The Korean War gave supporters of NSC 68 the opportunity they needed to gain acceptance of this policy and its military implications. Before this war, supporters of NSC 68 realised that the US Congress and the general public wanted reduced taxation and that it would require an important event to change this. Essentially, Truman, the US military and the right in general used the Korean War as an opportunity to launch a new, much more aggressive Cold War policy. In many ways, the Korean War marked the start of the Cold War arms race – both conventional and nuclear – and of the more limited 'hot' wars involving client states in the developing world. After 1953, the Cold War clearly became a global phenomenon.

For the USA to take on the role of global 'policeman' against communism anywhere in the world, it had to maintain near-parity in conventional forces with the Soviet Union and clear superiority in nuclear weapons. Thus, huge increases in the military budget and a massive increase in military production were essential.

In 1950, after the start of the war, Truman asked Congress to approve a massive increase in military spending – $10 billion on the armed forces, $260 million for the H-bomb project and $4 billion in military aid for US allies across the world. In 1950, USA defence expenditure for the year was $13.1 billion; by 1953, it was $50.4 billion. Although this figure declined after the Korean War, it never dropped below an annual figure of $40 billion for the rest of the decade. By 1953, US military production was 700 per cent higher than it had been in 1950.

Asia

Apart from having an impact on US policy in Europe, the Korean War also affected developments in Asia. Japan's economy was greatly helped by servicing the needs of the large numbers of US troops stationed there. It also benefited from the signing of the San Francisco Peace Treaty in September 1951 with the USA and 48 other states. This restored sovereignty to Japan and promised the end of US occupation by 1952. In return, Japan signed a mutual security agreement with the USA, guaranteeing US military bases could stay. Japan also agreed to sign a trade boycott – the Yoshida Letter – against communist China, intended to bring about the weakening and eventual collapse of Mao's regime.

The Yoshida Letter also promised that Japan would trade with Jiang's Taiwan which, since the start of the Korean War, had become more important to the USA. In June 1950, Truman sent the Seventh Fleet to defend Taiwan from any possible Chinese invasion. In addition, massive US military and economic aid was given to Jiang, as it was believed that Taiwan was now important in blocking any expansion of communist China in Asia (China could not risk expanding into Asia for fear of Taiwan attacking its rear). To confirm this, the USA signed a mutual defence treaty with Taiwan in 1954. US intervention in Korea and its recognition of Taiwan (representing the whole of China) in the UN led to a 20-year period of Sino-American hostility. The Korean War also had a significant impact on US policy in Indochina (see Chapter 18).

What was the Yoshida Letter?

Cold War treaties

The Korean War also led to the signing of two new Cold War treaties. In August 1951, the USA signed a military alliance with the Philippines; in return for defending the Philippines, the USA would be able to set up military and naval bases on the islands. The building-up of Japan by the USA worried both Australia and New Zealand, which saw Japan as an economic competitor and as a potential military threat. To allay these fears, the USA proposed the Anzus Pact – this offered US support against any military aggression and promised on the part of Australia and New Zealand to help the USA against any communist activities in the Pacific region. This was signed in September 1951.

These new developments had been considered by the USA before 1950, but the start of the Korean War speeded up their implementation. It is also significant that by the end of the Korean War all the key proposals of NSC 68 had been put into operation. Any hesitations or doubts that the USA had about its Cold War policies in the period 1945–50 were dispelled by the Korean War. Few now doubted that a communist victory anywhere in the world posed a serious threat to the USA's global interests as the North Korean attack seemed to prove that communism was intent on expansion. By 1953, the USA was committed to a global military strategy of opposing communist 'aggression' and defending the 'free' world whenever necessary, up to and including putting US troops into combat situations. This was to remain the keystone of US Cold War policy for the next two decades.

What two new Cold War treaties were signed by the USA after the Korean War?

1 Khrushchev's comments on the origins of the Korean War

Kim returned to Moscow when he had worked everything out . . . Stalin had his doubts. He was worried that the Americans would jump in, but we were inclined to think that if the war were fought swiftly – and Kim Il-sung was sure it could be won swiftly – then intervention by the USA could be avoided.

Nevertheless Stalin decided to ask Mao Zedong's opinion about Kim Il-sung's suggestion. I must stress it wasn't Stalin's idea, but Kim Il-sung's. Kim was the initiator. Stalin, of course, didn't try to dissuade him . . . Mao Zedong also answered him affirmatively. He approved Kim Il-sung's suggestion and put forward the opinion that the USA would not intervene since the war would be an internal matter which the Korean people would decide for themselves.

E. G. Rayner, *The Cold War*, London, 1992, p. 27

2 The historian Isaac Deutscher's view on Stalin's attitude to the Korean War (for a time Deutscher was a supporter of Trotsky)

The risks seemed negligible. It was about two years since the Soviet occupation armies had left Northern Korea; and by the end of 1948 the American troops had withdrawn from the South. Moreover the Americans had declared they had no vital interest to defend in Korea and hinted that they considered the country 'expendable'. Stalin had, therefore, some reason to assume that what Kim Il Sung was starting was a local war that would not turn into a major international conflict.

I. Deutscher, *Stalin*, Harmondsworth, 1966, p. 584

Historical-source questions

1 What, according to Krushchev in Source 1, was Stalin's attitude to the plans of North Korea?
2 To what extent does Source 2 support the view presented in Source 1?
3 Why must the reliability of these two sources be questioned?
4 Use the sources and your own knowledge to explain why Stalin believed the USA would not intervene if war broke out in Korea.

Summary question

1 Identify and explain any *two* reasons for the outbreak of the Korean War.

2 Compare the importance of at least *three* ways in which the Korean War affected US foreign policy in Asia.

18 Indochina and Vietnam, 1954–63

Focus questions

◆ Why did the USA get involved in Vietnam?

◆ What impact did Indochina have on the Cold War?

Significant dates

1946	Fighting begins between France and the Viet Minh
1949	France grants limited independence to Vietnam, under Bao Dai
1950	USSR and China recognise Ho Chi Minh as legitimate ruler of Vietnam
1954	*January* Berlin Conference
	May USA decides to increase aid to France in its war against the Viet Minh; French defeated at Dien Bien Phu
	July Geneva Accords
	September USA sets up SEATO; first Taiwan Straits Crisis
1956	South Vietnam, backed by USA, refuses to hold unification elections, as promised at Paris in 1954
1958	Viet Cong set up in South Vietnam and begin guerrilla war against the government
1958	Second Taiwan Crisis
1959	*June* Soviet technicians withdrawn from China
	September Sino-Indian border dispute
1960	NLF set up and receives aid from North Vietnam
1961	*January* Kennedy becomes US president
1963	*November* Diem murdered after CIA-assisted military coup; Kennedy assassinated and replaced by Vice-President Johnson

Overview

As we have seen in Chapter 16, the USA was, at first, against the French returning to Indochina as a colonial power. However, the combination of the outbreak of war between the communist-led Viet Minh and the French in 1946 and developments elsewhere in Asia in 1949–50 (the communist victory in China and the Korean War), caused the USA to decide to give aid to the French in order to contain communism.

The 1954 Berlin Conference between the USA, the USSR and France seemed to promise agreements on Korea and Indochina, but then the French suffered a heavy defeat at Dien Bien Phu. Later that year the Geneva Accords made provision for the temporary division of Vietnam into North and South along the 17th parallel, with unification elections to be held in 1956. The USA then immediately set up a military mission to give economic and military aid to South Vietnam.

Convinced that the communist leader of North Vietnam, **Ho Chi Minh**, would win the elections, the US-backed South refused to hold them. In 1958, the Viet Cong began a guerrilla war against the government of South Vietnam and in 1960 the National Liberation Front was set up and included all those who were against the South Vietnamese government. The USA increased its military aid to the South and, with Kennedy's approval, the CIA helped the South Vietnamese army to overthrow the corrupt Diem in November 1963.

Why did the USA get involved in Vietnam?

Containment and the domino theory

As we have seen, US policy towards the Soviet Union and communism had been based on the Truman Doctrine and the policy of containment since 1947 (see page 139). This policy was further entrenched after Mao and the communists came to power in China in October 1949. However, Truman was only prepared to make a military stand in Asia along what was known as the defensive perimeter (see pages 214–15).

US policy regarding the Asian mainland, including south-east Asia, was to give economic aid to anti-communist forces. Indochina and especially Vietnam were seen as vital in blocking communist access to the rice-growing areas of the region. The outbreak of the Korean War in June 1950 was a turning point in US policy towards Vietnam. Once North Korea began its invasion of the South, Truman and Dulles quickly began to implement the NSC 68 proposals as Truman and his administration believed that the USA and the West could not afford to lose significantly more population, territory and resources to the other side. Within a short time, Truman decided to increase aid to the French in their struggle against the communist-led Viet Minh forces in Vietnam (the USA had been giving military aid to the French since March 1950); soon this aid reached $1 billion a year.

Born in 1890, **Ho Chi Minh** (real name Nguyen That Thanh) joined the French Communist Party in 1920. In 1930, he founded the Communist Party of Vietnam, but was forced into exile. By 1945, his Viet Minh controlled most of Vietnam and he was declared president of an independent Vietnam. At first, the USA supported him in his struggle against the Japanese and in his call for independence from France. But as the Cold War developed, the USA soon backed the return of the French. When the South refused to hold the elections which had been promised in 1954, he encouraged and then assisted the South Vietnamese communists (Viet Cong) in their resistance. He established a communist one-party state in the North, but died in 1969 before the reunification of his country. He was a popular nationalist leader (despite his political repression of opposition views) and was nicknamed Uncle Ho.

Why did the USA decide to help the French stay in control of Indochina after the Second World War?

The French and Indochina

Which three countries made up French Indochina?

Before the Second World War, Indochina (comprising Vietnam, Cambodia and Laos) had been part of the French empire. During the war, Indochina was taken over by Japan and after 1945 the French were keen to regain their south-east Asian colonies.

Initially, the USA had wanted these countries to be independent and allied to the USA and had applied pressure on France to withdraw. In addition, France faced strong opposition from the **Viet Minh**, a communist–nationalist movement seeking Vietnamese independence. Led by the communist Ho Chi Minh, the Viet Minh had liberated much of the country from Japanese occupation before 1945.

The **Viet Minh** (the Vietnam League for Independence) was set up by Ho Chi Minh in 1941, while in exile in China. After the Japanese invaded, the Viet Minh set up its own army and, from 1943, conducted a military campaign against the Japanese army. By 1945, the Viet Minh had liberated much of the country.

Ho felt encouraged by the USA's stance and had asked them for aid, but he was turned down because of his communist leanings. In 1946, fighting between the French and the Viet Minh began in what turned out to be a long guerrilla war, first against the French and then against the USA.

As the Cold War developed and national communist movements seemed to be growing in popularity, the USA decided to help the French stay in Indochina, but they pushed France into granting some concessions to non-communist Vietnamese nationalists. At first the aid was financial, but military aid was given as the situation became more serious.

In 1949, the French (who were experiencing economic difficulties at home) offered a form of limited independence to Vietnam, in part to satisfy the USA who were pressing for a more liberal regime. Under this scheme, Bao Dai was appointed head of a new government which was, however, rejected by the Viet Minh who were demanding total independence.

In 1950, Ho was recognised by Stalin and Mao as the legitimate leader of Vietnam. The USA then recognised Bao Dai as ruler of Vietnam. The USA concluded that Ho, like Kim in North Korea, was acting on instructions from Moscow and was merely an instrument of international communism. Beginning in March 1950, the USA began to send military aid to the French, in the hope that they could defeat the Viet Minh. The USA saw a French victory in Vietnam as important for European security, as a defeat for France might strengthen the **French Communist Party**. At the same time, US support for the French in Vietnam was seen as 'buying' French acquiescence to the rebuilding of West Germany's economic and military strength, which the USA believed was crucial to containing communism in Europe.

It was believed that a French defeat in Vietnam would weaken the government and lead to a political crisis which, in turn, would increase support for the **French Communist Party**.

Eisenhower and the New Look

As we have seen, Eisenhower's New Look foreign policy was supposed to be significantly different from Truman's pursuit of containment. Eisenhower (like Truman) saw Ho as an instrument of international communism and believed that the 'loss' of Indochina would have drastic results for the rest of south-east Asia (the domino theory), which was seen as vital to US interests.

This policy was particularly associated with Dulles and it placed a great emphasis on the USA obtaining a clear nuclear superiority in order to have the power to pressurise the USSR and China into making concessions. This was part of the doctrine which Dulles called 'massive retaliation'. There is some evidence to suggest that Eisenhower was much more prepared than Truman to sanction covert operations to contain communism as such methods were quick, cheap and beyond the scrutiny of Congress; however, the evidence is inconclusive.

By now, it was clear that the French were finding it increasingly difficult to maintain their position in Vietnam as a result of the Viet Minh's determined resistance. Eisenhower and Dulles feared that, if France was defeated, communism would triumph in Vietnam and then, according to the domino theory, the rest of Indochina (Cambodia and Laos) would follow, with Malaya, Indonesia, Taiwan and South Korea being the next communist targets.

Initially, Eisenhower continued giving massive aid to French forces in Vietnam and sending US 'advisers' (but no troops). Although these advisers were there only to train and give advice, in fact they took part in military operations. By 1954, the USA was paying about 70 per cent of the French military budget in Indochina and had given over $4 billion in aid. At this stage, the USA had no desire to get involved in another war, as they had in Korea, with its likely price of heavy US casualties (which had proved unpopular with the American public), especially as Eisenhower calculated that direct US involvement might provoke the Chinese into intervening.

Then, in March 1954, a critical stage was reached: the French were clearly facing a heavy defeat in the battle of Dien Bien Phu and the USA believed that the French would soon be requesting direct military support from the USA. Eisenhower ruled out sending US troops as Congress had made it clear they wanted 'no more Koreas' and Britain said it was not prepared to get involved either. At this point, the Pentagon suggested that three tactical nuclear weapons should be dropped to destroy the Viet Minh troops, led by General **Giap**, who were surrounding the French forces at Dien Bien Phu. Although the French also made this request, it was rejected. Instead, Eisenhower decided that the USA would not intervene without congressional approval and the support of the USA's allies. As Churchill, the British prime minister, remained opposed, no action was taken to save the French at Dien Bien Phu. It fell to the Viet Minh on 7 May 1954, effectively ending French colonial rule of Indochina.

From this we can see that although, in practice, Eisenhower's New Look seemed little different from Truman's containment policy, Eisenhower had great reservations about nuclear warfare.

What was Eisenhower's New Look foreign policy?

Born in 1912, Vo Nguyen **Giap** was a Vietnamese communist and a brilliant general. He was familiar with the guerrilla warfare tactics used by the Chinese communists, but also developed his own strategies over many years of war. He commanded the Viet Minh troops which entered Saigon after the defeat of Japan and was responsible for the defeat of the French at Dien Bien Phu in 1954. He commanded North Vietnam's armies during the Vietnam War and organised the Tet Offensive in 1968. After reunification in 1975, he became deputy prime minister.

The division of Vietnam

After their defeat at Dien Bien Phu, the French decided to withdraw from Vietnam. The USA, the USSR and China were prepared to arbitrate between the Vietnamese government and the Viet Minh to end the conflict. The Soviet leadership put pressure on Ho to accept the temporary division of Vietnam into North and South along the 17th parallel, even though the Viet Minh controlled about two-thirds of the country. The provisional government appointed by the French before their withdrawal and Ho's representatives finally agreed to these terms (known as the Geneva Accords) at a conference held in Geneva in July 1954. Ho accepted this compromise in order to stop the fighting and because it was agreed that national elections to bring about reunification would be held within two years. In Laos, the pro-communist Pathet Lao forces (though not in power) were left alone, while national elections were allowed in Cambodia.

However, the USA did not sign the Accords because it believed that the communists would win the elections, although it did promise not to break them by the use of force. In the meantime, Ho concentrated on establishing a one-party communist state and on rebuilding the economy in the North. This reconstruction was achieved partly with Soviet assistance.

At the same time, the USA began to train a South Vietnamese army and set up a military mission to give advice. The USA started to prop up South Vietnam to block communism from advancing from the North in what was effectively the start of US involvement in the longest war in its history (see Chapter 19).

Even before the French left, the USA were by-passing them and giving aid directly to any South Vietnamese movements prepared to work with the USA (as long as they were not communist). By July 1955, most of the French troops had been withdrawn. The USA quickly removed the French-backed Bao Dai and appointed Ngo Dinh **Diem** to head a new government for South Vietnam. Following Eisenhower's instructions, one of his first acts was to announce that the national reunification elections would not be held (several estimates predicted Ho would win about 80 per cent of the vote). The USA's main aim now was to create a viable state in South Vietnam that would be able to prevent the advance of communism. But the South had been devastated by years of warfare and was in political turmoil.

Diem's rule soon became corrupt and increasingly repressive, and communists in the South began to organise resistance and guerrilla warfare – they became known as the Viet Cong, a term of abuse used by both Diem and the USA. Diem's troops, who were not trained to fight a rural insurgency, found it almost impossible to cope with these communist guerrillas who had spent years fighting the Japanese and then the French.

What was agreed about Vietnam in the Geneva Accords of 1954?

Why were the reunification elections, promised for 1956, not held?

Born in 1901, Ngo Dinh **Diem** was a nationalist who was opposed to both the French and the communists. In 1954, he was appointed as prime minister of South Vietnam. At first, he was supported by the USA, but his regime alienated the mainly Buddhist population, leading to increased support for the Viet Cong.

In 1959, North Vietnam announced its intention to reunite Vietnam, and in 1960 Ho encouraged the Viet Cong to form the National Liberation Front, in alliance with other anti-Diem forces. This acted as the political arm of the Viet Cong.

Who were the Viet Cong?

Despite the growing unpopularity of Diem's regime in the years 1955–60, the USA continued to give him massive economic and military aid (totalling over $1 billion in this period) in order to prevent a communist victory in South Vietnam. Though this propped up Diem's increasingly unpopular regime, it did nothing to solve the problems faced by the **South Vietnamese peasants**.

The **South Vietnamese peasants** faced lack of land ownership and high rents, while Diem's regime backed the landlords.

Kennedy's 'flexible response'

The 1960 presidential elections were won by J. F. Kennedy. Although he was a Democrat, he shared Eisenhower's world view. Since the late 1940s, he had been a staunch Cold War warrior: he had attacked Truman over the 'loss' of China, had supported McCarthy's campaign and had even accused Eisenhower of allowing the USSR to open up a 'missile gap' with the USA. In fact, on taking office, Kennedy found out that the USA still had a clear lead, which he was determined to maintain.

By the time he assumed office in January 1961, Cold War tensions had reached a dangerous level and the USA had come to regard Vietnam – and south-east Asia in general – as indispensable for US security. Although Eisenhower was prepared to concede the loss of North Vietnam, he had not wanted to be the president who lost Indochina, and Kennedy was equally reluctant to be remembered this way. He was fearful that the Democrats would lose the next presidential elections, due in 1964, if South Vietnam fell to the communists and immediately appointed fervent anti-communists to key posts, including some Republicans. Also important were appointees such as **Dean Rusk** and **Robert McNamara**, who believed that China was behind North Vietnam and that behind China was the Soviet Union.

Born in 1909, **Dean Rusk** was a Democratic politician. In 1950, he was involved in the US decision to enter the Korean War. From 1961 to 1969, he was secretary of state and both advocated and defended US involvement in Vietnam.

Born in 1916, **Robert McNamara** was US secretary of defence from 1961 to 1968. However, he began to develop serious doubts about US policies and actions in Vietnam and eventually resigned. He later went on to be president of the World Bank.

They rapidly drew up and adopted a new containment strategy, known as the 'flexible response'. This was based on increasing US conventional military forces to enable it to fight limited wars in Asia and, if necessary, in Europe. It was presented as a criticism of Eisenhower's public reliance on nuclear weapons and 'massive retaliation'. The flexible response strategy was also seen as a way of bringing some control and stability to warfare in the new nuclear age.

What were the main aspects of Kennedy's 'flexible response'?

Kennedy's first crisis in Indochina was in Laos. Towards the end of Eisenhower's presidency, in 1960, the pro-US government there, set up in 1958 with CIA involvement, was overthrown by a neutralist group. Kennedy was determined to take action, as he believed that a communist victory in Laos would threaten the survival of South Vietnam as an anti-communist state. He

SEATO (the South East Asia Treaty Organisation) was set up by the USA in 1954 in Manila, with its HQ in Bangkok. Designed to contain the spread of communism in Asia, it had no standing forces of its own, but did undertake joint military exercises. As well as the USA and various Asian states, it also included Britain and France. In 1965, both Pakistan and France withdrew, as they did not wish to become involved in the Vietnam War. It was decided to end SEATO in 1975 and its last military exercise took place in 1976.

'Search and destroy' was one of the military strategies used by the USA in Vietnam. After Vietnamese civilians had been 'persuaded' to move into 'strategic hamlets' in areas controlled by the South Vietnamese army and the USA (to remove them from contact with the Viet Cong), US troops were then sent into these cleared areas to 'search and destroy' the Viet Cong. It was assumed that any Vietnamese who remained in such areas must be members or supporters of the Viet Cong, so troops were encouraged to achieve a high 'body count'. It was this strategy which led to the My Lai Massacre in 1968.

protested at Soviet aid to the Pathet Lao, sent the Seventh Fleet to the Gulf of Thailand and put all US forces in the Far East on alert. At the same time, Kennedy persuaded several **SEATO** members to pledge military support for any US-led action.

Khrushchev then decided that Laos was not of great importance and agreed to put pressure on the Pathet Lao to conclude a ceasefire. In 1962, in Geneva, the USSR and USA signed an agreement accepting and guaranteeing the neutrality of Laos. Kennedy accepted this, even though pro-communist forces remained in a dominant position. In fact, fighting was resumed almost immediately – the USA resorted to covert operations and the Soviet Union renewed military aid to the Pathet Lao. The CIA used Thai mercenaries and local tribesmen to create an anti-communist guerrilla army, almost 50,000 strong, and set up a theoretically private company (Air America) to bomb the Pathet Lao as, officially, they were not at war with Laos. Despite this, the Laotian communists continued to increase their strongholds.

The situation in Laos renewed Kennedy's determination to hang on to South Vietnam. Consequently, Kennedy increased economic aid to Diem and sent extra military 'advisers' to South Vietnam. The number of these advisers rose from 2,000 in 1961 to 11,000 in 1962; by the time of his assassination in November 1963, there were 16,000 US advisers in Vietnam, equipped with 300 planes and 120 helicopters. He also allowed them to engage in combat (such as flying South Vietnamese troops into battle) and authorised counter-insurgency operations such as the 'strategic hamlets' programme, designed to grind down the NLF by a policy of attrition, and even **'search and destroy'** missions. By 1963 over 100 US soldiers had been killed in Vietnam.

By then, it was clear that such strategies were not working, mainly because Diem's repressive policies and his refusal to carry out reforms continued to alienate the majority of the population, some 90 per cent of whom were Buddhists. Diem and his brother, Ngo Dinh Nhu, the head of the secret police, tended only to appoint Catholics (who were a minority) to positions of authority. In the summer of 1963, Buddhists organised massive protests against the government, which were fired on by the police. In protest, a Buddhist monk set himself on fire in Saigon – this practice soon spread. The Taylor–Rostow Report then suggested sending 8,000 US troops, ostensibly as a flood relief team.

However, twice in 1961 Kennedy rejected advice to send in regular US combat troops, even though his vice-president, Lyndon B. Johnson, was in favour of this course of action. Just before his assassination, though, Kennedy authorised the CIA to assist a group of South Vietnamese generals in a coup against the increasingly corrupt and inefficient Diem. This was because the USA had come to realise that the battle against communism needed to be

One of the many Buddhist priests who burned themselves to death as a protest against the corrupt government of South Vietnam in the early 1960s.

more than just a military one – it also required political, economic and social reforms. Hence, they went along with the South Vietnamese generals and gave their support to one who, they believed, would be less corrupt. On 1 November 1963, Diem was overthrown and he and his brother were murdered. Thus Kennedy consciously followed his own policy of flexible response (as did Johnson later).

Why did Kennedy agree to the overthrow of Diem?

What impact did Indochina have on the Cold War?

The search for new alliances

Tensions over Indochina led the USA to create another NATO-type alliance for Asia, in order to contain the spread of communism there. On 8 September 1954, the South East Asia Treaty Organisation (SEATO) was set up by Dulles. Its members, apart from the USA, were: France, Britain, Australia, New Zealand (these last two states were already allied to the USA via the Anzus Pact of 1951), Thailand, the Philippines and Pakistan. These members of SEATO were united in seeing South Vietnam, Laos and Cambodia as strategically important. Significantly, three states – Burma, Indonesia and India (the last two being two of the most important states in the region) – rejected membership, as they believed the USA was exaggerating the communist threat to the area.

These countries agreed that they would intervene in states where communists were poised to take power by force. Dulles assured the US Congress that intervention would only be considered if communist forces were clearly dominant. He also stated that the first military action would be taken by the airforce, not by ground troops, and promised that no interventions would take place without the approval of the Senate. However, another clause in the treaty stated that intervention might also take place in a country in which a communist party seemed likely to win elections – although the other member states refused to help the USA in such circumstances.

The Soviet response to SEATO and to growing US influence in Asia was to give its support to the non-aligned grouping of African and Asian states which had been set up at the **Bandung Conference** in Indonesia. This was a movement dedicated to opposing racism and colonialism and to finding a 'third way' (neither capitalism nor communism) between the two sides of the Cold War. During November and December 1955, Khrushchev and the Soviet prime minister, Bulganin, visited India, Burma and Afghanistan. Sukarno of Indonesia visited Moscow and was promised economic and military aid, even though he also received aid from the USA.

The **Bandung Conference** was the meeting held in Bandung (the capital of the Indonesian island of West Java); it was attended by 29 non-aligned Asian and African states. They were opposed to colonialism and racism and wanted to gain recognition of the developing world as well as stay out of the Cold War. They agreed to accept only 'no strings attached' aid and not to become involved in Cold War disputes.

Taiwan Straits Crisis

Mao was alarmed by the announcement of the formation of SEATO and calculated that the USA would now try to separate Taiwan permanently from mainland China. Jiang had recently announced an imminent attack on China in what was to be a new 'holy war' against communism. Mao retaliated by shelling some of the offshore islands – the Jinmen (Quemoy) and Mazu (Matsu) groups – in September 1954 to persuade the USA not to commit too closely to Jiang Jieshi's regime, which had troops in these islands. In 1955, China also began shelling the Tachen Islands, also occupied by Jiang's troops. During this Taiwan Straits Crisis in the years 1954–55, which resulted from Mao's attempts to take control of these islands, the US military once again recommended the use of nuclear weapons and once again (after some hesitation) Eisenhower refused, as he believed it would prove difficult to limit such action.

Though Dulles suspected Jiang might be trying to provoke a war with China so that, with US help, he could retake the mainland, the USA refused to agree to communist China being allowed to regain the offshore islands. The USA believed it had to be seen as standing by Taiwan. The result was the conclusion of a firm mutual defence pact between the USA and Taiwan, though it contained secret clauses that Jiang was not to attack China without US consent and that the USA would not commit itself to defending the disputed offshore islands.

The USA then attempted to get China to commit itself never to use force to regain Taiwan. Mao at first refused, pointing out that the island belonged to China and that the dispute was merely a leftover from the Chinese civil war. However, when China seized the Tachen Islands, Eisenhower threatened to use nuclear weapons if China attacked Taiwan, and Congress passed the Taiwan Resolution, which authorised Eisenhower to take whatever military action he deemed necessary. Zhou Enlai, the Chinese premier, then said China would only use peaceful means to regain Taiwan and a de facto ceasefire came into effect in the Taiwan Straits.

Tensions flared up again in 1957, when continuing Sino-American talks about the islands and Taiwan were broken off by the USA because of Mao's intransigence – Sino-American relations reached rock-bottom. In 1958, a second crisis broke out when China resumed its shelling of the Jinmen and Mazu Islands. Dulles declared it to be the first stage in a Chinese invasion of Taiwan and the Seventh Fleet was sent to the Taiwan Straits, US forces were placed on alert and the USA once again began to threaten the use of nuclear weapons. However, both China and the USA were prepared to negotiate and another ceasefire was arranged. Dulles once again made it clear to Jiang that though the USA would support the independence of Taiwan it would not help him in any invasion of mainland China. Dulles also put pressure on Jiang to reduce his troop levels in the disputed islands.

The USSR and China

This tension over SEATO and the situation in Asia also led to worsening relations between the USSR and China. When the USA broke off talks with China in 1957, Mao asked Khrushchev for Soviet support for a Chinese offensive to regain the islands of Jinmen and Mazu. Khrushchev, however, refused to provide any offensive military aid and said that the Soviet Union would only intervene if China was directly invaded by the USA. At the same time, the US threat of a nuclear response if the attacks persisted forced Mao to back down. This resulted in increased bitterness between the two communist powers (especially as the Soviet Union still refused to give China access to atomic bomb technology) and to a growing split which soon affected the communist movement around the world. Also important in this split was the process of limited de-Stalinisation being undertaken in the USSR after Khrushchev's secret speech of 1956, as Mao and the CCP believed the old Stalinist methods of rule should be maintained.

In fact, as early as the first Taiwan Straits Crisis in 1954, Dulles had realised that a firm USA stance on these islands – as well as sending a clear signal to all concerned that the USA was prepared to take military action in southeast Asia – might help bring about a collapse of the Sino-Soviet alliance. He calculated that a strong US line would dissuade the USSR from actively supporting China and that this would drive a wedge between them. Nevertheless, he and Eisenhower were forced to stick to the 'Two Chinas' policy – supporting Jiang's nationalist regime against Mao's communist one – by the continued activity of the US China Lobby. This group persisted in pressuring the US government to help Jiang invade mainland China. Had it not been so vociferous, it is possible that direct Washington–Beijing negotiations might have taken place long before they eventually did in 1971.

On 20 June 1959, this growing Sino-Soviet split resulted in the USSR suddenly withdrawing all its experts from China, at a critical time for the Chinese economy, leaving many uncompleted projects. Soon another tension developed in Asia, this time when on 9 September 1959 Chinese and Indian troops clashed over disputed border territory. Mao was infuriated by the Soviet Union's decision to stay neutral. This led to an open split at the Congress of the Romanian Communist Party in June 1960 which quickly resulted in the communist movement splitting into either pro-Moscow or pro-Beijing parties.

Historical sources

1 Extract from a speech by J. F. Kennedy to the American Friends of Vietnam in June 1956

Vietnam represents the cornerstone of the Free World in South-east Asia, the keystone to the arch, the finger in the dike. Burma, Thailand, India, Japan, the Philippines, and, obviously, Laos and Cambodia are among those whose security would be threatened if the red tide of communism overflowed into Vietnam . . . Moreover the independence of Free Vietnam is crucial to the free world in fields other than the military. Her economy is essential to the economy of all South-east Asia; and her political liberty is an inspiration to all those seeking to obtain or maintain their liberty in all parts of Asia – and indeed the world.

E. G. Rayner, *The Cold War*, London, 1992, p. 54

2 Extract from a television interview given by President Kennedy to Walter Cronkite in September 1963

Kennedy: I don't think that unless a greater effort is made by the government [of South Vietnam] to win popular support that the war can be won out there. In the final analysis, it is their war. They are the ones who have to win it or lose it. We can help them, we can give them equipment, we can send our men out there as advisers, but they have to win it, the people of Vietnam, against the Communists.

Cronkite: Hasn't every indication from Saigon been that President Diem has no intention of changing his pattern?

Kennedy: If he does not change it, of course, that is his decision. Our best judgement is that he can't be successful on that basis . . .

O. Edwards, *The USA and the Cold War*, London, 1997, p. 112

Historical-source questions

1 What do you understand by the term 'Free World' in Source 1?

2 How reliable is Source 2 concerning US attitudes to Diem and his regime in South Vietnam?

3 Use the sources and your own knowledge to explain the role played by the 'advisers' mentioned in Source 2.

Summary questions

1 Identify and explain any *two* reasons why the USA decided to become involved in the war in Vietnam.

2 Compare the importance of at least *three* ways in which Kennedy increased US involvement in Vietnam.

19 The Vietnam War, 1964–75

Focus questions

◆ Why did US involvement in Vietnam increase after 1964?

◆ Why did the USA decide to withdraw from Vietnam?

◆ What effect did the Vietnam War have on US foreign policy after 1975?

Significant dates

1964	*August*	Gulf of Tonkin Incident; Tonkin Gulf Resolution
1965	*March*	Start of Operation Thunder; first US troops sent to South Vietnam
	July	180,000 US troops sent to South Vietnam
1968	*January*	Tet Offensive
	March	My Lai Massacre; peace negotiations start in Paris
	October	Johnson announces temporary halt to US bombing of North Vietnam
1969	*January*	Nixon becomes president; My Lai Massacre exposed
	June	First US troops withdrawn
1971		USA allows China to take seat in UN
1972	*February*	Nixon visits China; large offensive by North Vietnamese and Viet Cong
1973	*January*	Ceasefire agreed; US troops start to withdraw; Congress vetoes Nixon's plans to invade Cambodia
1974		Nixon forced to resign because of Watergate scandal
1975	*March*	North Vietnam launches attack on South Vietnam
	April	North Vietnamese victory ends war; Vietnam reunited

Overview

What was the significance of the Gulf of Tonkin Incident in 1964?

Unlike Kennedy, Johnson was prepared to commit US troops to the war in Vietnam which had become a major Cold War issue. The Gulf of Tonkin Incident in 1964 led to the US Congress passing the Tonkin Gulf Resolution – this resulted in the bombing of North Vietnam and regular US combat troops being sent to the South. Under Johnson, US involvement and the war soon escalated. By late 1967, over 540,000 US troops were in South Vietnam. However, US tactics were unsuccessful and even counterproductive. In the USA and elsewhere massive anti-war protests began to take place. After the Viet Cong's and the Viet Minh's Tet Offensive in January 1968, the first peace talks took place between the USA and North Vietnam. Nixon, who became president in 1969, promised to end the war and soon began the process known as **Vietnamisation**. In 1973, partly through combined pressure from the Soviet Union and China, the North agreed to a ceasefire and US troops began to withdraw from South Vietnam. In 1975, the North launched an invasion of the South and the war ended with the defeat of the South in April 1975.

Why did US involvement in Vietnam increase after 1964?

Johnson and escalation

By the time of Kennedy's assassination in November 1963, the Viet Cong were in control of more than half of rural South Vietnam. In the cities, they launched a terrorist campaign against government officials and police commanders. When Vice-President **Johnson** took over, he was determined to step up US involvement in the war in South Vietnam. During the presidential elections in November 1964, he declared he would not see south-east Asia 'go the way China went', thus indicating his belief in containment and the domino theory.

In August 1964, a US destroyer (close to the North Vietnamese coast in the Gulf of Tonkin, and so in North Vietnam's territorial waters) was attacked by North Vietnamese ships. Although no serious damage was done, Johnson used this Gulf of Tonkin Incident as an excuse to order the bombing of the North's naval bases, even though no state of war had been declared. The US Congress was then persuaded to pass the Tonkin Gulf Resolution, which gave the president the power to 'take all necessary steps, including the use of armed force', to defend the South. This was, in effect, a blank cheque for Johnson to conduct the war as he saw fit, without having to consult Congress further. In March 1965, US bombers were flying regular massive bombing missions against the North, in a campaign known as Operation Rolling Thunder, and thus the conflict between the USA and the Viet Cong escalated into full-blown war.

For several years, Johnson had favoured sending a large US army into the South to destroy the Viet Cong. In March, he sent some US ground forces to South Vietnam, initially to protect the US airbase at Da Nang. Then in July 1965, Johnson ordered in 180,000 **US troops**. By 1968, the number of US troops in Vietnam was 540,000. Although the arrival of such large numbers of American soldiers helped prevent the total collapse of the South Vietnamese

Vietnamisation was the US policy to get the ground fighting in the Vietnam War done by the South Vietnamese army, so that US troops could be withdrawn. The first US troops were withdrawn in 1969; by 1970, the USA had mostly ceased its direct involvement in the ground fighting, though it continued to give air support.

Born in 1908, Lyndon B. **Johnson** was a Democrat and, as a member of the House of Representatives (1937–48) and then the Senate (1948–60), he became known as a liberal. However, this reputation – and his 'Great Society' programme – were overshadowed by his escalation of the USA's involvement in the Vietnam War, which he began after he became president in 1963, following Kennedy's assassination. Under him, the war became increasingly costly and unpopular and, in March 1968, he announced that he would not stand for re-election.

Under Johnson about 10 per cent of **US troops** comprised young men who were conscripted to fight in Vietnam. Their average age was 19 and many did not want to be there.

Napalm is a gelatinous petroleum, developed during the Second World War, that was widely used by the USA in the Vietnam War. This inflammable jelly is put into bombs – when they explode, the flaming petrol spreads widely and sticks to anything it touches. When it was discovered that victims jumped into water to try to put out the flames, phosphorous was added so that the jelly would continue to burn under water. Many Vietnamese civilians as well as Viet Cong soldiers were horribly burnt or killed.

Agent Orange was one of several chemical **defoliant** sprays developed and used by the USA in Vietnam. They were designed to remove the leaves from the trees in the jungle, to deprive the Viet Cong of cover and to expose the Ho Chi Minh Trail to American bombers. However, these defoliants also damaged the peasants' crops and timber (an important export crop); they also had serious effects on unborn babies, resulting in still-births and deformities. Napalm and agent orange had been authorised earlier by Kennedy.

Anti-personnel bombs are bombs which throw out smaller bombs that lie around until someone steps on them or picks them up. During the

What was the purpose of defoliants (such as Agent Orange) used by the USA in Vietnam?

military regime (headed by General Thieu), the increasingly heavy fighting did not succeed in destroying the Viet Cong. The US bombing of both North and South Vietnam was repeatedly stepped up – it is estimated that more bombs were dropped on North Vietnam in three years than the total number of bombs dropped on Germany, Italy and Japan during the whole of the Second World War.

The Viet Cong – aided by equipment and troops from North Vietnam which was itself receiving military equipment from the Soviet Union – were able to survive by digging a vast network of underground tunnels. Furthermore, the vast experience of the Viet Cong in guerrilla warfare meant they frequently outmanoeuvred the US troops. Unable to match the expertise of the Viet Cong in setting ambushes and booby traps, US military commanders decided to rely on their massive fire-power advantage. In addition to traditional bombing, the USA made heavy use of **napalm**, **defoliants** and **anti-personnel bombs**. These, however, frequently killed civilians and caused mounting opposition to US involvement and tactics, both in Vietnam and abroad, including in the USA itself. Johnson's hope of fighting and winning a limited war, without provoking the entry of the USSR and China, was foundering on the firm resistance mounted by the Viet Cong and the North.

The Tet Offensive, January 1968

The lack of success being achieved by US tactics was shown dramatically in January 1968. During the Tet religious festival (during which only a skeleton staff of security guards would be on duty), Viet Cong and North Vietnamese troops launched a massive attack against many towns and US military bases across South Vietnam. They even attacked the US embassy in Saigon, the capital of South Vietnam. The communists hoped that this would spark off an urban insurrection in the South, but this did not happen. For the next three months, there was intense and bitter fighting, as the USA attempted to recapture the towns taken in January. By the end of March 1968, over 50,000 communist troops had been killed and virtually all their gains had been lost.

Despite this, the Tet Offensive turned out to be a turning point in the Vietnam War. Though in the short term it proved to be a defeat for the communists, in the long term it marked the beginning of a reappraisal in the USA of its involvement in this war. Some of Johnson's advisers, such as Acheson, began to think that the USA could not prevent the communists from winning in the South. The Tet Offensive showed that the USA was far from achieving a victory and that the communists' resistance was as determined as ever. Many US politicians became disillusioned with the war and the anti-war movement in the USA grew considerably.

One more immediate result was that, in March 1968, Johnson announced his decision not to stand for re-election as the Democrat candidate in the November elections. The war, with its mounting civilian casualties, had made Johnson the USA's most unpopular president. A common chant by anti-war protestors was: 'Hey, hey LBJ, how many kids did you kill today?' Despite massive expenditure – which had helped undermine Johnson's **Great Society** project – it was clear that the USA was slowly losing the war. By then, the war was costing $28 billion a year and over 300 US soldiers were being killed each week. Johnson announced that the bombing would be scaled down and called for peace talks with Hanoi. The North Vietnamese government agreed and negotiations began in Paris in May 1968, but no real progress was made, despite Soviet pressure on the North. However, in October 1968, Johnson did call a temporary halt to the bombing of North Vietnam to help along the peace talks (and also to counter protests).

Why did the USA decide to withdraw from Vietnam?

Nixon's search for peace

The November presidential elections was won by Richard Nixon, the Republican candidate. He was determined to end the war, but wanted a peace that would not humiliate the USA by forcing it to totally abandon South Vietnam. At first, he suggested at the Paris peace talks that North Vietnamese troops should withdraw from the South, at the same time as US troops were pulled out. If the North did not agree, he threatened to launch a massive new bombing campaign. However, the North refused and, in the end, Nixon did step up the bombing of the North and of Viet Cong strongholds in the South. Nixon also tried to persuade the Soviet Union and China to put pressure on North Vietnam to agree to a compromise. In return, Nixon promised US economic help for the USSR. Though the Soviet Union made some attempts to persuade North Vietnam to comply – for instance, it refused to supply the North with its most effective surface-to-air missiles – the North was reluctant to compromise.

More practically, Nixon decided on a policy of Vietnamisation of the war. This involved putting more and more of the burden of fighting the war on to the South Vietnamese army, by withdrawing US troops; US financial aid, however, continued. In April 1969, the number of US troops in South Vietnam was 543,000; by 1971, Nixon had reduced this figure to 157,000.

By then, however, the USA had been shocked by the exposure, in 1969, of a US war atrocity. In March 1968, a US unit on a 'search and destroy' mission led by Lieutenant William Calley, massacred about 400 civilians (mostly children and old men and women) in the small village of My Lai in South

Vietnam War, some were brightly coloured, apparently to attract the interest of children. Some bombs in this category were covered in plastic which exploded into thin slivers and so could not be detected by X-rays when the victim went to hospital.

Why was the Tet Offensive of 1968 important?

The **Great Society** was President Johnson's attempt to do something about the great poverty and inequality which existed for millions of people (white and black) in the USA. In order to build 'a great society', in 1964, he initiated the most ambitious legislative programme since Roosevelt's New Deal. This included a 'War on Poverty', the Medical Care for the Aged Act, the Social Security Act, educational and urban renewal initiatives, as well as measures to give real civil rights to African-Americans. Much of this was, however, undermined by the escalating costs of the Vietnam War.

What were the main points of Nixon's Vietnamisation policy?

This photograph, taken on 16 March 1968, shows some of the 400 women and children massacred at My Lai by US troops on a 'search and destroy' mission in South Vietnam.

What happened at My Lai?

Vietnam. Calley was eventually sentenced to 20 years imprisonment for the murder of 109 civilians (in fact he only served 5 years). The revelations increased anti-war sentiments and protests, especially after it emerged that the My Lai Massacre was not an isolated incident.

Part of the process of Vietnamisation of the war involved increased bombing of the Ho Chi Minh Trail (see map on page 239) in order to prevent fresh supplies of troops and equipment reaching the communists in South Vietnam. In practice, this had little effect on the ability of the Viet Cong to wage their guerrilla war and only resulted in spreading the conflict to the neighbouring countries of Laos and Cambodia, through which the supply trails ran. Between 1969 and 1973 alone, the USA dropped over 500,000 tonnes of explosives on Cambodia – the effect was only to increase the support for, and determination of, the Cambodian communists, the Khmer Rouge. In Laos, too, the Pathet Lao received increased support.

Rapprochement with China

As part of his strategy to get the Soviet Union to put pressure on North Vietnam to accept a compromise peace, Nixon made an attempt to improve relations with China. China (which, in the previous century, had ruled Vietnam) was unhappy about Ho Chi Minh's close links with the USSR even though China itself gave limited support to North Vietnam. Kissinger believed that an agreement with China would allow US troops to leave Vietnam and south-east Asia in general. China could also be used as a check on the USSR and on

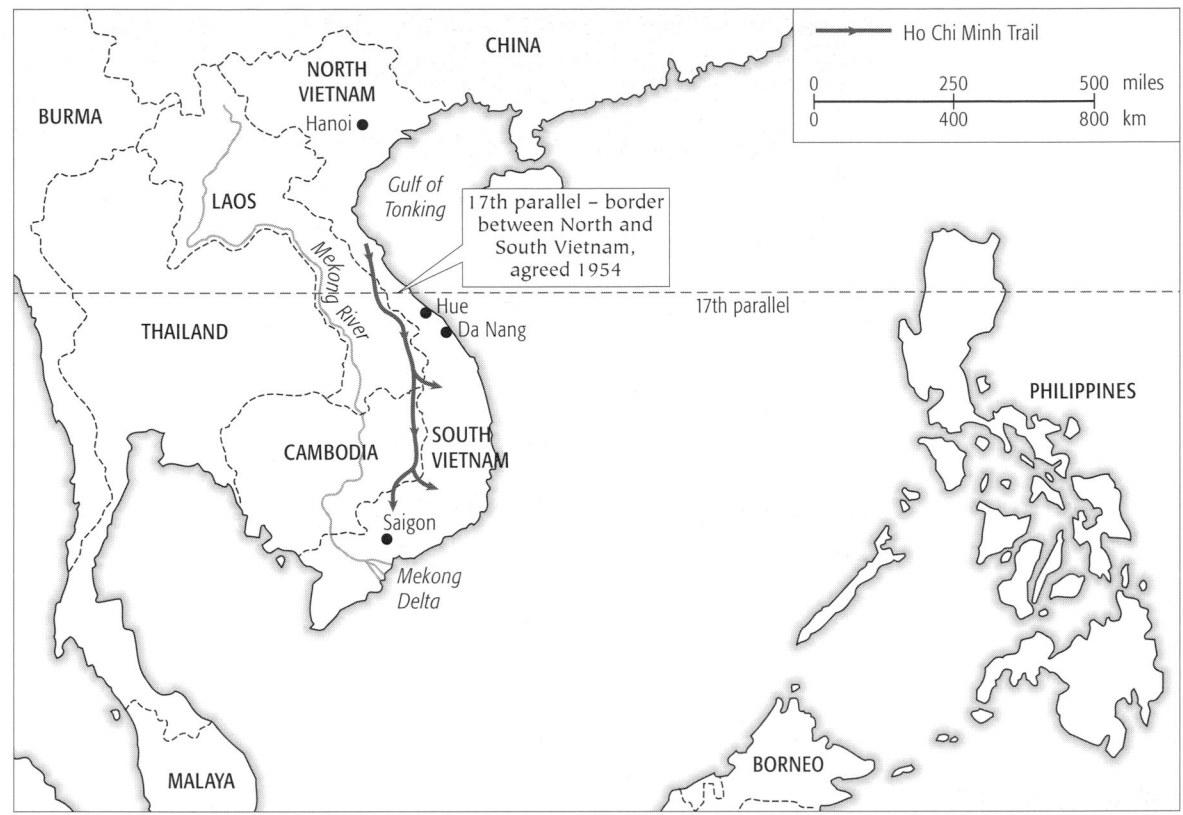

Map of Vietnam and south-east Asia, showing the division of Vietnam and the various routes of the Ho Chi Minh Trail, along which North Vietnam sent supplies to the Viet Cong.

Vietnam – as China had little influence globally, this policy was not seen as involving any risks for US interests. All this would allow the USA to concentrate its efforts on dealing with the Soviet Union.

In 1971, Nixon announced his intention to visit communist China even though he still refused to recognise its government. In the same year, the USA allowed China to join the United Nations. The visit, which took place in February 1972, was a success, with Nixon agreeing to withdraw US troops from Taiwan and promising to promote the idea of Chinese unification if China would help it get out of Vietnam without 'losing face' and refrain from any military actions in the Taiwan Straits.

This improvement in Sino-American relations was slowed down by Nixon's growing political embarrassment during the **Watergate** scandal of 1973–74. It was also hindered by the right in the USA, whose opposition forced Nixon to delay US recognition of China (it did not take place until December 1978) and to maintain the defence treaty with Taiwan.

By causing concern in the USSR over the 'loss' of a communist ally, the USA helped create the framework for a settlement over Vietnam in particular and

Why was China reluctant to give more than limited aid to North Vietnam?

Watergate was the political scandal which involved the Nixon administration and which finally led to his resignation as president in August 1974, in order to avoid being impeached by Congress. It arose from an attempt to burgle and bug the Democratic Party's national HQ (the Watergate building) in June 1972 – this was only five months before the presidential elections, in which Nixon was standing for re-election. Nixon and his advisers tried to cover up their involvement but, by June 1974, 17 members of his government had been found guilty of various crimes (his vice-president, Spiro Agnew, had also had to resign because he had been fiddling his tax returns – he was replaced by Gerald Ford). When Nixon resigned, Ford became president; one of his first acts was to grant Nixon a pardon.

What did Kissinger mean by 'linkage' when discussing a possible peace in Vietnam?

the process of detente in general (see pages 169–71). Kissinger favoured the idea of 'linkage': if the Soviet Union would help the USA out of its predicament in Vietnam and agree to 'stabilise' other developing world tensions, the USA would accept its eastern European sphere of influence and offer it financial and technical assistance.

Ceasefire and withdrawal

While this was happening, Vietnamese peace talks in Paris had continued to drag on inconclusively. In the summer of 1972, the communists launched another all-out offensive, this time on the urban centres in the South. This proved to be more successful than the Tet Offensive, even though the main population centres were not taken. The offensive resulted in the peace negotiations becoming more serious, with Kissinger for the USA and Le Duc Tho for North Vietnam. In January 1973, they agreed a ceasefire. Later that year, Congress refused to give Nixon permission to send US troops to defend Cambodia from North Vietnamese incursions – Nixon had hoped that this action would speed up the peace talks by hitting communist supply routes in Cambodia. Congress also passed an act preventing any president from deploying US troops before declaration of war, ordered an end to the bombing of Cambodia and ruled that US troops should not be sent to Vietnam again. Once the ceasefire was signed, the USA began to withdraw its remaining troops.

The war in Vietnam soon flared up again between the communists and the South Vietnamese forces. In March 1975, the North launched another major attack. This time, lacking US air support and troops, the South was unable to withstand the attack. The Viet Cong and the North Vietnamese army pushed southwards and, on 29 April 1975, the communists marched into Saigon. After almost 30 years of warfare, the communists at last controlled the whole of Vietnam. By then, over 2 million Vietnamese had been killed.

Less than two weeks before, the Khmer Rouge had taken power in Cambodia and, on 9 May, the Pathet Lao finally took over in Laos. Later, in 1978, communist Vietnam sent its army into Cambodia to remove the Pol Pot regime; it also intervened in Laos. This in turn led to China invading Vietnam in January 1979 in an attempt to limit the power of Vietnam which, in 1978, had signed a treaty with the Soviet Union.

Why did China invade Vietnam in January 1979?

What effect did the Vietnam War have on US foreign policy after 1975?

The failure of the USA to win the war in Vietnam – and the fact that a nation from the developing world had forced the world's most powerful superpower to withdraw – was a deep shock for US politicians and public alike. Not only had the war cost $150 billion, more than 55,000 US soldiers had been killed and many more were seriously wounded or maimed. Despite all this, South Vietnam had been 'lost' to communism, as had the neighbouring states of Laos and Cambodia.

More disturbing as far as containment was concerned was the fact that these communist successes were seen to be as much the result of popular support as of the 'outside pressure'. Consequently, Nixon and his chief adviser, Kissinger, decided to pursue the new policy of detente as regards the communist world. Kissinger argued that the USA was focusing too much on communist activity in one area of the world at the expense of the total global balance of power. He also saw that the world had shifted from a **bi-polar international situation** to a multi-polar one.

The rift between the Soviet Union and China presented new opportunities for developing US foreign policy. This approach was continued by Nixon's successors, Ford and Carter, until the end of the 1970s. The defeat in Vietnam also contributed to a US reluctance to commit its own troops to other developing-world conflicts. The USSR took advantage of this, during the remainder of the 1970s, to attempt to increase its influence in those parts of the world where it was weak, especially in the Middle East and Africa.

A bi-polar inter-national situation existed when the USA and the USSR were the two superpowers; a multi-polar situation came into existence when three or more powerful nations emerged.

Historical sources

1 Part of President Nixon's television broadcast to the nation on 23 January 1973, announcing the end of the Vietnam War

At 12.30 pm Paris time today, 23 January 1973, the agreement on ending the war and restoring the peace was initialled by Dr Henry Kissinger on behalf of the United States and by Le Duc Tho on behalf of the Democratic Republic of [North] Vietnam . . . The cease-fire will take effect at 24.00, GMT, 27 January 1973 . . .

Throughout these negotiations we have been in the closest consultation with President Thieu and other representatives of the Republic of [South] Vietnam. This settlement meets the goals and has the full support of president Thieu . . .

The United States will continue to recognise the Government of the Republic of Vietnam as the sole legitimate government of South Vietnam . . .

E. G. Rayner, *The Cold War*, London, 1992, p. 57

2 A comment on the effect of the anti-war movement on the US decision to withdraw from Vietnam, made by Senator Eugene McCarthy (who, in 1968, was one of the leaders of the anti-war movement)

I'm inclined to believe that the war would have ended just about when it did, even if there had been no protest, if I had not campaigned, because they didn't end it on policy finally: they just ended it because they were losing it and . . . the soldiers wouldn't fight.

A. Pollock, *Vietnam*, Melbourne, 1995, p. 126

Historical-source questions

1   What position was held by Henry Kissinger, referred to in Source 1?
2   How accurate is Source 1 about the attitude of President Thieu of South Vietnam concerning the Paris peace agreement?
3   Why are the views expressed by Eugene McCarthy in Source 2 on the role played by the anti-war movement in ending the Vietnam War so significant?

Summary questions

1   Identify and explain any *two* ways in which US involvement in Vietnam increased after 1964.

2   Compare the importance of at least *three* reasons behind the decision of the USA to withdraw from the Vietnam War.

20 The Cuban Revolution and the Americas

Focus questions

◆ Why did the USA see Cuba as being so important?

◆ Why did the Cuban Missile Crisis happen?

◆ What impact did the Cuban Revolution have on the Cold War?

Significant dates

1947   Rio Pact

1948   *March* OAS formed

1951   Arbenz elected president of Guatemala

1953   Arbenz nationalises some American-owned land (including some owned by the United Fruit Company) to begin land reform

1954   *June* CIA helps Armas to overthrow Arbenz

1956   *December* Castro's force lands in Cuba to begin guerrilla war against Batista

1959   *January* Castro's revolutionary government takes control of Cuba

1961   *January* USA breaks off diplomatic relations with Cuba
        April Bay of Pigs: attempted invasion of Cuba

1962   *October* Cuban Missile Crisis
        November Kennedy authorises Operation Mongoose to be resumed

1963   *June* Hot line established
        August Nuclear Test Ban Treaty

1965   Che Guevara goes to Bolivia to help revolution there

1967   Guevara captured and shot

1975   Cuban troops help MPLA in Angola

1977   Cuban troops sent to help Ethiopian government

1979   *January* Iranian Revolution
        March Grenadan Revolution
        July Nicaraguan Revolution

Overview

Historically, the USA had always claimed its right to see the Americas as its sphere of influence and had fought a war against Spain in 1898 which established its control of the region. This attitude was strengthened by the development of the Cold War and resulted in the Rio Pact and the formation of the Organisation of American States in the period 1947–48.

Concern about the reform policies of Arbenz, the president of Guatemala, resulted in the CIA helping to topple him in a coup in 1954. US domination of Cuba seemed threatened by a revolution led by Fidel Castro, in 1959. Pressure from the USA led Castro to turn to the USSR for assistance and soon Cuba became part of the Cold War. After a failed attempt by US-backed forces to overthrow Castro in 1961, Cuba appealed to Khrushchev for protection. He responded by sending intermediate-range ballistic missiles, which were spotted by US spy-planes, and led to the Cuban Missile Crisis. Despite the real risk of nuclear war during this crisis, Kennedy and Khrushchev were able to agree a compromise.

Afterwards, Soviet–US relations were improved by the establishment of a hot line between Moscow and Washington and the signing of a partial Nuclear Test Ban Treaty. However, the USA maintained its hostility to Cuba.

Cuba tried to encourage other revolutions in the Americas and, during the 1970s, sent troops to help sympathetic governments and movements in Africa involved in wars against US-backed groups. However, the Soviet Union's growing problems meant that Soviet military and economic aid declined and, under Gorbachev, came to a complete end.

Why did the USA see Cuba as being so important?

The USA, Latin America and the Caribbean

The USA had always seen Latin America and the Caribbean as its 'backyard'. The **Monroe Doctrine** of 1823 then made it abundantly clear that the USA intended to be the overwhelmingly dominant power in the region. In the 1890s, Britain had conceded that the Caribbean region was a US sphere of influence and the USA had gone on to occupy Cuba and Panama and set up a protectorate over the Dominican Republic. In 1904, President Theodore Roosevelt – who said that, in dealing with Latin America, the USA should 'speak softly and carry a big stick' – had announced what became known as the Roosevelt Corollary to the Monroe Doctrine. This justified intervention in Latin and Central America on the grounds of protecting private property, maintaining order or protecting American lives. There were, in fact, several armed interventions in the years before 1933, when the USA adopted the **'Good Neighbor' policy** under Franklin D. Roosevelt.

As soon as the Cold War began, the USA took steps to ensure that no communist or pro-communist state would be established in the Americas. In 1947, the USA signed its first post-war security treaty, the Rio Pact, which

The **Monroe Doctrine** was the US foreign policy statement made by President James Monroe in December 1823. This made it clear that the USA would not tolerate any interference in the Americas by any European nation – any such involvement would be treated as an act of war against the USA. From then on, the USA looked on the whole of the Americas as its own 'backyard'. This policy continued and, by the outbreak of the First World War, was firmly established. The start of the Cold War then gave it an extra political element. The USA acted on this in the 1950s and 1960s (especially as regards Cuba) and, even as late as 1983, carried out a military intervention against the small Caribbean island of Grenada.

The **'Good Neighbor' policy** was intended to move away from aggressive military intervention in the Americas. Instead, large amounts of US money were invested in Latin American countries: $3 billion by 1939. Some saw this as a form of 'dollar imperialism'.

stated that any attack on any country in the American continent would be treated as an attack on all, meaning that the USA would prevent any other country from interfering in the area. In March 1948, the USA set up the Organisation of American States (OAS) as the political arm of the Rio Pact signatories. Its charter included a clear, unequivocal statement that 'international communism' was incompatible with 'American freedom'.

Why did the USA set up the OAS in 1948?

Guatemala

The first apparent challenge to the USA's policy in the region was presented by developments in the Central American state of **Guatemala**. In 1950, the elected reforming president handed over power to the defence minister, Colonel Jacobo Arbenz Guzman, because of large demonstrations for reform. Arbenz then headed a centre-left coalition that won the election later in the year and he was installed as president in 1951. Arbenz intended to carry out land reform and, in June 1952, pushed through an act allowing the government to nationalise uncultivated areas of land in the large plantations. He made provision for compensation to be paid for any land so taken. Over the next 18 months, over 1.5 million acres of such land were redistributed to over 100,000 families. Then, in 1953, some unused land owned by the American United Fruit Company (UFCO) was taken. They owned huge areas of land in Guatemala, 85 per cent of which was unused and, in order to avoid paying tax, had consistently undervalued the land they owned.

Eisenhower, who became president in 1953, had – like Truman before him – been worried by Arbenz's election in 1951 and his land-reform programme. The fact that Arbenz was supported by the communists was used by Eisenhower as an opportunity to take action. According to revisionist historians, the issue was complicated by the fact that many in Eisenhower's administration were closely involved with or connected to UFCO. Other historians have pointed out that the planned American coup (see page 246) was actually opposed by UFCO and that Eisenhower's justice department eventually prosecuted UFCO under the anti-trust laws, which attempted to prevent large businesses from establishing monopolies.

The USA alleged that Arbenz was 'soft' on communism and that, whatever his intentions, he was a 'stooge' for the Soviet Union. Eisenhower claimed that his land-reform programme was the first step in a communist takeover, even though there were only four communists in the Guatemalan parliament.

In August 1953, Dulles tried to get the members of the OAS to agree that action should be taken under the terms of the Rio Pact, citing outside influence in Guatemala and claiming that, if Guatemala fell, the rest of Central America was in danger. However, at a meeting in early 1954, the OAS failed to support the USA's call for action and instead only affirmed that communist

Guatemala was a poor agrarian country, where most of the land was in the hands of a wealthy minority – over half the population owned only 3 per cent of the land.

domination of a member's government would, in theory, require joint action. As a result, Eisenhower opted for covert action and authorised the CIA to develop a plan to overthrow Arbenz's government. This plan (known as Operation P B Success) centred on a coup, to be led by Castillo Armas, a fervent anti-communist. Armas was given funds for a small group of mercenaries and provided with a base in neighbouring Honduras from which he could launch his coup.

Meanwhile, the US government kept up its demands for massive compensation for the loss of American property. Arbenz, aware of the growing threat, decided to buy small arms from the Eastern bloc. In June 1954, Armas launched his 'invasion' – the CIA also provided him with two planes, flown by US pilots, which bombed civilian targets. This led Arbenz to believe that there was a large invasion force. In the ensuing panic, the armed forces deserted him and he fled to Mexico. Armas installed himself as military dictator and ordered the execution of hundreds of political opponents, even though only one member of his mercenary force had been killed. Once installed as military dictator, Armas proved to be a corrupt but reliable ally for the USA – but only for a short time, as he was soon overthrown himself.

Cuba

A more obvious challenge to US hegemony in the region occurred following events in Cuba, a Caribbean island about 150 km south of Florida. Since the Spanish–American War of 1898, Cuba had been dominated by the USA (as had Puerto Rico and the Philippines). Initially, Cuba had been under US military occupation but, in 1901, the USA allowed Cuba to draft a constitution into which, however, it was forced to include the Platt Amendment, which stated that the USA had the right to 'oversee' the Cuban economy, veto any international agreements it made and intervene in Cuba's domestic politics. Thus Cuba was, in practice though not in law, a US protectorate.

By 1933, when Roosevelt ended the Platt Amendment, the Cuban economy was highly dependent on sugar and effectively controlled by US business interests. Since 1934, after the defeat of a left-of-centre reforming government, Cuba had been ruled by a right-wing military dictator, General Fulgencio **Batista**, supported by the USA, with a series of puppet presidents until 1940. From 1940 to 1948, Batista ruled directly, then from 1948 to 1952, he reverted to using nominal presidents to give the impression that he (and the army) was no longer running the country. Then, in 1952, he carried out a coup and ruled openly as a military dictator.

Under his rule, the USA acquired increasing control of both the Cuban economy and political developments on the island. Soon, most of Cuba's land, industries and even public utilities were owned by US companies, and

What was the Platt Amendment of 1901?

Born in 1901, Fulgencio **Batista** was a sergeant in the Cuban army, before leading a successful coup in 1933. At first, he ruled through a series of puppet presidents until, in 1940, he took full control after being 'elected' president himself. He retired in 1944 and moved to Florida, but organised a military coup in 1952 and ruled as a dictator until he was overthrown by Castro in 1959.

Havana, its capital, was a playground for rich American businessmen and the Mafia. In addition, the USA retained an important naval base at Guantanamo.

Many were opposed to Batista's regime and to Cuba being little more than a US 'satellite'. Such people looked back fondly to the short-lived reforming government of 1933. One group was led by a young student radical called Fidel **Castro** – though left-of-centre, he was not associated with the larger and better organised communist student group. On 26 July 1953, his group carried out an attack on the army's Moncada Barracks. This was a total failure and Fidel and his brother Raul surrendered themselves in an attempt to halt Batista's slaughter of suspects. Castro was sentenced to 15 years in prison but was amnestied in 1954. He then went into exile in Mexico where he met up with a young Argentine doctor and revolutionary called Ernesto 'Che' Guevara and together they formed the **26th of July Movement** and plotted Batista's overthrow.

In December 1956, a small force of revolutionaries, led by Castro, landed in Cuba, with the intention of overthrowing Batista's regime. After being almost totally defeated at the start, they retreated to the Sierra Maestra mountains. At this stage, the revolutionaries were still essentially middle-class liberal reformers, which reassured the Cuban bishops sufficiently for them to issue a call for a government of national unity in February 1958.

In March, the USA (embarrassed by public criticism of its support for Batista's repressive regime) placed an embargo on arms shipments to both sides. After a bitter guerrilla war – during which Eisenhower's government came increasingly to believe that continued support for Batista was actually endangering its interests in Cuba – Batista suddenly decided, on New Year's Eve 1958, to flee to the Dominican Republic. On 1 January 1959, Castro's forces were able to enter Havana.

Castro's revolution

At first, the new government was headed by Urrutia (president) and Cardona (prime minister), but real power rested with Fidel Castro, who was commander-in-chief of the armed forces. In February, Cardona resigned in protest at his lack of power and Castro took over his post.

Initially, Castro looked to the USA for aid, especially as the USA was the chief purchaser of Cuba's main exports, sugar (under a quota system, the USA imported 40–60 per cent of its sugar from Cuba) and tobacco. In April 1959, he visited the UN headquarters in New York and tried to convince the USA to support his plans for reform, in exchange for which the USA could keep its naval base at Guantanamo. However, Eisenhower refused to meet him, although Vice-President Nixon did.

The USA was seriously worried by Castro's Agrarian Reform Law of May

Born in 1926, Fidel **Castro** was the son of a wealthy sugar plantation owner, and studied law at the University of Havana from 1945 to 1948. He practised law from 1950 to 1952, and stood for Congress in 1952.

The **26th of July Movement** was the name of Castro's political group, formed in May 1955. Castro and several others had been imprisoned after their unsuccessful attack on the Moncada Barracks. The attack had taken place on 26 July 1953 – hence the name of the movement founded following their release from prison. Once in Mexico, the group issued two official manifestos. Though they wanted a radical social revolution, Castro made great efforts to establish their lack of involvement with communism. It was this group which began the struggle against Batista in December 1956.

1959. Not only did it limit all estates to 1,000 acres – with compensation in bonds based on 1958 tax valuations (which were always deliberately under-valued by the rich landowners in order to avoid paying taxes) – but it also said that foreigners would no longer be allowed to own agricultural land in Cuba. Of particular concern was the fact that Castro appointed Nunez Jimenez, a communist, as head of the National Institute of Agrarian Reform (INRA). The USA began to see Castro, with his plans for land, health and welfare reforms, as another Arbenz.

In June 1959, the commander of the Cuban airforce resigned in protest at growing 'communist' influence in the military and in July the president, Urru-tia, also resigned. Eventually, Castro strengthened his position and, in Septem-ber, he announced at the UN that neutrality was the only realistic position for developing states in the Cold War. This was a clear rejection of US influence over Cuba.

With Cuban exiles already flying bombing missions from Florida and firing sugar-cane fields, Castro began to accuse the USA of plotting the return of Batista. This was not an unfounded accusation: from late 1959, the CIA were making use of Cuban exiles and hatching plans to disrupt the economy and destabilise Castro's government. During 1960, tensions increased when Castro ordered the American-owned oil refineries in Cuba to process Soviet crude oil, which was cheaper than the oil normally purchased from Venezuela. When they refused to do so (so breaking Cuban law), Castro nationalised the US oil companies. In response, Eisenhower suspended the Cuban sugar quota with the USA in July 1960 and cut it off permanently in December. Castro replied by nationalising almost all US-owned companies in Cuba, and the USA placed an embargo on virtually all trade to Cuba. In February 1960, Cuba had signed a trade agreement with the USSR, which gave Cuba $100 million credit for the purchase of equipment while the Soviet Union promised to purchase 2 million tonnes of sugar a year for the next four years. Castro further upset the USA by concluding a trade agreement with communist China.

Later in 1960, Castro began a general programme of nationalisation of the Cuban economy and, in response to his government's growing fears about the possibility of imminent counter-revolution and invasion, many political freedoms were removed, most notably the freedom of the press. During this period, Castro – although not a member himself – came to rely increasingly on the Cuban Communist Party to provide administrators for his reform programmes.

In March 1960, the CIA persuaded Eisenhower to approve the training of an invasion force of right-wing Cuban exiles to overthrow Castro; training began in earnest in July. Based in Guatemala, these exiles were given US weapons and training. The USA were further angered (and the USSR

Why was the USA's cancellation of the sugar quota in 1960 so important for Cuba?

disappointed) when, in September 1960, Cuba became the first Latin American state to establish diplomatic relations with Mao's China.

As Castro moved closer and closer to the Soviet bloc, Eisenhower broke off diplomatic relations with Cuba in January 1961. A small island in the USA's 'backyard' seemed to be offering a direct challenge to the USA's containment policy and thus became an important factor in the Cold War. By mid 1961, Castro had established diplomatic and trade relations with every communist state, including both North Korea and North Vietnam.

Why did the Cuban Missile Crisis happen?

The Bay of Pigs, 1961

Eisenhower's economic blockade against Cuba and his invasion plans were inherited by Kennedy, who won the presidential election in November 1960. Not only did Kennedy share Eisenhower's hostility towards Castro's government, he had even accused him of having 'lost' Cuba by being too passive. He authorised the CIA to continue with their project, despite warnings from the joint chiefs of staff and the secretary of state that it might backfire, strengthen Castro and damage the USA's image in the rest of the developing world.

On 15 April 1961, the Cuban exiles (with CIA pilots) carried out preliminary air-raids to knock out the Cuban airforce. For some time, Castro had been expecting the USA to attempt to repeat its Guatemalan intervention of July 1954. Castro's immediate response, on 16 April, was to announce that Cuba now intended to follow a 'socialist' road in order to complete its revolution. At the same time, negotiations continued with the Soviet Union for a large aid package, including weapons. Most historians now believe it was US actions like these, not genuine ideological commitment, that pushed Castro towards Marxism.

Since 1959, Castro's attempts to purchase small arms in order to build up a Cuban army strong enough to resist any attempt by Batista to return had been blocked by the USA. From February 1960, the USSR began to provide such weapons, along with military advisers. These weapons and advisers proved useful in dealing with the land invasion, which followed the air-raids, on 17 April 1961. The landings, of about 1,400 exiles, took place in the Bahia de Cochinos (Bay of Pigs) in a remote part of the island. The Cubans always refer to this event as the *Playa Giron*, the name of the beach on the eastern side of the bay where the main body of would-be invaders landed. Though Kennedy had ordered that no Americans take part, the USA provided the transport and weapons and, in fact, the first invader to touch Cuban soil was an American.

This attempted invasion was quickly defeated and the whole venture became a deeply humiliating fiasco for the new president of the USA. In all,

What happened at the Bay of Pigs in 1961?

1,179 of the Cuban exiles were captured – in order to have them returned, the USA had to give $53 million worth of aid in the form of baby food, medicines and medical equipment to Cuba. Not only had the CIA seriously underestimated the strength of the Cuban armed forces, they had also failed to realise the extent of popular support for Castro's regime.

The Cuban Missile Crisis, 1962

Though US plans clearly suffered a serious setback with the Bay of Pigs incident, Kennedy was still determined to bring about Castro's overthrow, so he authorised CIA operations to continue. These included bizarre schemes to assassinate Castro, with exploding cigars or diving wetsuits coated with a deadly poison, as well as using 'private' planes to bomb or napalm sugar and tobacco fields. CIA agents also sabotaged oil refineries and sank Cuban merchant ships. As early as 30 November 1961, Kennedy authorised another attempt to overthrow Castro, known as Operation Mongoose. Cuban security police also captured documents which said that, if Castro had not been overthrown by October 1962, then the USA would have to take more drastic action. In addition, the USA had Cuba expelled from the OAS, while 40,000 US troops staged a 'mock' invasion of Puerto Rico in a military exercise clearly intended as a warning to Castro of how easy it would be for the US to invade Cuba.

Fearing another possible US-backed invasion, Castro appealed to Khrushchev for protection. From May 1962, Soviet weapons deliveries to Cuba increased dramatically. Castro's request came at a time when the Soviet Union was becoming increasingly concerned about the nuclear missiles which the USA had placed in Turkey on the Black Sea coast close to the Soviet Union. Khrushchev was also worried in general about the 'missile gap' between the USSR and the USA.

During a visit to Bulgaria in May 1962, Khrushchev began to consider how placing Soviet missiles on Cuba might serve a dual purpose. Castro would get the protection he had requested against further US aggression, while the Soviet Union would be able to counter the threat posed by the US missiles in Turkey with a similar threat against the USA. By September 1962, the Soviet Union had begun to install and equip missile sites in Cuba as well as increase the number of tanks, bombers and fighters supplied to Castro's armed forces. There were soon over 5,000 Soviet technicians and engineers working on the missile sites which were, however, under Soviet – not Cuban – control. The total Soviet presence on Cuba eventually reached 42,000.

On 11 September, Kennedy warned Khrushchev that the USA would prevent the installation of Soviet nuclear missiles in Cuba by 'whatever means might be necessary'. Khrushchev replied that the Soviet Union had no intention of providing such missiles for Cuba. Khrushchev felt able to take such a risky step as the crisis over Berlin had subsided after the building of the Berlin Wall in 1961, thus leaving him free to concentrate on other problems. More importantly, the failure over Berlin led him to seek a success elsewhere. However, these Soviet short- and intermediate-range missiles were seen by Kennedy as altering the strategic balance of forces in a region long seen as being a US sphere of influence.

On 14 October, a US U-2 spy-plane flew over Cuba and came back with photos of an intermediate-range ballistic missile (IRBM) site being constructed in Cuba. These missiles, with a range of over 1,600 km, turned most of the USA's major cities into potential targets. For six days, a few members of the US government (the Executive Committee of the National Security Council or ExComm) discussed the various response options, without consulting any allies. As a first step, Robert McNamara, the US defence secretary, ordered preparations for an invasion of Cuba to be ready by 20 October. Only on

> Why was the USA so concerned about the presence of Soviet missiles in Cuba?

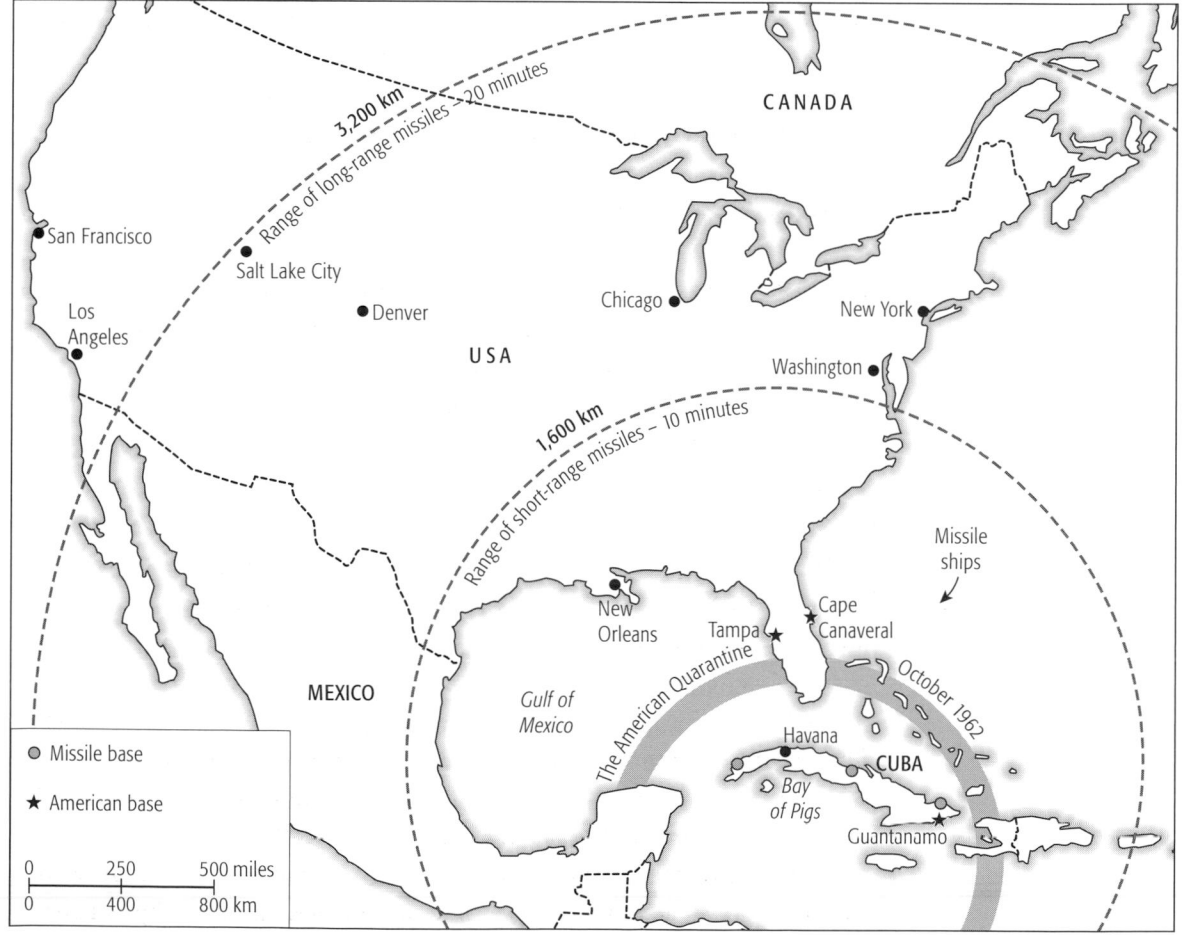

The Cuban Missile Crisis, October 1962.

21 October, after Kennedy had decided on what action to take, was Britain informed about the missiles.

Kennedy had decided on two responses: the USA would first mount a naval blockade of Cuba, then US troops would invade the island. The blockade, or 'quarantine', was announced publicly on 22 October; the USA stated that, from 24 October, it would stop and search all ships bound for Cuba. On 23 October, Khrushchev replied by saying Soviet ships would not respect the blockade. Opinion continues to be divided on whether or not the USA's actions were technically an act of war.

On 24 October, 18 Soviet ships (possibly containing warheads for the missiles) were stopped or turned back just before reaching the limit set by the USA. The risk of nuclear war breaking out was increased when the USA announced that, if the missiles were not removed at once, Cuba would be invaded. On 25 October, the USA began to put into effect plans for an air-strike against the missile sites, to take place on 29 or 30 October. Castro – and even some Soviet generals – urged Khrushchev to launch some missiles in order to prevent the threatened US invasion of Cuba. Khrushchev, however, rejected these calls and instead, on 26 October, sent a letter to Kennedy.

This letter offered the withdrawal of Soviet missiles from Cuba and promised no more would be sent if the USA would lift its blockade of Cuba and promise not to invade the island. Then, on 27 October, without having had a response from the USA, Khrushchev sent a second letter, with different demands. This time, the Soviet Union offered to remove its missiles from Cuba if the USA would reciprocate by removing its own Jupiter missiles from Turkey. Khrushchev further suggested that this be done via the UN. This presented difficulties for the USA as it had never publicly admitted it had missiles in Turkey.

The US military chiefs pressed Kennedy to launch an air attack on Cuba but he was hesitant. After some intense discussions, it was agreed that Khrushchev's second letter should be ignored; instead, Kennedy replied to the first letter and offered to give a commitment not to invade Cuba, provided the Soviet missiles were withdrawn first. Later that same day, Robert Kennedy, the president's brother, was sent to have discussions with Anatoly Dobrynin, the Soviet ambassador in the USA. Robert Kennedy was instructed to give an unofficial ultimatum and offer to the ambassador. The ultimatum was that, if the Soviet Union had not promised by 28 October to remove its missiles, the USA would attack and destroy them; the offer was that, once the missiles were withdrawn, the USA would remove its missiles from Turkey in the near future, but it was stressed that this would not be part of any public deal. Dobrynin reported back to Khrushchev, who accepted this compromise, so ending the crisis.

Results of the crisis

The end of what proved, for 13 days, to be the most serious crisis of the entire Cold War was portrayed in the West as a victory for Kennedy and a defeat for Khrushchev, as the deal over the US missiles in Turkey was kept secret. In April 1963, the US missiles were removed, but the American public were not told about this until 1969. In fact, the Soviet Union gained very little from the deal on US missiles, as the USA had already decided to remove them, as land-based sites had been made obsolete by the introduction of SLBMs, which were much more difficult to detect and hence to destroy.

Although Khrushchev had secured unofficial promises about US attacks on Cuba, many leading Soviet communists were unhappy at the USSR's public climb-down. The Cuban Missile Crisis undoubtedly played a part in Khrushchev's removal from power in 1964. At the same time, Khrushchev's agreements confirmed the Chinese communists' belief that he was unwilling to stand up to the USA. The Chinese therefore continued to develop their own independent foreign policy, thus widening the split in the world communist movement.

In western Europe, there was some anger at how little the USA had consulted its allies during this emergency, despite the risk that any conflict between the USA and the USSR would probably have involved other NATO members. France, in particular, was resentful and this was one of the reasons why de Gaulle eventually decided to withdraw France from NATO and tried to encourage the rest of western Europe to adopt an independent foreign policy.

The hot line and the Nuclear Test Ban Treaty

Both sides had been shocked by how close they had come to a nuclear third world war over the Cuban Missile Crisis and were determined to avoid such serious tensions in the future. It was agreed, almost immediately, to install a special telephone 'hot line' between the Kremlin and the White House, so that its leaders could communicate quickly and directly with each other during any future crisis. This was in operation by June 1963. Though the Cold War continued, the level of tension between the USA and the USSR never again reached that of October 1962. Such brinkmanship was seen as being too dangerous in the nuclear age.

This crisis also helped bring about a partial thaw in East–West relations. In what came to be seen as the first step towards halting the nuclear arms race, the Soviet Union and the USA signed the Nuclear Test Ban Treaty in August 1963. Though it did not limit or reduce the building and deployment of nuclear weapons, it did attempt to control the testing of such devices. In addition, and separate from the treaty, the USA agreed to sell the Soviet Union surplus grain worth $250 million. The Treaty for the Non-Proliferation of Nuclear Weapons, though drawn up, was not actually signed until 1969 during the era of detente. However, from 1962, Cold War conflict remained confined to the developing world.

What impact did the Cuban Revolution have on the Cold War?

Cuba and Latin America

Despite the 1962 agreements, the USA remained extremely hostile to Cuba; as early as June 1963, Kennedy ordered the resumption of Operation Mongoose. The CIA also continued to carry out acts of sabotage and small military raids and to plot Castro's assassination.

Because of continuing US hostility to Cuba after the Missile Crisis of 1962, Castro hoped the example of the Cuban Revolution would inspire similar revolutions in Central and Latin America and the Caribbean, as such a development would end Cuba's isolation in the region. This is precisely what the USA – and many Latin American rulers – feared, especially as the Cuban revolutionaries had a strong commitment to the idea of international revolution. The first attempt by Castro to spread revolution in the region came in 1959, with an unsuccessful intervention in the Dominican Republic. However, despite the appearance of several groups claiming inspiration from the Cuban Revolution and the supply of weapons and training by Cuba, nothing significant happened. Even a personal attempt by Che **Guevara** – who had spearheaded the drive to spread revolution in the region – to help stimulate a revolution in Bolivia in 1965 failed.

One of Guevara's aims – and Castro's hopes – had been to create 'many Vietnams', in order to weaken the USA's ability to intervene in the developing world and crush incipient revolutions. Up until 1968, Cuba's foreign policy tended to be somewhat at variance with that favoured by the USSR, despite its economic and military dependence on the communist superpower. In particular, the Soviet Union did not approve of Castro's attempts to 'export' revolution. One of the reasons behind this difference was that, since the Cuban Missile Crisis of 1962, Castro had come to realise that the USSR had used Cuba in its global contest with the USA.

After Guevara's failure and death in Bolivia, Castro began to follow a line more in keeping with Moscow's preferences. The first sign of this came in 1968, when Castro publicly supported the Warsaw Pact's invasion of Czechoslovakia. This shift was intensified after Cuba experienced serious economic problems in 1969 and 1970, and so became increasingly dependent on Soviet aid. However, Castro still remained committed to the idea of internationalism,

Born in Argentina in 1928, Ernesto **Guevara** was usually referred to as 'Che'. He qualified as a doctor in 1953. He met Castro in Mexico in 1955 and was part of his group of revolutionaries who landed in Cuba in December 1956. Like Castro, he was not, at first, a communist, though he was a Marxist by the time of the Cuban Revolution in 1959. During the guerrilla war, he proved to be an astute commander. After the overthrow of Batista in 1959, he was eventually put in charge of economic planning. However, life as a government minister did not suit him so, in 1965, he left Cuba to give assistance to a small group of revolutionaries in Bolivia. In 1967, he was captured and shot by US-trained counter-insurgency forces. His image became a widespread symbol of revolution during the 1960s and the 1970s.

though he was now a much more reliable ally of the Soviet Union in the developing world.

Cuba and Africa

In the mid 1970s, Castro became increasingly prepared, despite the crippling economic blockade maintained by the USA, to assist developing world liberation struggles taking place outside the Americas. This was especially true of the former Portuguese colonies in Africa: Mozambique, Guinea-Bissau and, particularly, Angola. All of these had been granted independence in 1975, following the Portuguese Revolution of 1974. In Angola, a bitter civil war broke out in 1975 between the MPLA or Movement for the Popular Liberation of Angola (backed by the Soviet Union), the FNLA (backed by the USA and China) and UNITA (backed by China, South Africa, Israel and, later, the USA).

Until the late 1960s, the Soviet Union had had little influence in Africa, even though Khrushchev had publicly announced his intention to support 'wars of national liberation' in Africa and elsewhere. During the 1960s, the USSR had been loosely linked to Ghana and Mali; however, in 1966 and 1968 respectively, the rulers of Ghana (Nkrumah) and Mali (Keita) had fallen from power. For most of this time, the USA, the Soviet Union and, increasingly, China had competed against each other for influence in Africa. But the collapse of the Portuguese empire after 1974 had destabilised the situation, especially in southern Africa.

Angola was rich in oil and minerals and was thus of both economic and strategic importance. The USSR-backed MPLA was the biggest and most popular group, so China and then the USA increased their supply of weapons to the FNLA; the Soviet Union then did the same for the MPLA. China later ended its involvement in Angola and the USA swung its weight behind UNITA. Castro decided to help the MPLA's struggle by sending in 17,000 Cuban troops. The victorious MPLA was able to form a government, which signed a treaty of co-operation and friendship with the USSR in 1976, as did Mozambique the following year. (The MPLA government worried the USA to such an extent that **Ford**, the US president, banned the word 'detente' from his vocabulary.)

In 1977, the USA was further alarmed by events in Ethiopia. The Soviet Union gave support and aid to the Ethiopian government in its struggle to expel Somalia from the Ogaden region. Once again, Castro provided about 17,000 Cuban combat troops. After a military coup, Ethiopia became a pro-Soviet socialist republic. One result of Cuba's involvement, however, was that the USA became even more determined to find ways to undermine Castro's position. This continued under Carter who, in 1980, agreed to the establishment of the Rapid Deployment Force for interventions in the developing world.

What impact did the Cuban Missile Crisis of 1962 have on the Cold War?

Born in 1913, Gerald **Ford** trained as a lawyer and served in the US navy during the Second World War. He entered the House of Representatives as a Republican in 1948. He became vice-president in 1973, and replaced Nixon as president when the latter had to resign because of the Watergate scandal. He was defeated by the Democrat Jimmy Carter in the 1976 presidential elections.

How did Cuba aid several African countries in the 1970s?

Sandinistas refers to those opposed to Somoza's dictatorship in Nicaragua who, in 1961, set up the Sandinista Front for National Liberation (FSLN). The name relates to General Augusto Sandino, who led a liberal nationalist uprising in the early 1930s against the Nicaraguan government and the US marines stationed there almost continuously since 1912. Sandino's guerrillas gained widespread support and, in 1933, accepted a ceasefire – but his terms were not acceptable to the government or to the USA. In 1934, while leaving the presidential palace after more peace talks, Sandino was seized and murdered by the US-trained National Guard of Nicaragua, at that time commanded by Anastasio Somoza.

The Somoza family had been **supported by the USA** in its control of Nicaragua since 1936. Before then, from 1909 to 1933, Nicaragua had been a US protectorate, with US marines permanently stationed there.

The **Contra terrorist group** were those opposed to the new Sandinista government of Nicaragua, and included members of Somoza's hated National Guard. Claiming that the Sandinistas were using their power to supply weapons to the left-wing guerrillas in El Salvador, Reagan decided to give

In 1979, revolution broke out in Central America: in March, the left-wing revolutionary New Jewel Movement took power in the Caribbean island of Grenada. Then in July, a successful revolution in Nicaragua led to the victory of the **Sandinistas**, a coalition group which contained many Marxists, as well as liberals, radicals, priests and some businessmen. More importantly, it led to the defeat and expulsion of Somoza, a corrupt and brutal dictator, who had seized power in 1936 and had used the National Guard to suppress any opposition. He was allied to and **supported by the USA** (though at one point Carter had cut off US aid after receiving information about Somoza's corruption). When the Sandinistas took power in 1979, their government had two broad aims – an 'independent and non-aligned' foreign policy, and the creation of a 'mixed' economy in order to achieve social and economic justice. At first, the USA gave some economic aid and, though Cuba sent about 2,500 engineers, doctors, nurses and teachers, the Soviet Union did not offer aid. Much more substantial aid came from western Europe. However, Reagan (elected in 1980) decided to undermine what he described as a 'Marxist takeover' of Nicaragua.

In 1979, the USA announced the 'discovery' of a Soviet combat brigade in Cuba – in fact, Soviet troops had been in Cuba for many years. Such developments led Carter and, later, Reagan, to give increased US support to the military dictatorship in El Salvador and to the **Contra terrorist group** in Nicaragua as part of the policy to aid all anti-communist forces in the region in order to 'contain' the spread of communism. When the news spread of

A US marine guarding prisoners during the US invasion of the tiny Caribbean island of Grenada in October 1983. Reagan claimed the left-wing government was turning the island into a 'Soviet–Cuban colony'.

mounting Contra acts of terrorism against civilians, Congress voted to end any military support. However, Reagan attempted to continue his support by illegally using money received from other, non-official, sources – including arms deals with Iran (also banned by Congress) to fund the Contras. This was discovered and led to the Contragate scandal.

These attempts to put pressure on developing countries opposed to the USA was part of the new Reagan Doctrine, which recognised that the direct deployment of US troops entailed too many risks. Although Reagan did send a US invasion force to overthrow the left-wing rulers of Grenada in October 1983, Grenada was just a tiny island with a population of only 80,000. The Soviet Union, despite Castro's fears about the USA's immediate intentions about Cuba, did nothing in response to this US invasion. In all, the years 1974–80 witnessed a whole series of revolutionary upheavals in the developing world, resulting in fourteen changes of regime. It was developments such as these which helped contribute to the end of detente and the start of the Second Cold War as the USA grew increasingly uneasy at the loss of previous allies and the Soviet Union's subsequent increased presence in the developing world.

money and CIA assistance to the Contras. Later, as continued US threats and Contra terrorist acts against economic targets, literacy teachers and FSLN members led to increasing restrictions of certain freedoms (e.g. the opposition press), some of the original supporters of the Sandinistas began to support the Contras.

Gorbachev and the end of the Cold War

As well as disengaging from Afghanistan and eastern Europe (see pages 189–93), Gorbachev eventually decided to reduce Soviet support for the Cuban economy and Cuba's interventionist foreign policy. As Soviet economic aid was withdrawn, Cuba's ability to support sympathetic governments and movements was reduced. In the Americas, Castro had to reduce support for the Nicaraguan government and for the left-wing rebels in El Salvador. One result of this was elections being held in Nicaragua which ended the Contras' terrorist activities and led to the formation of a coalition government.

In Africa, Gorbachev's new policy also affected Cuba's world role. He negotiated an agreement with the USA concerning the civil war in Angola, which had been going on since 1975. In 1991, Cuban troops were withdrawn and the civil war was suspended, although it has flared up on several occasions since then. In the Horn of Africa, the Soviet Union also ended its support of Ethiopia, with Cuban combat troops again being withdrawn. The USA then ended its support of Somalia and the war between Ethiopia and Somalia came to an end. The ending of wars in these 'hot spots' contributed to the eventual conclusion of the Second Cold War.

Conclusion

With the collapse of the Soviet Union in 1991, only one superpower from the Cold War remains. Even today, the USA maintains its hostility to Castro's

How did the collapse of the USSR in 1991 affect Cuba?

Cuba, which continues to be a communist island in the western hemisphere. Yet, despite being deprived of economic and political allies, Cuba still acts as an irritant to the USA, and an almost forgotten footnote to the Cold War which lasted for almost 50 years.

Historical sources

1 Extract from the memoirs of N. S. Khrushchev, *Khrushchev Remembers*, (ed. E. Crankshaw)

The fate of Cuba and the maintenance of Soviet prestige in that part of the world preoccupied me . . . We had to establish a tangible and effective deterrent to American interference in the Caribbean . . . The logical answer was missiles. We knew that American missiles were aimed against us in Turkey and Italy, to say nothing of West Germany . . .

We sent the Americans a note saying that we agreed to remove our missiles and bombers on the condition that the President give us his assurances that there would be no invasion of Cuba by the forces of the United States or anybody else. Finally Kennedy gave in and agreed to make a statement giving us such an assurance . . .

E. G. Rayner, *The Cold War*, London, 1992, pp. 50–1

2 Extract from the minutes of an ExComm meeting during the Cuban Missile Crisis of 1962, involving Kennedy and his national security adviser, McGeorge Bundy

Kennedy: He's [Khrushchev's] got us in a pretty good spot here, because most people will regard this as not an unreasonable proposal, I'll just tell you that. In fact, in many ways –
Bundy [disagreeing with Kennedy]: But what most people, Mr. President?
Kennedy: I think you're going to find it very difficult to explain why we are going to take hostile military action in Cuba against those sites – what we've been thinking about – the thing that he's saying is, 'If you'll get yours out of Turkey, we'll get ours out of Cuba.' I think we've got a very tough one here.

O. Edwards, *The USA and the Cold War*, London, 1997, p. 120

Historical-source questions

1 What was the 'American interference' concerning Cuba referred to by Khrushchev in Source 1?
2 In what ways does Source 2 support the comments made in Source 1?
3 To what extent are Sources 1 and 2 reliable evidence about the negotiations over the Cuban Missile Crisis? Use the sources and your own knowledge to explain your answer.

Further reading

General

There are several texts which deal with the general history of Europe in the twentieth century, though many either start before 1919 or finish before 1989. A straightforward read is J. Joll, *Europe since 1870*, Harmondsworth, 1976, while S. Lee, *Aspects of European history, 1789–1980*, London, 1982, has a useful introduction.

Comprehensive coverage of some of the main issues is provided by C. Culpin and R. Henig in *Modern Europe, 1870–1945*, London, 1997. Several specific topics are covered in P. Catterall and R. Vinen, eds., *Europe 1914–45*, Oxford, 1994. For an interesting overview, there is E. Hobsbawm, *Age of extremes*, London, 1994, which covers the period 1914–91.

International relations, 1919–39

There are many useful texts on this topic: for a comprehensive overview try R. J. Overy, *The inter-war crisis, 1919–39*, London, 1994, and F. McDonough, *The origins of the First and Second World Wars*, Cambridge, 1997. R. Henig's two books, *Versailles and after, 1919–1933*, 2nd edn, London, 1995, and *The origins of the Second World War, 1933–1939*, London, 1985, provide full coverage. More detailed is A. P. Adamthwaite, *The lost peace: international relations in Europe, 1918–1939*, London, 1980. As well as A. J. P. Taylor's classic *The origins of the Second World War*, London, 1961, worth reading are R. Overy, *The origins of the Second World War*, London, 1987, and E. Robertson, ed., *The origins of the Second World War*, London, 1971.

For specific countries, try W. Rock, *British appeasement in the 1930s*, London, 1977; K. Hildebrand, *The foreign policy of the Third Reich*, London, 1973; G. Roberts, *The Soviet Union and the Second World War*, London, 1995; and J. Haslam, *The Soviet Union and the struggle for collective security, 1933–1939*, London, 1984.

The USSR, 1924–53

There are many texts available for this topic. For a good general overview, try M. McCauley's two books: *The Soviet Union, 1917–1991*, 2nd edn, London, 1993, and *Stalin and Stalinism*, London, 1983. Also useful as an overview is D. Lane, *State and politics in the USSR*, Oxford, 1985. A much more detailed read is R. Service, *A history of 20th century Russia*, London, 1997. For the period up to 1932, sound coverage is provided by S. Fitzpatrick, *The Russian Revolution, 1917–1932*, 2nd edn, Oxford, 1994.

The historical debates are covered well in J. Grant, *Stalin and the Soviet Union*, London, 1998, and in the longer and more difficult C. Ward, *Stalin's Russia*, 2nd edn, London, 1999. For an idea of economic developments under Stalin, there is A. Nove, *An economic history of the USSR*, London, 1992, and for military history there is A. Beevor, *Stalingrad*, London, 1998. Although written by an opponent of Stalin, a useful and readable biography is I. Deutscher, *Stalin*, Harmondsworth, 1966; also useful on the power struggle is Deutscher's *Trotsky* trilogy (Oxford, 1970).

The Cold War in Europe, 1945–91

Good overviews are provided by M. Walker, *The Cold War and the making of the modern world*, London, 1993, and J. W. Mason, *The Cold War, 1945–1991*, London, 1996. Two short texts by M. McCauley, *Origins of the Cold War, 1941–1949*, 2nd edn, London, 1995, and *Russia, America and the Cold War, 1949–1991*, London, 1998, provide comprehensive coverage.

Particularly useful on Soviet motives are A. Ulam, *Expansion and coexistence: Soviet foreign policy, 1917–1973*, New York, 1974, and C. Kennedy-Pipe, *Stalin's Cold War*, Manchester, 1995. US policy is dealt with by J. L. Gaddis, *The United States and the origins of the Cold War, 1941–1947*, New York, 1972.

For the Second Cold War, see F. Halliday, *The making of the Second Cold War*, 2nd edn, London, 1986: this is particularly useful on the relative military strengths of the two superpowers.

The Cold War in Asia and the Americas, 1949–75

For the developing world in general, try J. F. Hough, *The struggle for the Third World*, Washington, 1986. R. Crockatt, *The fifty years war: the United States and the Soviet Union in world politics, 1941–91*, London, 1995, provides detailed coverage. M. Light, ed., *Troubled friendships: Moscow's Third World ventures*, London, 1993, and N. Miller, *Soviet relations with Latin America, 1959–1987*, Cambridge, 1989, examine Soviet motives. The USA is dealt with by G. Kolko, *Confronting the Third World: United States foreign policy 1945–1980*, New York, 1983, and by J. L. Gaddis, *Strategies of containment*, New York, 1982.

For Korea, there is P. Lowe, *Origins of the Korean War*, London, 1986, and M. Hastings, *The Korean War*, London, 1987. For Vietnam, there is G. Herring, *America's longest war: the US and Vietnam, 1950–1975*, New York, 1979. For Cuba, there is R. Garthoff, *Reflections on the Cuban Missile Crisis*, Washington DC, 1989. H. L. Matthews, *Castro*, Harmondsworth, 1970, is a somewhat dated but interesting biography.

Index